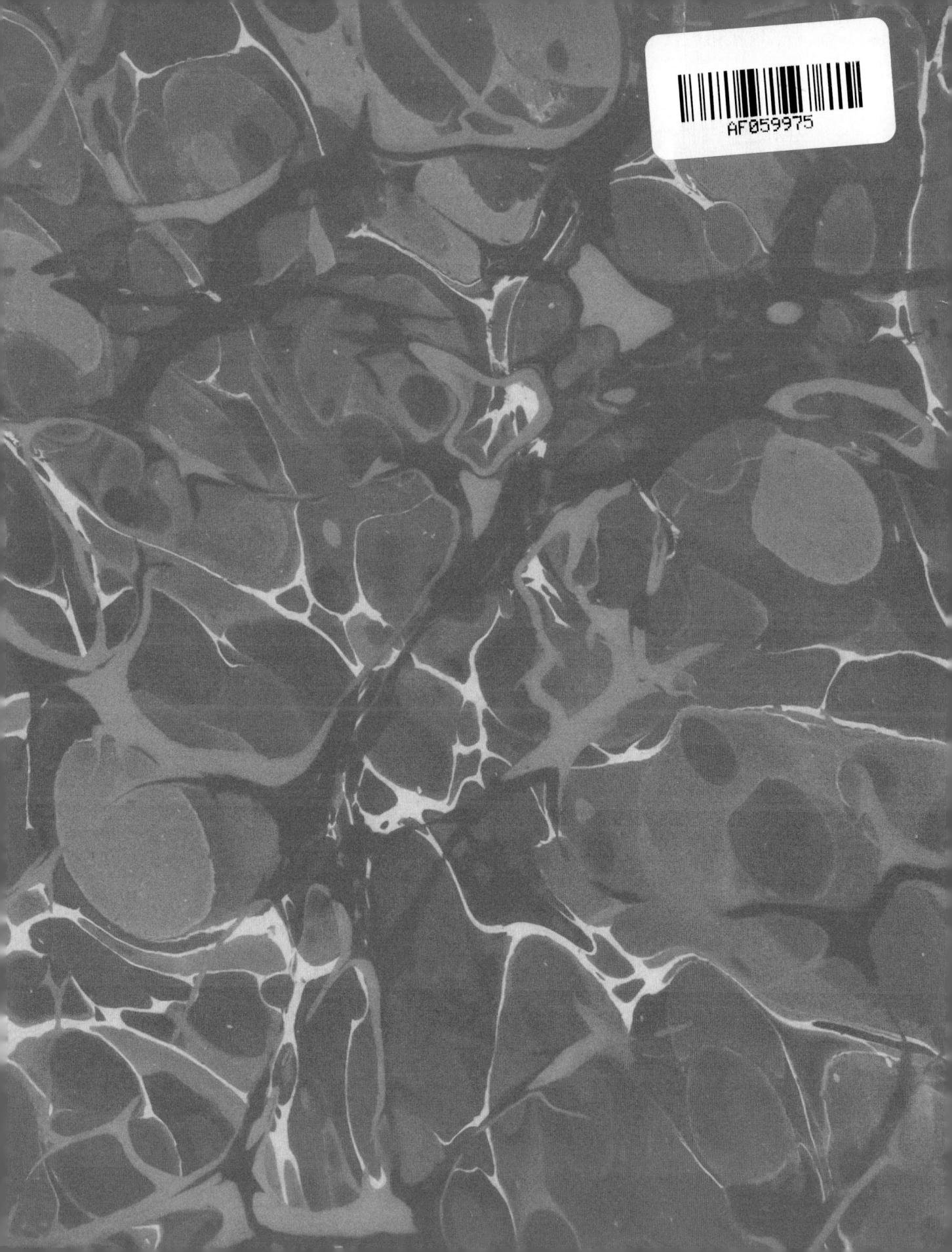

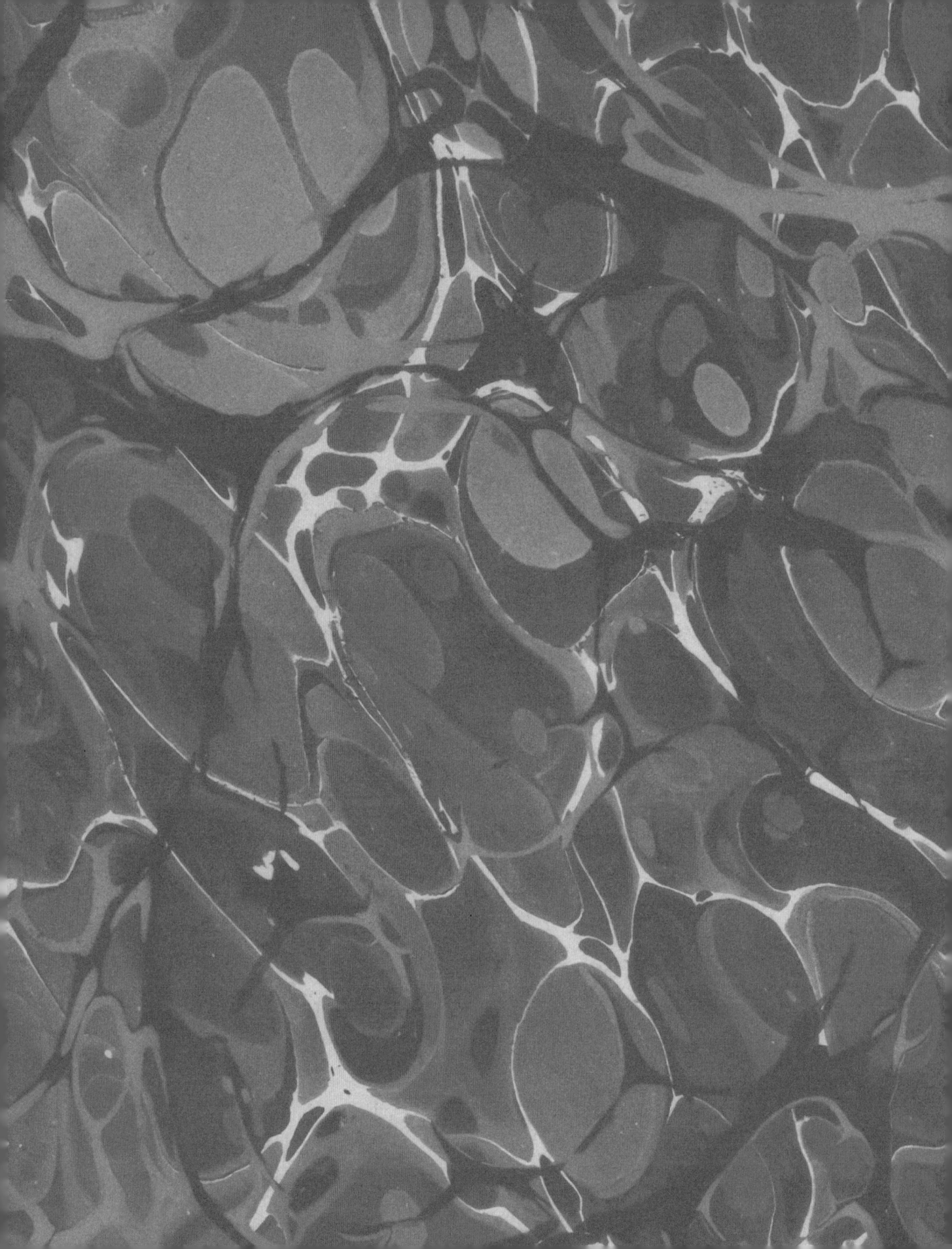

PROPHECIES

PROPHECIES

✠

OMENS

AUGURIES

DIVINATION

ORACLES

DREAMS

APOCALYPSE

✠

CHRISTOPHER
DELL

A PROPHETIC
PLANISPHERE

6

A BRIEF HISTORY
OF FUTURE-TELLING

10

FURTHER READING

308

SOURCES OF QUOTATIONS

310

SOURCES OF ILLUSTRATIONS

311

INDEX

314

I

ORACLES & SEERS 26

Augurs in Rome 30
Egyptian Oracles 32
Germanic Seeresses 34
The Sibyls 36
Pythia 40
Babaláwos 42
Oracles in India 44
The Japanese Bureau
of Divination 46
Merlin 48
Tibetan Oracles 50

II

OMENS & PORTENTS 52

Comets 56
Rainbows 60
Eclipses 62
Auroras 66
Bird Omens 68
Snake Omens 72
Physiognomic Omens 76
Auspicious &
Inauspicious Days 78
Superstitions around the World 82

III

PROPHETS & PRIESTS 86

Origins 92
Zoroaster 96
Abraham to Malachi 100
Christianity 104
Montanus 110
Mani 111
The Seal of the Prophets 114
The Book of Mormon 118
The Báb and Baha'u'llah 119

IV

PREDICTIONS & REVELATIONS 120

Tui Bei Tu 126
Hildegard of Bingen 130
Jayabaya the Javanese Prophet King 132
Nostradamus 134
Nguyen Binh Khiem 138
Luca Gaurico 140
Paracelsus 142
Mother Shipton 146
Edgar Cayce 148
Jeane Dixon 150
Baba Vanga 152

V

DREAMS 154

Mesopotamian
Dream Interpretation 160
Egyptian Dream Books 162
Buddhism and Dreaming 164
Dreams in the Bible 166
Artemidorus's Oneirocritica 168
Synesius on Dreams 170
The Great Book of Interpretation of Dreams 172
Native American Dreams 174
Maori Dreams 178

VI

ASTROLOGY 180

The Origins of Astrology 186
Astrology & Astronomy 188
The Basics of Astrology 192
Horoscopes 196
Astrology in India 200
Hellenistic Astrology 206
Astrology in East Asia 208
Astrology in Islam 212

VII

DIVINATION & FORTUNE-TELLING 220

Dice 228
Scrying 234
Haruspices 236
Bibliomancy 240
Sacred Lots 246
Tarot 250
Palmistry 254
I Ching 256
Scapulimancy & Plastromancy 260
Geomancy 262

VIII

WHEN PROPHECY FAILS 266

False Prophets 270
Early Christian Millennialism 272
The Floods of 1524 276
Joanna Southcott 278
Millerism and the
Great Disappointment 280
Harold Camping 284
Doomsday Cults 286
The 2012 Phenomenon 288

IX

THE END OF THE WORLD 290

The Maitreya in Buddhism 294
The Cycles of Hinduism 296
The Apocalypse 298
Ragnarök 304
The Five Suns 306

A PROPHETIC PLANISPHERE

A chart demonstrating the interconnectedness
of divinatory practices across history and cultures.

	I ORACLES & SEERS		II OMENS & PORTENTS		III PROPHETS & PRIESTS
i	Augurs in Rome	i	Comets	i	Origins
ii	Egyptian Oracles	ii	Rainbows	ii	Zoroaster
iii	Germanic Seeresses	iii	Eclipses	iii	Abraham to Malachi
iv	The Sibyls	iv	Auroras	iv	Christianity
v	Pythia	v	Bird Omens	v	Montanus
vi	Babaláwos	vi	Snake Omens	vi	Mani
vii	Oracles in India	vii	Physiognomic Omens	vii	The Seal of the Prophets
viii	The Japanese Bureau of Divination	viii	Auspicious & Inauspicious Days	viii	The Book of Mormon
ix	Merlin	ix	Superstitions around the World	ix	The Báb and Baha'u'lláh
x	Tibetan Oracles				

	IV PREDICTIONS & REVELATIONS		V DREAMS		VI ASTROLOGY
i	Tui Bei Tu	i	Mesopotamian Dream Interpretation	i	The Origins of Astrology
ii	Hildegard of Bingen	ii	Egyptian Dream Books	ii	Astrology & Astronomy
iii	Jayabaya the Javanese Prophet King	iii	Buddhism and Dreaming	iii	The Basics of Astrology
iv	Nostradamus	iv	Dreams in the Bible	iv	Horoscopes
v	Nguyen Binh Khiem	v	Artemidorus's Oneirocritica	v	Astrology in India
vi	Luca Gaurico	vi	Synesius on Dreams	vi	Hellenistic Astrology
vii	Paracelsus	vii	The Great Book of Interpretation of Dreams	vii	Astrology in East Asia
viii	Mother Shipton	viii	Native American Dreams	viii	Astrology in Islam
ix	Edgar Cayce	ix	Maori Dreams		
x	Jeane Dixon				
xi	Baba Vanga				

	VII DIVINATION & FORTUNE-TELLING		VIII WHEN PROPHECY FAILS		IX THE END OF THE WORLD
i	Dice	i	False Prophets	i	The Maitreya in Buddhism
ii	Scrying	ii	Early Christian Millennialism	ii	The Cycles of Hinduism
iii	Haruspices	iii	The Floods of 1524	iii	The Apocalypse
iv	Bibliomancy	iv	Joanna Southcott	iv	Ragnarök
v	Sacred Lots	v	Millerism and the Great Disappointment	v	The Five Suns
vi	Tarot	vi	Harold Camping		
vii	Palmistry	vii	Doomsday Cults		
viii	I Ching	viii	The 2012 Phenomenon		
ix	Scapulimancy & Plastromancy				
x	Geomancy				

REVELATION
Information about the future may be actively sought out or passively received.

CHANNEL
Prophecy may be communicated by a god, fate or a spiritual force; it may manifest itself through omens; or in the arrangement of celestial bodies; or people may harness objects or systems to access it.

INTERMEDIARY
Those who interpret or convey information delivered by various channels.

CONTEXT
Prophecy can have official status in forms of government, be widespread within societies or be part of personal beliefs.

A PROPHETIC PLANISPHERE

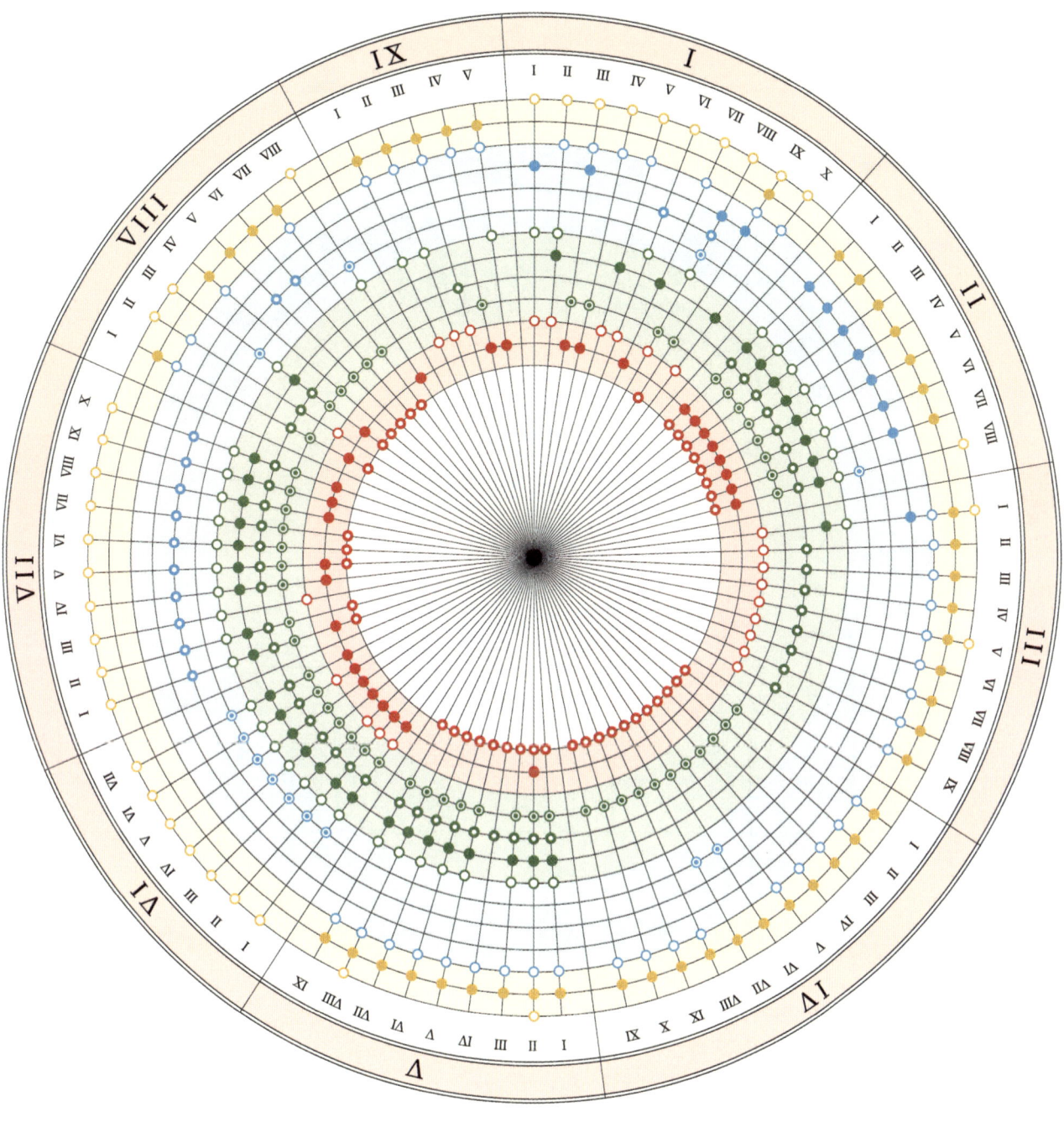

REVELATION
○ Active
● Passive

CHANNEL
○ Divine communication
● Signs
◎ Tool
⊙ Celestial

INTERMEDIARY
○ Priest
● Oracle
◎ Prophet
⊙ Mystic

CONTEXT
○ Official
● Societal
◎ Personal

ဆို့လက္ခဏာဘဝတ်လျှောက်သောအခါရှိက်သုဒ္ဓေါဒန မင်းကြီးကသင်တို့သည်အဘယ်သို့သော
ရှင်သားရဟန်းပြုလိမ့်မည်ဆိုသနည်းဟုမေးရာကော ဈည်ပုဏ္ဏားကအရှင်မင်းကြီးဖွားသည်
သူသော "ရဟန်း"ဉာဏ်မိတ်လေးပါးကိုမြင်၍ရဟန်းပြု လိတ်ဆိုကြောင်းကိုလျှောက်ကြားနေဟန်

A BRIEF HISTORY OF FUTURE-TELLING

THERE is an ancient belief, handed down to us even from mythical times and firmly established by the general agreement of the Roman people and of all nations, that divination of some kind exists among men; this the Greeks call *mantike* – that is, the foresight and knowledge of future events. A really splendid and helpful thing it is – if only such a faculty exists – since by its means men may approach very near to the power of gods.

CICERO, *ON DIVINATION*

PRECEDING PAGES

King Suddhodana consults 108 Brahmins to predict the future of his newborn son and learns that his son will become the Buddha.

OPPOSITE

The mythological Greek hero Odysseus meets with the blind prophet Tiresias in the underworld.

THE future is a place that both exists and does not exist. While we can differ over how to interpret the past, there will always be some facts that everyone can agree on – particularly after the emergence of written history. And to understand the present we can rely on and trust in our own senses and experiences. But the future is ripe for speculation and probing, while also holding the keys to our hopes, dreams and anxieties: will our crops be sufficient, will we be successful in war, will our finances improve, will we recover from illness, will we find love?

Throughout history humans have invested huge energies into trying to foretell the future. With great ingenuity they have attempted to divine, discern, predict, forecast and uncover what will happen next, hoping to establish control. The structured form of future-telling that informs many of the present-day practices of divination, omen-reading and astrology most likely emerged in ancient Mesopotamia – the area between the Tigris and Euphrates rivers roughly correlating to modern-day Iraq – before spreading to India, Egypt, Europe and China, where it blended with indigenous practices. However, many other distinct traditions have existed, and continue to exist, around the world – for example, spider divination in Cameroon, or the mirror-scrying practices of the Aztecs. And while today forecasting is often a scientific discipline of data and probability, here we explore the many *supernatural* practices, stories and myths relating to prophecy, divination and omens, also taking in an array of related topics such as visions (induced or otherwise), shamanism, oracles, and fortune-telling.

There are many different methods used to prise open the stubborn jaws of the future, and we can categorize them into two types: 'active' and 'passive'. The first kind, active, is when knowledge of the future is deliberately sought out – this is the realm of divination, of the intercessions of priests, soothsayers and oracles. We often find such intermediaries in a religious context, frequently even being central to the religion. They have held high positions of influence in the Shang courts of ancient China, in the temples of Egypt and in the shrines of the Indian subcontinent. Mediators between the material world and

LEFT

The Chinese zodiac signs appearing in an astrology book from Mongolia, *c.* 1900.

ABOVE LEFT

The prophecies of the famous French seer Nostradamus are still widely consulted today.

ABOVE RIGHT

The prophet Ezekiel, miniature in a fifteenth-century Dutch manuscript.

the great beyond, they were relied upon by rulers and commoners alike in their planning. This is also where future-telling and magic can overlap, though with an important distinction – whereas prophecy and divination are about *understanding* our futures, magic is more concerned with controlling our environments and fortunes, interacting with the supernatural realm in order to influence things in a way that is favourable to us.

The second kind of communication about the future is passive. These are the messages or signs that come to humanity unannounced, even against our will: dreams and visions, revelations, portents and warnings. And like the forms of active divination, they can be sometimes very clear or sometimes very ambiguous – and in many cases still require an intermediary to interpret them.

The boundary between 'active' and 'passive' is porous. For example, in ancient Egypt people would sleep in specific temples that were known to cause prophetic dreams, thereby proactively putting themselves in situations where they could receive messages. Similarly, shamans and seers as found in Korea, Finland or Peru could use music, dancing, psychoactive substances or chanting to put themselves in a state more receptive to revelations, visions and insights. So, in practice, there is a continuum from prophecy (divinely inspired visions of the future) to mysticism (revelations about the present or the future) to divination (the proactive process of discovering the future), and these categories of convenience simply allow us to impose some structure on a naturally amorphous topic.

The word 'prophet' can also be somewhat misleading. In the Abrahamic traditions that inform language in the West, a prophet is someone with a message from God. The word translates directly from the Greek, a 'forth-teller' or 'interpreter' (i.e. not necessarily with a future meaning). In the context of the Bible, the term 'prophecy' refers to an often future-facing moral message. In this sense, a prophet is similar to a priest or even more so a mystic or shaman – someone who has a direct connection with the divine. Connection with the mystical realm is central to all types of prophecy and divination – indeed, it is impossible to believe in the efficacy of the methods discussed here without recourse to a divine or supernatural realm.

This is a useful reminder, then, that the word 'prophet' can have various meanings, and we should also be wary of assuming that terms such as 'oracle', 'shaman' and 'prophet' are used in precisely the same way around the world.

Divination, in particular astrology, can be a central part of religious practice. This is particularly true in the Vedic traditions of South Asia, where there is the concept of *rta* – the cosmic order of things, the way that things should be. One of the ways to understand this cosmic order is through astrology. Since the stars are (apparently) eternal and cyclical in their movement, it is logical, so the reasoning goes, that they could represent unchanging principles. And, therefore, it is logical to try to divine in the stars what might happen next.

This same sense of what might be called 'destiny' can also be found in the religion of ancient Greece in the form of the Moirai – the Fates – who ensured that each god and each mortal lived the life they were destined to live. What the Fates had dictated was impossible to overcome, as in the story of Oedipus, who was condemned to kill his father and marry his mother despite all efforts to avoid it. Or in Norse mythology we find another trio of spinners of fate, the Norns, who represent the interconnectedness of past, present and future. Such predeterminism has been a common discussion in religion and in contemplating the predicted end of the world.

All early civilizations, from ancient Egypt, Mesopotamia and Shang China to the Aztecs, Maya, Inca and the Yoruba, have practised some form of divination. The first evidence we have of omens and divination dates from the early second millennium BCE in Mesopotamia, home to the Sumerian, Akkadian, Babylonian and Assyrian civilizations. The ancient Babylonians were keen collectors of omens, which they compiled in compendia on clay tablets. A famous example of this is *Enuma Anu Enlil* ('When [the gods] Anu and Enlil ...'), most likely compiled in the period 1595–1157 BCE, which contains between 6,500 and 7,000 different omens derived from observing the moon, weather, earthquakes, eclipses and stars. Another is called the *Shumma alu* ('If a city is set at a height'), which contains 10,000

ABOVE

The Hindu figure Nanda requests a horoscope for his foster son, the god Krishna.

RIGHT

A multi-armed figure representing the planet Saturn from a Mughal Indian book of omens, c. 1580.

omens, including: 'If ... snakes are coiling in the ... foundations, ... the owner of that house ... will be imprisoned' and 'If fungus is seen on an exterior wall, a servant will die.' There is good evidence that these compendia made their way into Greek, Sanskrit and Hebrew – for example, in the textual formation of omens in Greek that follows the Mesopotamian formula of 'if X, then Y will happen' and the Roman adoption of haruspicy. In fact, the Mesopotamian region remained associated with divination for many centuries, with the term 'Chaldean' (after a part of Babylonia) being used in Mediterranean cultures much later to refer to diviners and astrologers.

Returning to the topic of astrology in the Vedic traditions of India, the first written mentions appear in the *Vedanga Jyotisha*, which has been dated to as early as *c.* 1400 BCE, based on the solstices mentioned (though in its current form is probably from some centuries later). It is said that Valmiki, traditionally identified as the author of the *Ramayana* (probably seventh to fifth centuries BCE), also wrote a treatise on palmistry – attesting to its status as a worthy subject matter.

In China, oracle bones used in divination have been carbon-dated to as early as 1900 BCE, though the majority can be dated to the late Shang dynasty (around 1600 to 1050 BCE). These bones (actually sometimes pieces of turtle shell, but often ox shoulder bones) had a request or question inscribed upon them before being put into a fire; the bones cracked under the heat, and then the cracks were interpreted, either by a named diviner or even the king himself. Strikingly, oracle bones constitute the earliest and largest corpus of ancient Chinese writings. The topics covered included hunting, childbirth, campaigns, harvests and sickness. A little later, in around 1000–750 BCE, the *I Ching*, or *Book of Changes*, emerged, one of the oldest of the classic Chinese texts. In this system of divination, yarrow stalks are cast to create patterns that are then interpreted against a set of hexagrams in the book, with each pattern having a meaning.

At the same time as the Mesopotamian, South Asian and Chinese civilizations were flourishing, there was emerging a new

BELOW
A tablet of commentaries on parts of the Mesopotamian divinatory series *Shumma alu* devoted to snake omens.

OPPOSITE
In the Bible, King Saul consults with the Witch of Endor to divine the future and aid decision-making.

religion that would have a significant impact on how divination was seen. Proto-Judaism as a monotheistic religion has been dated variously to the Exodus from Egypt (c. 1300–1200 BCE) or as late as the sixth century BCE. The Tanakh – the Hebrew Bible – attacks divination and related practices and was deeply suspicious of all forms of magic since these practices all threatened to usurp the authority of a single sovereign god. In the Bible there is a strong sense of resistance to the many cultures around the Israelites, who all practice some sort of divination, and from whom they want to distinguish themselves.

However, this does not mean that such practices don't occur in the Bible – they do, quite frequently. In 1 Kings 22:6, for example, Ahab assembles four hundred prophets to ask whether he should go to war. One of them, Micaiah, informs the king that the other prophets are false and his own prophecy is later proved correct, confirming that genuine prophets do exist. Elsewhere, in 1 Samuel 10:5, Saul meets a band of prophets 'with harp, tambourine, flute and lyre before them; they will be in a prophetic frenzy', giving some insight into the practices they used to provoke trances and revelations.

In the Bible, dreams are seen as a valid way of understanding the future, though they still require interpretation as in Genesis when Joseph predicts a seven-year famine on hearing the pharaoh's dream of seven lean cows. Elsewhere reference is made to the Urim and Thummim, which were divinely sanctioned tools for casting lots, although their precise form and method of use is very unclear. In 1 Samuel, Saul seeks advice from prophets and the Urim and Thummim, but he receives no insights and so he consults the Witch of Endor, who summons the spirit of the prophet Samuel. While the Bible may not approve of every path to future-telling, it seems to acknowledge that multiple paths exist.

The later parts of the Old Testament and all of the New Testament overlap temporally with the world of the ancient Greeks and Romans, which – unlike Judaism and

ABOVE AND OPPOSITE

A selection of Chinese oracle bones from the Shang dynasty. The bones were inscribed and then burned to answer questions about the future.

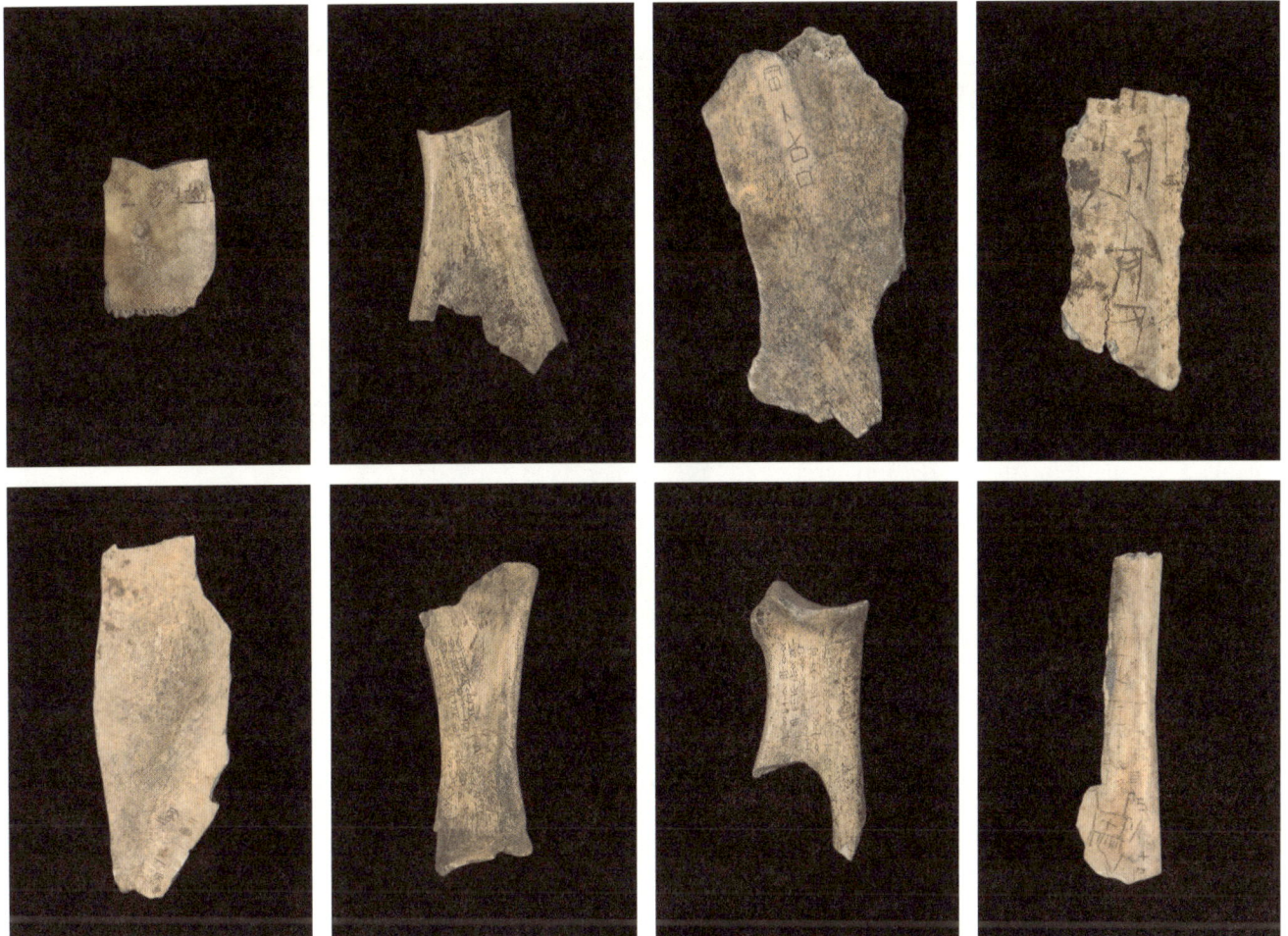

Christianity – embraced many forms of divination and future-telling. Indeed, divinatory practices were at the heart of classical religion. In Greece in particular there flourished many oracles, perhaps the most famous of them being the oracle of Apollo at Delphi, which was consulted on matters of state. In Rome, priests known as *haruspices* would consult the entrails of sacrificial victims, and augurs would consult other signs, particularly birds. Cicero, in *On Divination*, claimed that Romulus, the founder of the city, had been a skilful augur. Of course, there was also healthy scepticism. Cicero distinguished between 'inspired' divination, such as dreams, and those forms of divination that required some skill, such as haruspicy, augury and astrology.

The rapid spread of Islam that followed the death of Muhammad in 632 CE had considerable implications for future-telling. While Muhammad was seen as the Seal of the Prophets – that is, the last in a long line of prophets sent by God, which also included Abraham and Jesus – in this context 'prophet' refers less to future-telling than to the receiving of divine revelations. As a result, early Islam was strongly opposed to magic, and this led to a severe clampdown on divination practices. However, it also led to a growing interest in astrology, since an accurate understanding of the position of the moon and stars was critical to determining the time for prayer. The establishment of the first observatory in Baghdad in the eighth century led to the creation of a remarkable library of works on astrology, and Islamic scholars in the Middle East, North Africa and Spain were prolific authors on the topic of astrology, ultimately informing many European perspectives in the Middle Ages, largely through Spain.

In China, the second half of the first millennium CE was a time of growing power and cultural consolidation. The Tang dynasty (618–907 CE) saw the invention of *ziwei doushu* ('purple star astrology'), supposedly by Lu Chun Yang. This, like the *bazi* ('Four Pillars of Destiny') system, assigned each person characteristics dependent on when they were born, down to the hour. Chinese interest in astrology reached its peak during the Song dynasty (960–1279 CE). At the same time,

ABOVE

A first-century CE Roman depiction of the mythological figure of Orestes consulting the oracle at Delphi in his mission to avenge his father's murder.

Korea also had its own tradition of mostly female *mudang* (sometimes called shamans), who could also undertake *jeom* (divination) for individuals, employing techniques such as casting rice or coins. Much later on, Korea would adopt an anti-superstition Confucian philosophy, although fortune-telling remains popular even today.

The Middle Ages in Europe generally saw the world (the microcosm) as being deeply linked to the universe (the macrocosm). Considering the belief in a connection between the terrestrial and the celestial, a belief in astrology was logical. However, anyone straying too close to magic could expect to encounter the Catholic Church's Inquisition, which was first established in 1184 to root out heretical thinking and which grew significantly after the mid-thirteenth century. Similarly, the medieval Christian world was full of miracles, visions and predictions, with

TOP

An Ottoman celestial map showing the zodiac signs and lunar mansions, 1583.

ABOVE

A seventeenth-century illustration of the concept of the 'great chain' linking life on Earth to the celestial bodies and ultimately to God.

stories of saints and mystics receiving visions – such as those of Hildegard of Bingen or St Catherine of Siena. Thanks to preservation and translation by Islamic scholars, philosophical and astrological texts from ancient Greece and Rome – including Ptolemy's *Tetrabiblos* – became available. The themes of the Book of Revelation became regularly depicted in Christian art in all their apocalyptic detail. The apocalypse loomed large in people's minds as the end of the world was widely predicted for the year 1000 CE, since it marked a millennium from Christ's birth, leading to mass panic.

We might imagine that with the European era of science that started in the sixteenth century, belief in fortune-telling and prophecies might recede, but this was not the case. The best-known practitioner in these times was the French astrologer Nostradamus, whose prophecies continue regularly to be reprinted and pored over around the world. But he did not exist in a vacuum – throughout Europe there remained strong interest in astrology and mysticism. For example, Tarot card reading only really started growing in popularity from the late eighteenth century through publications by figures such as the French Etteilla.

However in the seventeenth and eighteenth centuries, the burgeoning Enlightenment forced prophecy towards the realm of literature and fantasy. For example, Samuel Madden's *Memoirs of the Twentieth Century*, published in 1733, is a set of predictions disguised as letters transported back in time. The birth of a new gothic literature took more and more interest in the occult, but alongside this growing fantasy genre there were emerging in the United States real-life prophets such as Joseph Smith (the founder of Mormonism) and William Miller. The latter predicted that 1844 would see the end of the world and the Second Coming of Christ. When this failed to happen, it led to what was called the Great Disappointment among his followers.

The nineteenth century also saw the growing fame of fortune-tellers who now became celebrities, including Evangeline Adams, sometimes called America's first astrological superstar, whose fortune-telling practices (then illegal) led her to be taken

ABOVE

A Millerite pamphlet from Boston from 16 October 1844 announcing the end of the world in six days' time.

LEFT

A modern-day psychic in the East Village, New York City.

BELOW RIGHT

A fortune-teller using Tarot cards, captured by Brassaï in 1933.

OVERLEAF

A priestess consults with a preserved human head oracle in this painting by John William Waterhouse, 1884.

to court (and acquitted) three times. Even though her credibility was undermined when she advised her followers to invest in the stock market shortly before the infamous crash of 1929, public interest in psychics and astrologers grew. Americans Edgar Cayce and Jeane Dixon and the Bulgarian Baba Vanga all achieved worldwide renown for their predictions.

Today, even if mainstream scientific thinking rejects divination and prophecy as superstitions, future-telling has lost none of its appeal. Horoscope astrology is as popular as ever, portents are still taken seriously and conspiracy theories about the future abound. A 2003 survey in China found that 25 per cent of respondents believed in fortune-telling, and astrology was reintroduced to the academic curriculum in India around 2000. While ostensibly entertainment, Paul the Octopus in Germany gained huge international coverage when he predicted results of the 2010 World Cup with over 85 per cent accuracy. And there was brief panic when some New Age thinkers claimed that the Mayan calendar predicted the end of the world in 2012. The reality is that, even with all our data and the ability to plot trajectories with ever-greater accuracy, we still keep asking the same question: 'what will happen next?'

I.

ORACLES & SEERS

ONLY a few people can truly understand and interpret signs sent from the supernatural realm – today we might call them oracles or seers. These men and women (and occasionally animals) stand between humankind and the divine as mediators, conduits, channels, interpreters of signs and keepers of rituals. Each, however, takes a slightly different approach.

OPPOSITE

A romantic imagining of the first-century CE Germanic seeress Veleda, who was treated as a deity by her tribe.

LEFT

A nineteenth-century image of the priestess of Delphi perched on her tripod and inhaling vapours from the chasm beneath.

ORACLES do not *interpret* signs from gods, rather they access the divine directly and relay the message unmediated (the word oracle comes from the Latin meaning 'to speak'). They tend to be tied to a specific place, typically a place of magic or significance, which enhances their power. The most famous example is that of the oracle of Apollo at Delphi in ancient Greece. Seers, on the other hand, are involved in interpretation and divination; their fundamental role is to interpret and discern supernatural messages. This does not mean that they lack supernatural skills.

Both oracles and seers are called upon in the making of big decisions, often in the service of the ruling elite. As the first-century BCE Roman statesman Cicero noted in *On Divination*: 'what colony did Greece ever send into Aeolia, Ionia, Asia, Sicily or Italy without consulting the Pythian [Delphic] or Dodonian oracle or that of Jupiter Ammon [Amun]? Or what war did she ever undertake without first seeking the counsel of the gods?'

Egyptian rulers would also defer to the gods on larger decisions. There is an inscription on the mortuary temple of Hatshepsut at Deir el-Bahari (near modern-day Luxor) that details her consulting an oracle of Amun before sending an expedition to Punt, and she frequently used oracles to legitimize her reign. In China and Japan, divination was highly formalized and brought under the direct control of the government. In China, diviners had official positions in the court during the Shang and Zhou dynasties (1600–256 BCE), since power rested to a large extent on the ability to commune with the divine. In Japan, the *Onmyoryo* (Bureau of Divination) was created in 676 CE to oversee the practices of *I Ching*, the divination of good and bad days, and astrology.

Despite being tied to a place, oracles are often valued outside of their own immediate culture, for example, Croesus, king of Lydia (r. 560–546 BCE), had a sacrifice made to the Egyptian god Amun in order to learn whether he should attack the Persians. Alexander the Great was confirmed by the same god's oracle at Siwa to be a legitimate pharaoh.

Oracles and seer-type figures are also found extensively in mythology. In Norse mythology, the *Völuspá* ('Prophecy of the *völva*') has an unnamed *völva* (female seer) tell the deity Odin about the future destruction of the gods. Odin himself is said to have carried around the severed head of the knowledgeable Mimir, which could let him know the future.

The overlap between priesthood and seer remains considerable. For example, the Dalai Lama, leader of Tibetan Buddhism, relies on a figure called the Nechung oracle, who can commune directly with the gods, to make governmental decisions. And in the *Ifá* divination practices prevalent among the Yoruba people in West Africa, a *babaláwo* ('father of secrets') is a priest who conducts divination using chains or seeds to understand the will of the gods.

AUGURS IN ROME

REVELATION
Active

CHANNEL
Signs

INTERMEDIARY
Priest

CONTEXT
Official

The augurs of ancient Rome were a kind of priest belonging to a specific religious college, of which there were never more than around twenty-five members at any one time. They were responsible for determining the will of the gods.

AUGURS were a vital part of running Rome and empire. They observed the world around them, looking for and interpreting signs from the gods about specific future events. These signs could take the form of natural phenomena such as lightning, but typically the augurs focused on the study of birds. The first augurs were said to be the city's founders, Romulus and Remus. Unable to agree on which of modern Rome's seven hills to found the city, they each sat on their preferred hill to see who could see the most vultures – this being taken as a sign of the gods' favour. Romulus won, and the city was founded on the Palatine hill.

Augurs operated from an *auguraculum*, a temple with a square courtyard that gave a limited view of the sky. The sky that they could see was divided into four sections, to allow for more precise observations – in what direction were the birds flying, or did phenomena appear?

OPPOSITE

The legendary founders of Rome, Romulus and Remus, used augury to determine the site of their city.

EGYPTIAN ORACLES

REVELATION
Active

CHANNEL
Divine communication

INTERMEDIARY
Priest, Oracle

CONTEXT
Official

Priests of the oracle of Amun at Siwa once refused to legitimize the claim of Cambyses II, ruler of the Achaemenid Empire in the sixth century BCE, to Egypt. He sent an army of fifty thousand men to destroy the oracle, but they were buried in a sandstorm on the way and never found.

LEFT

The Temple of Amun at Siwa was home to an oracle consulted by figures including Alexander the Great.

LEFT

A depiction of the barque of Amun from the Red Chapel of Hatshepsut, Karnak – the barque used to carry the oracle of Amun at Siwa may have looked like this.

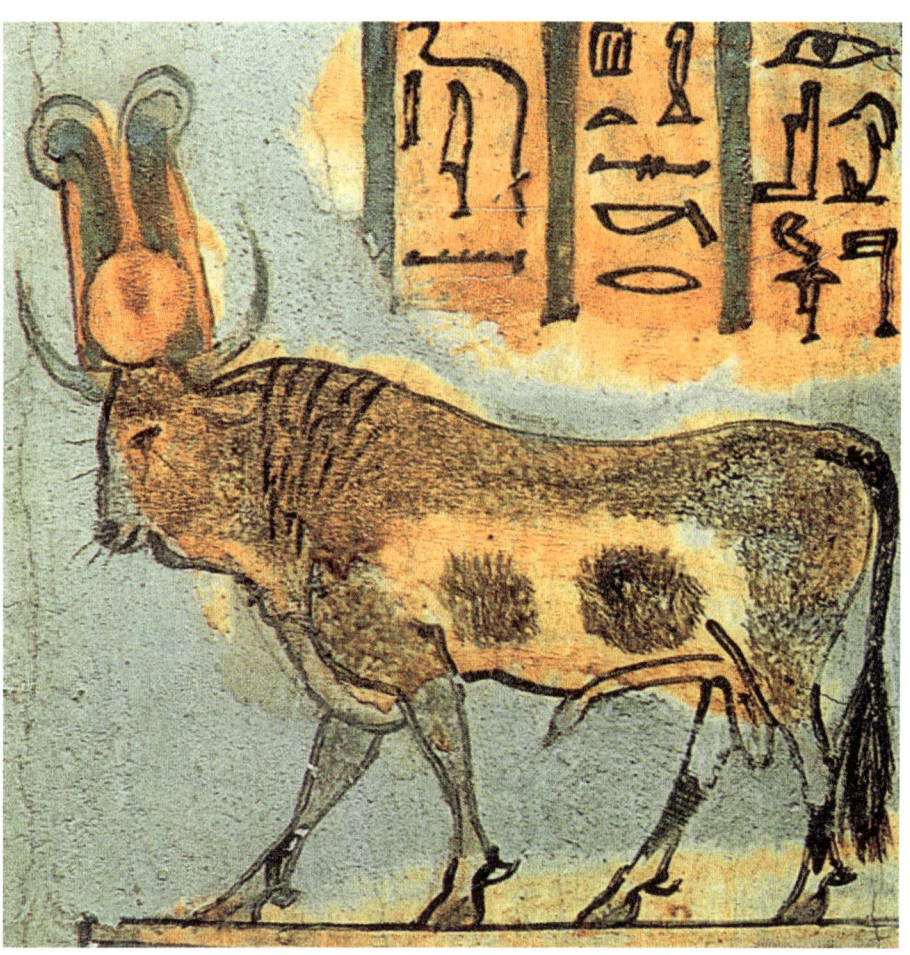

ABOVE

The Apis bull was consulted as an oracle at Memphis.

THE rulers of Egypt positioned themselves as mediators between gods and humankind, but they built a considerable official apparatus to bolster this, largely reliant on oracles that were accessed through priests. The role of priest in ancient Egypt was a regulated profession, and the most important priest was the High Priest of the Temple of Amun in Karnak (near the modern city of Luxor). This High Priest – also known as the First Prophet of Amun – interpreted the oracular decisions coming from the god.

At Siwa, western Egypt, the oracle of Amun – in the form of a statue of the god – was carried on a boat by eighty priests. The direction that the boat took as it swayed back and forth was interpreted as answering questions posed to the oracle.

At other Egyptian oracles, common people would ask questions, for example, seeking resolution in a dispute over ownership of cattle, and receive ritualized answers. Typically, the questions posed to an oracle were binary, necessitating a yes or no answer that lacked the depth of a prophecy or vision. In Memphis, a sacred bull known as Apis was used – it would choose between one of two doors to get to his favourite food, and the choice of door would indicate the will of the god. At some oracles, questions were answered by priests via a speaking tube, giving the impression that the gods themselves were answering.

GERMANIC SEERESSES

In Old Norse, female seers were known as *völvas*, which means 'staff bearers' and possibly references their carrying of magic wands.

REVELATION
Active

CHANNEL
Divine communication, Signs

INTERMEDIARY
Mystic

CONTEXT
Societal

LEFT

The seeress Veleda wielded huge power among her tribe in the first century CE and was famous even among her Roman enemies.

ABOVE LEFT

Yggdrasil, the vast ash tree that is central to Norse cosmology. The three Norns who control Fate live at its roots.

ABOVE RIGHT

A representation of Yggdrasil from a seventeenth-century Icelandic collection of Eddic writings that also contains the *Völuspá*.

THE Germanic religions (including the Norse traditions) of the north of Europe that were established by the mid-first millennium BCE, and survived in Sweden, Iceland and Norway until around 1000 CE, placed huge emphasis on fate, which neither humans nor gods could escape. Fate was created – spun into existence – by the deities called Norns, who sit at the base of the world tree Yggdrasil, which supports the universe with its branches. Understanding fate was a key theme of the mythology, and prophetic powers most often sat with seeresses or *völvas*. In the Old Norse poem *Völuspá* ('Prophecy of the *völva*') one such seeress, addressing the god Odin, foretells the destruction of the gods (see p. 304).

Völvas existed in real life as well as in mythology. Unearthed graves of seeresses in Sweden from the second half of the first millennium CE have shown that they were buried with their magic wands and hallucinogenic seeds. We know the names and stories of some of these early seeresses, mostly through their interactions with the Romans. The historian Cassius Dio records that one famous seeress, Ganna, from east of the River Elba, met the Roman emperor Domitian. In the second century CE, Waluburg, likely a student of Ganna, ended up at the First Cataract of the Nile in Egypt, as attested by an inscription on a pottery fragment. It has been speculated that she was there to interpret the swirling eddies of the river – something that seeresses were known to do.

THE SIBYLS

REVELATION
Active

CHANNEL
Divine communication

INTERMEDIARY
Mystic

CONTEXT
Societal

The sibyl with raving lips uttering things mirthless ... and unperfumed, reaches over a thousand years with her voice, thanks to the god in her.

Heraclitus, c. 500 BCE.

LEFT

Amalthea, the Cumaean sibyl, burns the Sibylline books when Tarquinius, the king of Rome, refuses her price.

LEFT

This fifteenth-century fresco blends two traditions by bringing together the Old Testament prophet Haggai and the classical Cumaean sibyl.

RIGHT

A medieval depiction from a Flemish prayer book of the twelve sibyls prophesying the birth of Christ.

SIBYLS – from the Greek *sibylla*, referring to a 'prophetess' – are semi-mythical figures associated with specific shrines. The very first sibyl is recorded by Pausanias (writing over a thousand years later) as living in Delphi as early as the eleventh century BCE. By the first century BCE there were approximately ten of them, according to the Roman historian Varro, spread across the Mediterranean at sacred sites. The most famous were the Cumaean, Delphic and Persian sibyls. The latter, also sometimes called the Hebrew sibyl, foretold the coming of Alexander the Great.

The Sibylline Books, a collection of prophecies, were purchased from the sibyl of Cumae by the semi-legendary last king of Rome, Tarquinius Superbus (534–509 BCE) and consulted in times of peril. When initially he refused the high price she was asking for, she burned six of the nine books. He then paid the same price for the remaining three books. The books seem to have existed in real life and were kept in the Temple of Jupiter on the Capitoline Hill until they were destroyed in a fire in 83 CE.

Renaissance artist Michelangelo included the sibyls in his fresco for the Sistine Chapel ceiling, where they are alternated with Old Testament prophets. It was believed that the Tiburtine sibyl had foretold the birth of Christ.

ABOVE AND OPPOSITE

A series of sibyls by Lucas van Leyden, *c.* 1530. Top row, left to right: Tiburtine sibyl, Libyan sibyl, Samarian sibyl, Delphic sibyl, Phrygian sibyl, Hellespontine sibyl.

Bottom row, left to right: European sibyl, Agrippine sibyl, Erythraean sibyl, Cumaean sibyl, Persian sibyl and a depiction of Ecclesia Christi, or the Christian Church.

PYTHIA

REVELATION
Active

CHANNEL
Divine communication

INTERMEDIARY
Oracle

CONTEXT
Official

Pythia, the title of the priestess of the Temple of Apollo at Delphi, derives from an epithet of Apollo who was said to have killed the mythical snake Python at Delphi.

LEFT

Lycurgus, legendary lawgiver of Sparta, consults the Pythia on the laws that he wanted to implement.

ABOVE LEFT

Orestes seeks sanctuary at Delphi, with the tripod and the oracle visible behind, c. 330 BCE.

ABOVE RIGHT

The theatre at Delphi with the ruins of the Temple of Apollo, home of the oracle, just beyond.

WHILE Delphi is famous for the sibyl, it is perhaps even more famous for the priestess known as the Pythia. While the sibyl was semi-mythical, the Pythia was very real – the two roles are frequently conflated since they were both strongly associated with the god Apollo.

A suitable candidate for the Pythia should be over the age of fifty and of relatively virtuous life, however she was not required to be an existing priestess and could come from common origins. She inhabited an underground chamber in the Temple of Apollo and sat on a three-legged stool, or tripod, over a fissure in the floor from which volcanic vapours emanated. It has been speculated that her 'powers' came from inhaling these vapours.

On one auspicious day per month (on one occasion a Pythia died after working on an inauspicious day), she received guests one at a time and would be consulted on a huge range of topics: family matters, plague, war, politics and religion. She would then give an answer which was often cryptic – and sometimes poetic.

BABALÁWOS

REVELATION
Active

CHANNEL
Tool

INTERMEDIARY
Priest

CONTEXT
Official

A *babaláwo* (literally 'father of secrets') is a priest in the *Ifá* system of divination in the Yoruba culture of West Africa.

LEFT

An *Ifá* divination vessel used to communicate with Orunmila, the *orisha* (divine spirit) of wisdom and prophecy.

ORACLES & SEERS

ABOVE LEFT

In the divination ritual, nuts or other items are cast onto a tray.

ABOVE RIGHT

The resulting arrangement is interpreted by a *babaláwo*.

BABALÁWOS help humans understand their destiny and make good decisions. The priest communicates through divination with Orunmila, who in turn communicates with the Olodumare, the high god. The process of divination itself involves either the casting of palm nuts or *opele* chains strung with shells, mango seeds or metal pieces. These objects are cast onto a special round wooden tray. If chains are used, then the chain is cast twice, and the orientation of the chains or items (known as an *odu*) is interpreted against a set of sacred verses, the *odu* corpus. The *babaláwo* is highly trained and needs to learn a staggering number of verses: there are 256 possible *odu* each with multiple verses associated with it.

ORACLES IN INDIA

REVELATION
Active

CHANNEL
Divine communication

INTERMEDIARY
Oracle

CONTEXT
Societal

The Malayalam word *velichappadu* translates as 'the one who sheds light' or 'the bringer of light' and refers to individuals who mediate between deities and religious devotees in Kerala.

LEFT

The goddess Bhadrakali being worshipped by the three principal gods of Hinduism: Brahma, Vishnu and Shiva.

RIGHT

An ecstatic temple oracle at the annual Kodungalloor Bharani festival in Kerala, dedicated to the goddess Bhadrakali.

BELOW RIGHT

A Theyyam ritual dance at a temple in Kerala.

SOME of the best-known oracles in India are the Velichappadu of Kerala in southwest India. In a tradition that may go back as many as three millennia, these oracles are typically dedicated to the goddess Bhadrakali. Made up of both women and men, they have long hair, dress in red, wear bells and carry sickle-shaped swords.

The Velichappadu can be found around Hindu temples. Through dancing, drumming and convulsive movements, they go into trances which they see as being possessed by god. Those keen to ask them questions can put coins on their swords, and in return worshippers receive (often cryptic) utterances. The responses sometimes require interpretation from assistants.

In the North Malabar region of Kerala, we find Theyyam (meaning 'incarnation of god') oracles. In this ritual performance, after fasting and prayer, artists transform themselves into incarnations of different Hindu deities. Accompanied by drums and chanting they dance ecstatically and sometimes make pronouncements on behalf of the god they represent. Today these popular rituals are held nightly over the winter, with the precise time often set by astrologers.

THE JAPANESE BUREAU OF DIVINATION

REVELATION
Active

CHANNEL
Signs, Tool, Celestial

INTERMEDIARY
Priest, Mystic

CONTEXT
Official

The *Onmyoryo* (Bureau of Divination) was a government ministry created in 676 CE to oversee divinatory practices in Japan. It was eventually outlawed in 1870 as superstition.

IN many cultures diviners work for the ruling powers, but in Japan this was taken to a new level. The *Onmyoryo* was made up of three parts: the *Onmyodo* (Bureau of Yin-Yang), *Tenmondo* (Bureau of Astronomy and Astrology) and *Rekido* (Bureau of Calendar Studies). The office also used *I Ching* divination (see p. 256), brought from China in the seventh century, and was staffed by civil servants called *onmyoji*. This official bureau existed alongside Shinto priests who would perform *bokusen* (plastromancy or tortoise-shell divination).

The most famous *onmyoji* was Abe no Seimei. An astrologer and magician of the tenth century CE, his job was to analyse strange occurrences, and he was gifted in divining the sex of unborn children. Legend has it that he was part *kitsune* (fox spirit), giving him supernatural powers, and he successfully predicted the abdication of Emperor Kazan in 982. Today he has become a popular figure in manga and anime.

OPPOSITE

Abe no Seimei, the most famous practitioner of magic and divination in Japan.

MERLIN

REVELATION
Active, Passive

CHANNEL
Divine communication, Signs

INTERMEDIARY
Mystic

CONTEXT
Personal

> Woe unto the Red Dragon, for his extermination draweth nigh; and his caverns shall be occupied of the White Dragon that betokeneth the Saxons whom thou hast invited hither. But the Red signifieth the race of Britain that shall be oppressed of the White.
>
> Merlin prophesies a war between the Britons and the Saxons, Geoffrey of Monmouth, *History of the Kings of Britain*, c. 1136.

THE story of Merlin, a powerful wizard and prophet, first appeared in Geoffrey of Monmouth's *Prophecies of Merlin* from 1130. Likely a conflation of early stories about the Welsh prophet Myrddin (who is said to have lived in the sixth century) and Ambrosius Aurelianus (a figure mentioned in a sixth-century work by Gildas), it was full of cryptic utterances that were said to have been translated from another (unspecified) language. It gripped the public's imagination to the point that the prophecies were believed as widely as French astrologer Nostradamus's were some four hundred years later.

Later stories added more and more lore to Merlin, as in *History of the Kings of Britain*, which includes the story of Merlin interpreting a vision of two dragons fighting each other. Over time such accounts attributed his future-seeing gifts to God and associated him ever more closely with the legendary King Arthur, whose birth and downfall Merlin had foreseen.

ABOVE

Merlin explains the prophecy of the dragons to King Vortigern in a fifteenth-century manuscript.

TIBETAN ORACLES

REVELATION
Active

CHANNEL
Divine communication

INTERMEDIARY
Oracle

CONTEXT
Official

In Tibet, oracles are men and women possessed by 'mundane' (meaning non-eternal) spirits who speak through their hosts. This is not a vocation chosen by the hosts, but rather they are chosen by the deity.

LEFT

The Nechung oracle wearing the heavy headdress used during divine possession.

RIGHT

The Nechung Monastery, located near Lhasa, is the home of the most important Tibetan oracle.

ORACLES, meaning spirits that temporarily inhabit a human body, have been an integral part of Tibetan culture for centuries. After the spirit enters the body there is violent shaking, and the voice of the host often changes dramatically. Typically, an oracle will wear a very heavy headdress – that of the Nechung oracle weighs around 14 kilograms (31 pounds). With the spirit speaking through them, what the oracles say is often unclear and can require a translator.

The Nechung oracle is the most influential, existing as part of the retinue of power in Tibet since the mid-seventeenth century, and the one consulted by the Dalai Lama. The possessing spirit is Pehar Gyalpo, who gives the host superhuman strength. The oracle answers questions posed to him directly. The second most powerful oracle is the Gadong oracle, whose possessing spirit is said to reside in a well until it inhabits a human body.

II.

OMENS & PORTENTS

HUMANS have often tried to understand the future by looking for signs in the present, working on the assumption that the physical world is closely linked to the supernatural world. These signs could be subtle and very well hidden – for example, in the entrails of an animal – or obvious, such as in the weather or night sky. And while the word 'omen' may have negative connotations today (as in the word 'ominous'), it can herald positive or negative news.

II

THE first documentary evidence of the interest in omens can be found in ancient Mesopotamia, in compendia such as the *Barutu* ('Art of the diviner'), which was written in the seventh century BCE, though it built on practices from the Old Babylonian period (*c*. 1894–1595 BCE). From Mesopotamia, these compendia made their way all over South Asia and the Middle East and eventually to the Mediterranean civilizations, perhaps prompting Moses to warn in the Old Testament against anyone 'who practices divination or is a soothsayer, or an augur, or a sorcerer' (Deuteronomy 18:10).

Of particular interest to the Mesopotamians was the weather. The *Enuma Anu Enlil* ('When [the gods] Anu and Enlil …'), a collection of omens from the mid-second millennium BCE inscribed on tablets, has many weather interpretations, covering cloud formations, thunder, lightning, rainbows, rain, fog and mist. Aeromancy – the name given to this sort of divination from atmospheric conditions – was also popular among the Etruscans in Italy (*c*. 900–200 BCE). However, the same phenomenon can have very different interpretations in different cultures. For example, for the Inca of Peru (early thirteenth to mid-sixteenth centuries) a rainbow was a bad omen.

On some occasions, signs may present themselves without being sought, their drama making them difficult to ignore. Into this category fall unusual phenomena such as comets, rainbows, eclipses or aberrations in the natural order of things. Congenital anomalies, called 'prodigies', were regularly seen as a warning of something terrible about to happen. A child born in early 1512 in Italy, known as the 'Monster of Ravenna', was seen as forewarning of the coming loss in the Battle of Ravenna. A comet, now known as Halley's Comet after English astronomer Edmund Halley, was sighted in 1456 and considered a bad omen everywhere from Italy (where it was associated with the fall of Hungary to the Turks) to Kashmir (where the poet Shrivara believed that it presaged the death of a sultan). The same comet had already previously been associated with the death of King Harold of England in 1066. Another comet seen by the Aztecs in the early 1500s was seen as foreshadowing the

TOP

An Etruscan model of a liver used in the interpretation of omens from entrails (haruspicy).

ABOVE

Fragment of a commentary on the *Enuma Anu Enlil* catalogue of omens.

downfall of their empire – and it wasn't the only warning of the impending Aztec doom. In 1510 Nezahualpilli, king of neighbouring Tetzcoco, had warned the Aztec emperor Moctezuma II that the empire would be threatened. Moctezuma, not believing him, challenged Nezahualpilli to a ball game, but when Moctezuma lost, he took it as a bad omen. Over the years leading up to the Spanish conquest of the Aztecs in 1519 there were several more omens including columns of fire, comets and temples destroyed by fire and lightning.

While omens are important in religion and mythology, they also find a place in day-to-day superstition. For example, the Romans believed that a broken mirror would bring seven years' bad luck; having your feet swept over by a broom in South America means that you will remain single for the rest of your life; and getting an itchy left palm in the Caribbean means that you will soon be receiving money. The same can apply even to days: Friday the 13th is widely seen as unlucky in the West (though in Italy it is Friday the 17th that is seen as unlucky), while in Japan there is a rotating six-day calendar that dictates which time of each day is lucky or unlucky. In China, copies of the Imperial Calendar or *Tung Shing* are often consulted before making momentous decisions and have existed in their current state since the Qing dynasty (1636–1912). They are used mostly for determining auspicious dates for key events such as marriage, signing contracts and starting new ventures. Today, *Tung Shing* can be consulted in the form of an app – while the form of omens and their place in society may evolve over time, the superstitious part of our brains remains active.

OPPOSITE

Nezahualpilli telling Moctezuma II of Mexico of the omens presaging the downfall of the Aztec Empire.

ABOVE RIGHT

Illustrations of disasters and 'monstrosities' associated with two comets sighted in 1456.

56 · II

COMETS

REVELATION
Passive

CHANNEL
Signs

INTERMEDIARY
Any

CONTEXT
Societal, Personal

Sightings of the comet now known as Halley's Comet, named in 1758 for English astronomer Edmund Halley, have been regularly identified in historical records since around 240 BCE.

OMENS & PORTENTS

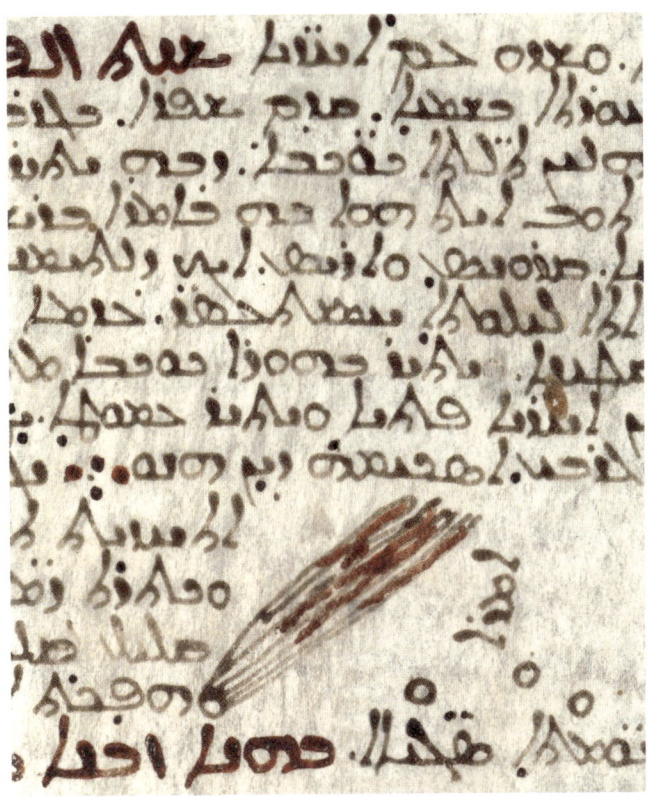

ABOVE

A photo of Halley's Comet from 1910.

OPPOSITE

Halley's Comet in 1066, as depicted in the Bayeux Tapestry from the late eleventh century, was seen as heralding the death of King Harold of England.

ABOVE LEFT

Halley's Comet depicted in a late eighth-century CE Syriac manuscript.

OF all the celestial phenomena, comets are among the most spectacular. Their appearance in earlier eras triggered dread and fear, in part because they followed paths that were so apparently unpredictable and unlike the stars. As a result, almost everywhere, from Mesoamerica to China, comets were seen as foretelling disaster.

Halley's Comet appears approximately every seventy-five to seventy-six years. In 12 CE it was believed to foretell the death of Roman general Marcus Vipsanius Agrippa, while its appearance shortly before the Battle of Hastings in 1066 was seen as a bad omen (and indeed the English king Harold was killed in the battle). It was sighted again in 1456, prompting the Italian writer Bartolomeo Platina to remark in his *Lives of the Popes* that 'a ... fiery star having then made its appearance for several days, the mathematicians declared that there would follow grievous pestilence, dearth and some great calamity'. The same comet was also seen at the same time in Kashmir, where the poet Shrivara believed that it signalled the demise of Sultan Zayn al-Abidin.

ABOVE AND OPPOSITE

Watercolours from a 'Comet Book' of 1587, which drew on sources including Ptolemy and Abu Ma'shar al-Balkhi.

RAINBOWS

REVELATION
Passive

CHANNEL
Signs

INTERMEDIARY
Any

CONTEXT
Societal, Personal

The rainbow is associated with the gods of many cultures and has a place in most mythological traditions, variously representing a bow, a bridge or a snake.

LEFT

Rainbows circling the sun as seen in Nuremberg in 1580 were taken as presaging a change of regime.

OMENS & PORTENTS

ABOVE LEFT

God, depicted as a hand, makes his covenant with Noah under a rainbow, marking the end of the Flood.

ABOVE RIGHT

Ngalyod the Rainbow Serpent, 1985, by Aboriginal Australian artist John Mawurndjul.

FOR the Maori of present-day New Zealand/Aotearoa, rainbows were associated with the spirit Uenuku and considered an omen – a war party would be defeated if a rainbow appeared above it. In Australian Aboriginal cultures a rainbow is associated with the Rainbow Serpent, a deity who can be both life-giving and desctructive.

One of the Irish names for rainbow, *tuar ceatha*, means 'rain-shower omen'. In the Book of Genesis in the Bible, a rainbow is God's guarantee of future peace, and in many Western traditions the appearance of a rainbow is a good time to make a wish. However, in areas as far-spread as South East Asia, South America and parts of Africa, despite its cheerful colours, a rainbow could signify an impending death or bloodshed – a predominance of red in the rainbow is a particularly bad sign. This was certainly the case in 651 BCE, when a rainbow was seen as foreshadowing the defeat of the Babylonian king Shamash-shum-ukin in conflict with his brother Ashurbanipal.

ECLIPSES

REVELATION
Passive

CHANNEL
Signs

INTERMEDIARY
Any

CONTEXT
Societal, Personal

There was an eclipse throughout England ... the obscuration of the Sun also was so remarkable, that persons sitting at table ... at first thought that Chaos was come again ... It was thought and said by many, not untruly, that the King would not continue a year in government.

William of Malmesbury, *Historia Novella*, 1140.

LEFT

A page from an Aztec manuscript showing a solar eclipse in Mexico in 1496.

ABOVE LEFT

A lunar eclipse depicted in a fifteenth-century astrology manuscript.

ABOVE RIGHT

Tinnin, the dragon who swallows the sun during an eclipse, analogous to Rahu in Hindu mythology. From a seventeenth-century Iranian manuscript.

AROUND the world eclipses are frequently seen as a powerful harbinger of doom. For the ancient Greeks an eclipse marked the beginning of difficult times, a sign of the gods' displeasure, while for the Incas it heralded the death of a prince. In England it was also taken as a bad omen, especially after Henry I died in 1135, just two years after a solar eclipse in 1133.

However, since eclipses are unavoidable, ways to counter their negative effects were developed. For Hindus an eclipse was a bad omen caused by the sun being swallowed by the *asura* Rahu. Mantras would be chanted to ward off the evil. In the Babylonian catalogue of omens *Enuma Anu Enlil* it was stated that so long as the planet Jupiter was visible during the eclipse the king would not be at risk. A unique ritual was used by the Assyrians: that of the *šar pūhi* ('substitute king'). To avoid any harm coming to the king, during a lunar eclipse, a commoner would be appointed and dressed as king for the period of the eclipse, while the real king went into hiding. After the eclipse the substitute king would be sacrificed, thereby appeasing the gods.

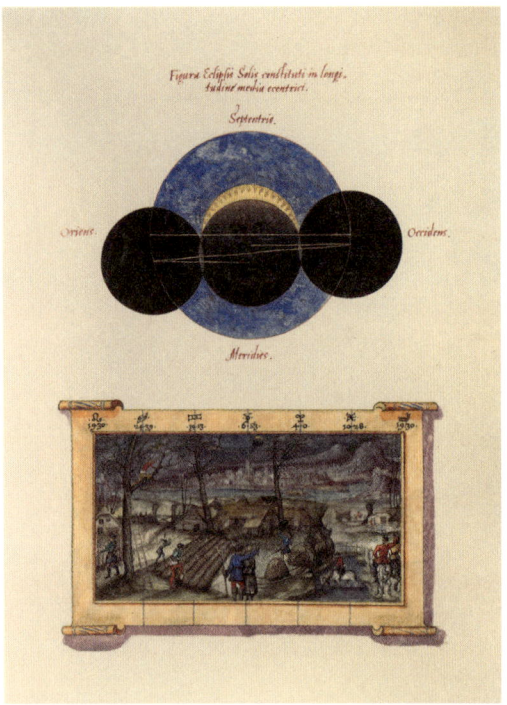
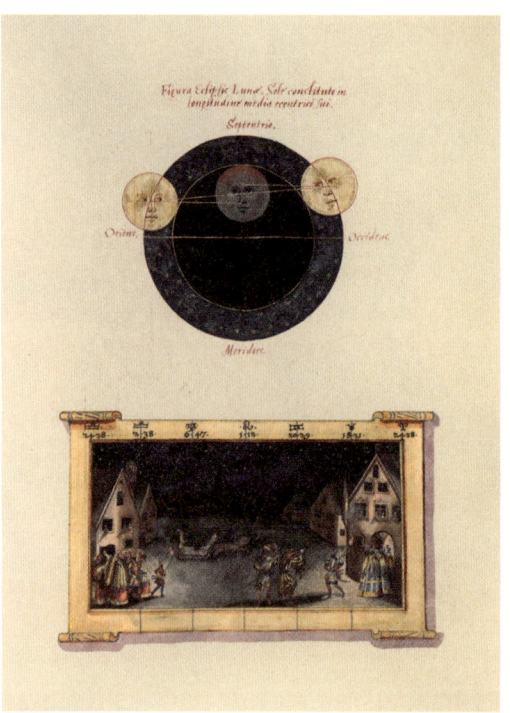
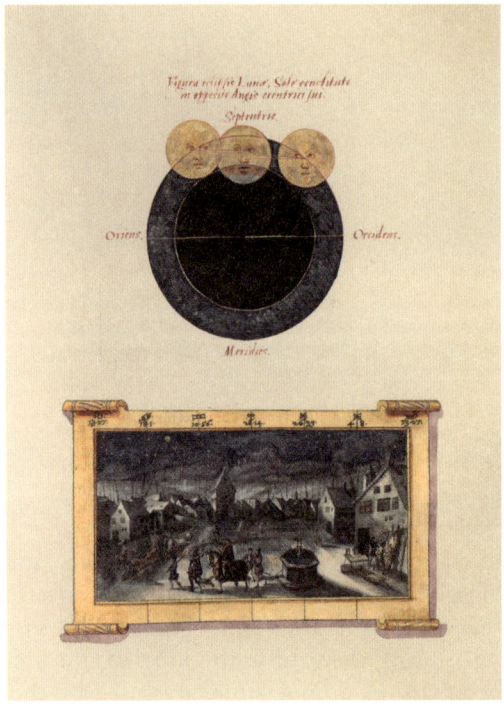

ABOVE AND OPPOSITE

Figures from Cyprian Leowitz's *Eclipses luminarium*, 1555, predicting eclipses up to 1600.

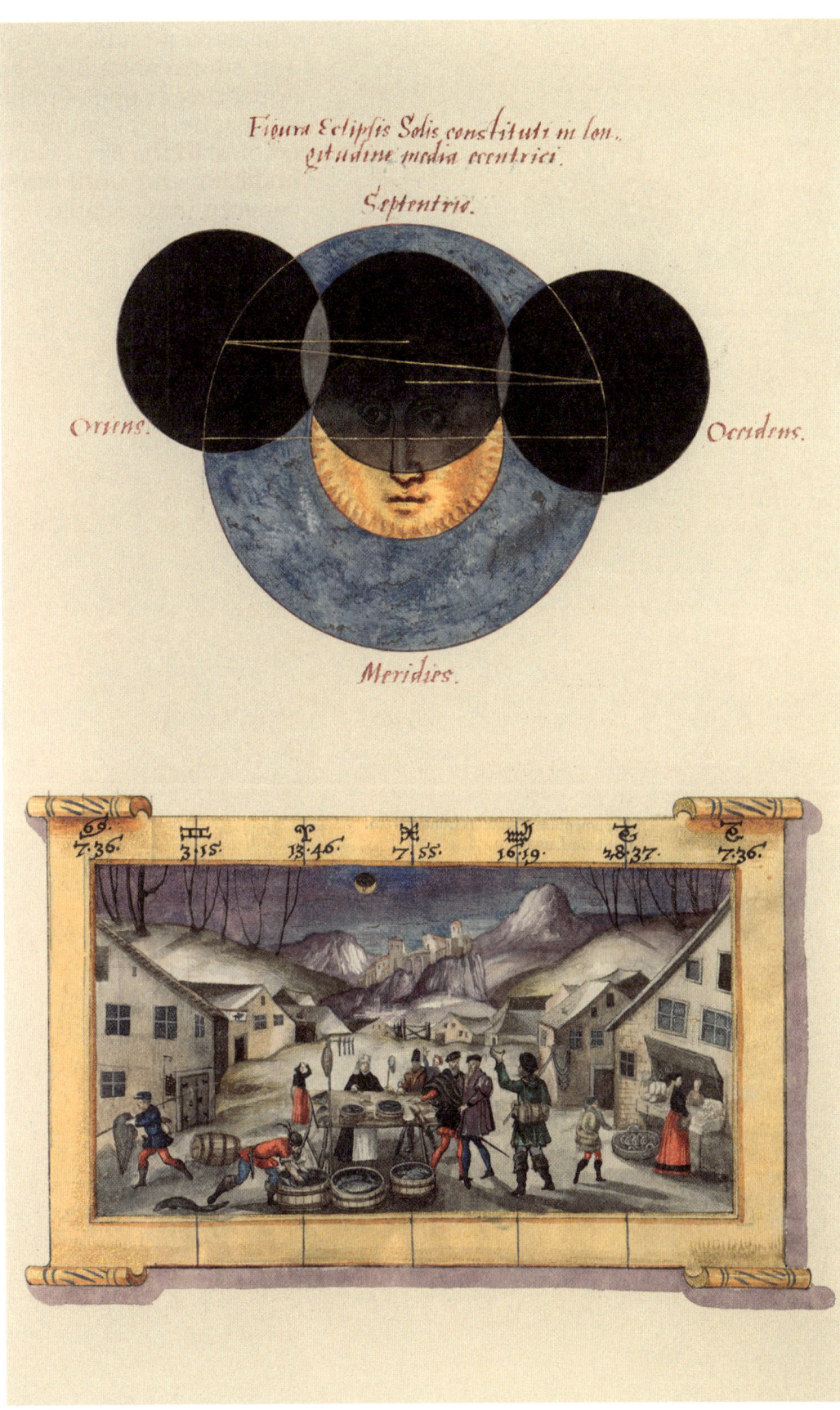

AURORAS

REVELATION
Passive

CHANNEL
Signs

INTERMEDIARY
Any

CONTEXT
Societal, Personal

The aurora borealis (Northern Lights) and aurora australis (Southern Lights), appearing at opposite poles, are atmospheric phenomena of swirling colours in the sky, beautiful, awe-inspiring and, until the nineteenth century, inexplicable.

LEFT

Aurora Borealis, 1865, by Frederic Edwin Church alluded to the fact that auroras were seen to portend a Union victory in the American Civil War.

RIGHT

Given the awesome nature of the aurora australis it is easy to understand why auroras were seen as omens.

ALMOST all cultures that live in the vicinity of auroras have sought meaning in them – and the meaning is typically negative. For the indigenous Sami people of northern regions of Norway, Sweden, Finland and Russia it was a bad omen that couldn't even be mentioned. They also believed that whistling at the Northern Lights would bring unwanted attention and misfortune. For the Maori of Aotearoa the lights were the campfires of ancestors, while for the Dieri people of southern Australia they were seen as a warning from an evil spirit.

Where the Northern Lights were less common, they were seen as a sign of something about to happen. Red light effects in particular were interpreted as coming war and bloodshed. For example, in the late eighteenth century, the Northern Lights were visible in England shortly before the French Revolution. Then a spectacular and unexpected display sighted across the United States in 1859 was believed to herald the American Civil War. A report from a newspaper in South Carolina in that year explains that the bells were rung, and people ran through the streets shouting 'day of judgment'.

BIRD OMENS

REVELATION
Passive

CHANNEL
Signs

INTERMEDIARY
Any

CONTEXT
Societal, Personal

Birds have long been studied to understand the future, perhaps because they inhabit the sky and therefore are seen as being closer to the metaphysical, leading to the distinct discipline of ornithomancy.

LEFT

Owls are often seen as evil omens, as seen in this print from Goya's series 'Los Caprichos', 1799.

ABOVE LEFT

Placing offerings on poles to omen-birds in Sarawak, Malaysia, where some communities believe that birds are messengers from spirits.

ABOVE RIGHT

St Athanasius predicts the future by the flight and scratching of crows.

RECORDS of Hittite bird oracles survive from as early as the thirteenth century BCE, in which the flight of birds was interpreted as communication of the will of the gods. The ancient Greek word for omen, *oionos*, also meant 'bird' and in the Greek epic the *Iliad* Calchas, a seer for Agamemnon, is called *oionopolos* or 'bird diviner'. He foretold that the Greeks would take Troy after ten years of war when he observed nine sparrows devoured by a serpent. In Greek mythology, Athena gave the blind seer Tiresias the gift of being able to receive prophecies from birdsong.

Different types of birds have their own omens: seeing or hearing an owl is bad luck in China and Sri Lanka, Roman author Pliny the Elder called it a 'direful omen' in his *Natural History*, and in the sixteenth century Shakespeare used owls to foretell death in *Macbeth* and *Henry VI*. In India seeing a peacock in the morning is auspicious, but at night is regarded as bad luck. In medieval Europe it was widely considered that peacock feathers were unlucky, with peacocks sometimes associated with the Devil. In other places they are believed to ward off the Evil Eye (bad luck cast on someone by another who wishes them ill). For mariners, to kill an albatross was seen as bad luck, since the giant sea birds were believed to hold the souls of dead sailors.

ABOVE AND OPPOSITE

A Hindi compendium of different birds and the omens associated with them. In Sanskrit, the antecedent of the Hindi language, the word for omen – *sakuna* – also means bird.

OMENS & PORTENTS

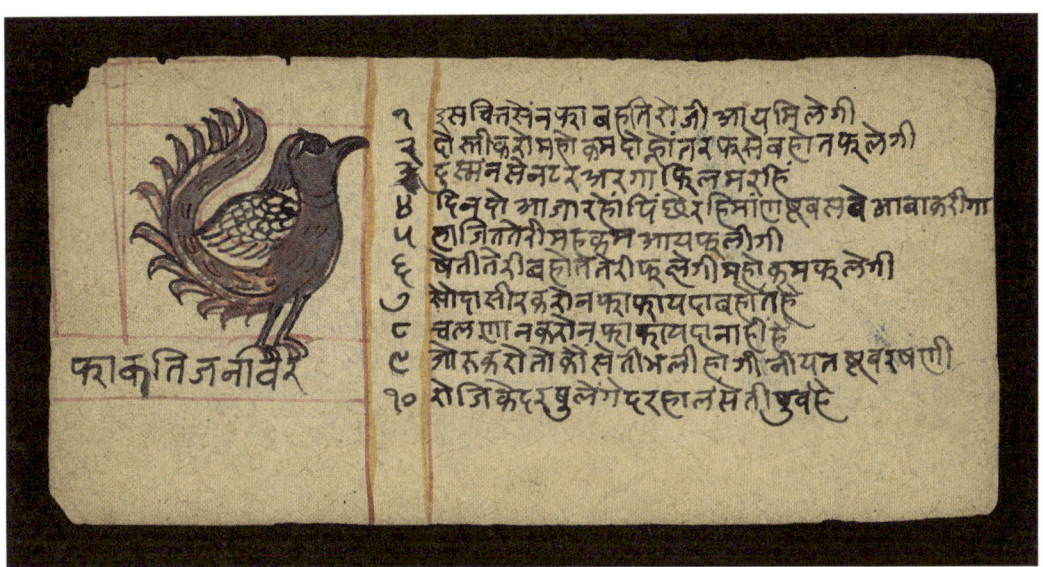

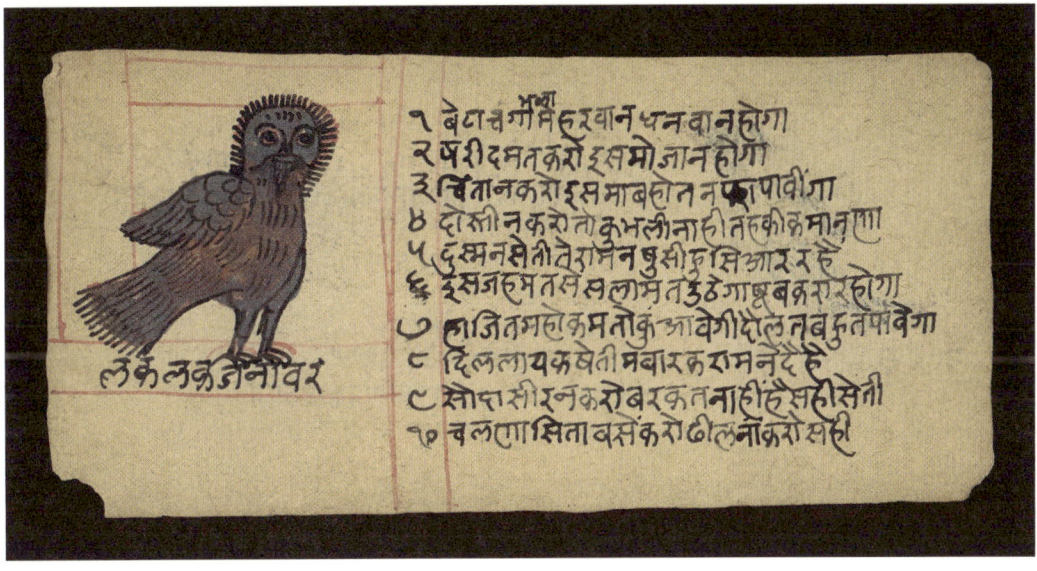

SNAKE OMENS

REVELATION
Passive

CHANNEL
Signs

INTERMEDIARY
Any

CONTEXT
Societal, Personal

If a snake lies on a man's bed, the man's wife will ... sell her children for money.

Omen from the *Shumma alu*, an Akkadian collection of cuneiform tablets.

SNAKES have a long association with prophecy, going back at least as far as ancient Egypt, where there was a renowned oracle at Per-Wadjet dedicated to the goddess Wadjet, who was often depicted as a cobra. In fact, snakes could have a range of meanings, sometimes associated with sovereignty and sometimes with chaos. One of the earliest sets of animal omens can be found in the Akkadian *Shumma alu* ('If a city is set at a height'), a collection of cuneiform tablets from ancient Mesopotamia. It covers pigs, cows, scorpions and lions, among other animals. But one of the most prominent animals in the *Shumma alu* omens is the snake – natural considering the ubiquity of snakes in that region. It offers remarkably clear outcomes for remarkably specific situations.

However, over time snakes got a more sinister reputation, in part due to the fact that they lived underground. Just as birds were closer to the gods, underground-dwelling creatures were closer to the underworld (at least this was how the Greek writer Artemidorus saw it in the second century CE). In Thailand, when King Rama I founded the capital of Bangkok in 1782 he erected a pillar to mark the centre of the new city. However, as the pillar was being lowered into its hole, four snakes slithered in and were crushed. Diviners and astrologers were summoned to explain the significance; the consensus was that this was a very bad omen. Seven years passed with nothing terrible happening – until 1789, when the Great Palace was struck by lightning and burned to the ground. The astrologers were again summoned and this time declared that the dynasty would last only 150 years. In 1932, the Siamese revolution brought absolute monarchy to an end.

OMENS & PORTENTS

ABOVE LEFT

The serpent-woman Cihuacoatl warning of the impending destruction of the Aztec empire, from the sixteenth-century Florentine Codex.

LEFT AND ABOVE RIGHT

The cobra is a symbol of the Egyptian goddess Wadjet, whose oracle was widely consulted.

ABOVE AND OPPOSITE

Pages from a 'Book of Wonders', containing a catalogue of animals mentioned in the Quran and their associations, including the meaning of dreams about certain animals.

PHYSIOGNOMIC OMENS

REVELATION
Passive

CHANNEL
Signs

INTERMEDIARY
Any

CONTEXT
Societal, Personal

> The woman having lines in her palm resembling a goad, a circle or a wheel, marries a king and gives birth to a son.
>
> *Garuda Purana*, an Indian text containing collections of bodily marks and their meanings.

OMENS & PORTENTS

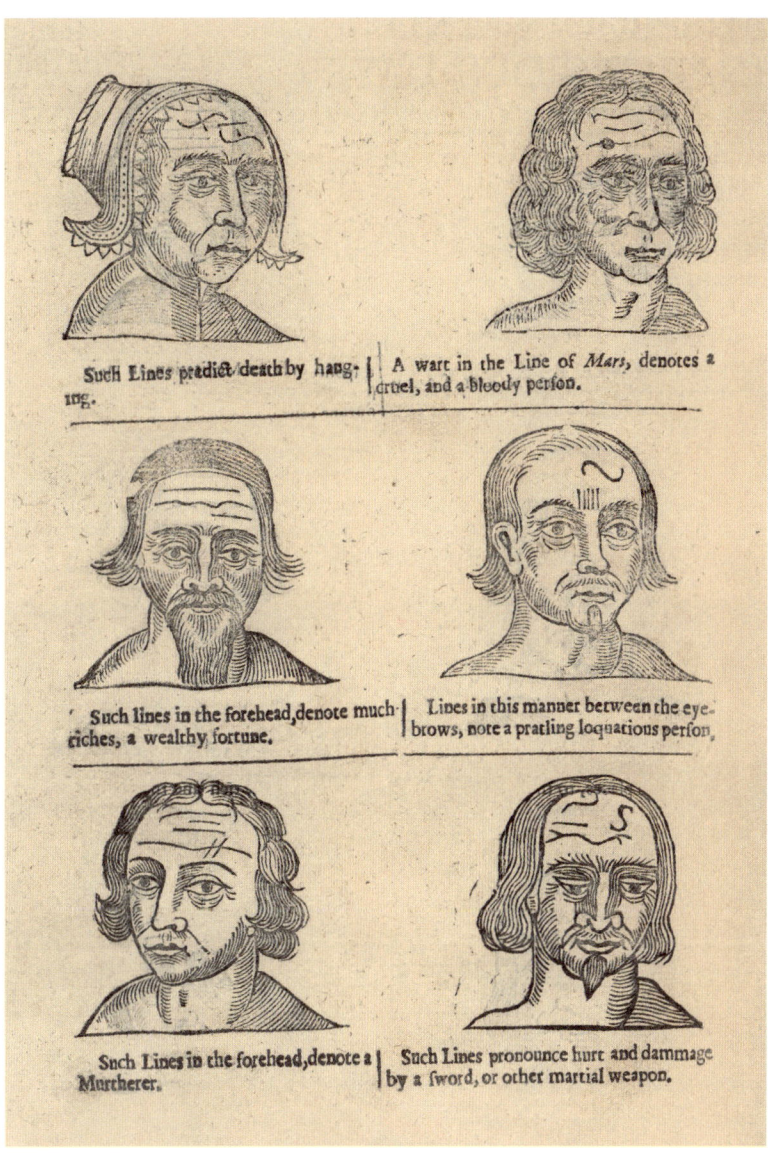

OPPOSITE

Analysis of facial features from a Thai fortune-telling manual, c. 1845.

ABOVE RIGHT

An English treatise, 1671, lists outcomes based on the position of moles and lines on the face, including, top left, 'Such lines predict death by hanging'.

HUMANITY has frequently been tempted to read something into people's features, characteristics and behaviour. This likely originated in ancient Mesopotamia as seen, for example, in the Akkadian text *Shumma sinnishtu qaqqada rabat* ('If a woman has a large head'). Later it was linked by the Greeks and Romans to theories of human tempers and humours, and astrology. In his *Natural History*, Pliny the Elder mentions practitioners of metoposcopy who could predict how long someone might live by studying the lines on their forehead.

In China there is the concept of *mien shiang* (face reading). For Taoists, the face records the past, reflects the present and predicts the future. With this technique, which is still sometimes used today, faces are analysed according to the principles of *wuxing* ('the five phases': Water, Earth, Fire, Metal and Wood). When a reading is conducted, every part of the face is studied, down to wrinkles, blemishes and bone structure. The upper part of the face is said to reflect an individual's fortune while young; the middle part of the face (eyebrows to the bottom of the nose) reflects their fortune between the ages of twenty and forty; and the bottom part of the face reflects their fortune when over forty.

AUSPICIOUS AND INAUSPICIOUS DAYS

REVELATION
Active

CHANNEL
Celestial

INTERMEDIARY
Any

CONTEXT
Societal, Personal

Hemerology is the name for the process of determining good and bad days for embarking on some new adventure – for example, starting a journey or getting married.

LEFT

A Tibetan chart indicating good and bad days for blood-letting.

RIGHT

The *Tonalpohualli* or 'day count' calendar was used in Mesoamerica to determine lucky and unlucky days.

OVERLEAF

A page from the Aubin *Tonalamatl* ('book of the days'), used by Aztec priests in divination rituals and containing the *Tonalpohualli*.

IN India, astrologers are still consulted to choose a wedding date, with the couple's horoscopes checked. In the case that one of them is born under the malign influence of Mars – *mangala dosha* – they are first 'married' to a tree, to ensure that the bad luck doesn't go to their actual spouse. In Chinese-speaking countries an auspicious wedding date is picked using the *Tung Shing* (the Imperial Calendar), while in Japan some patients will ask to be discharged from hospital on a lucky day.

There are also clearly inauspicious days. In many parts of the world Friday the 13th is seen as unlucky (harking back to Christ being killed on a Friday and there being thirteen people at the Last Supper); however, in Mexico it is Tuesday the 13th that is said to be unlucky. In China, dates containing the number four are avoided (since 'four' sounds like the word for 'death'). In Thailand, Wednesday is an inauspicious day to get a haircut, although there is disagreement as to why. Some believe that it is because only the king should have his hair cut on a Wednesday, while others believe that Wednesdays are associated with agriculture, and therefore one should be growing, not cutting.

The Aztecs were very keen observers of calendars. Diviners used their 260-day calendar or *Tonalpohualli* ('counting of the days') to determine when crops should be sown or harvested, or what sort of luck a person might have depending on when they were born.

ABOVE

How they Met Themselves, c. 1850/60, by Dante Gabriel Rossetti. Meeting one's double was traditionally seen in many countries as an omen of death.

SUPERSTITIONS AROUND THE WORLD

Belief in good and bad omens still persists around the world, even if they are usually dismissed as superstitions. Nevertheless, it speaks to a lingering concern with what the future may hold.

✠

SOME AUSPICIOUS OMENS FROM AROUND THE WORLD

CHINA
If bats nest in your home, you will become wealthy

THAILAND
Seeing a white elephant

TURKEY
Dreaming of scorpions

VIETNAM
If your first customer spends well, business will be good

SIOUX, CHEROKEE, COMANCHE AND NAVAJO
If you encounter a white bison, it means that change is coming

✠

AND SOME BAD LUCK OMENS FROM AROUND THE WORLD

A CUNEIFORM TABLET FROM 850 BCE
Eating garlic in the seventh month of the year could risk a death in the family

EUROPE
Seeing your doppelgänger, or 'double'

THAILAND
Hearing a gecko during the day

PREVALENT AT LEAST AS FAR BACK AS ANCIENT ROME
Spilling salt

JAPAN, THAILAND AND TURKEY
Whistling at night

ABOVE AND OPPOSITE

This pocketbook was likely used by astrologers in India to decipher the meanings of encountering different animals.

III.
PROPHETS & PRIESTS

From the rich cultural mix of ancient Mesopotamia emerged a set of religions that gradually transitioned from polytheistic roots to a belief in a single god complemented by a group of intermediaries that they called 'prophets'. These religions, all emerging between the eastern Mediterranean and modern-day Iran, included Judaism, Zoroastrianism, Christianity, Manichaeism and, later, Islam, and they were to change how we thought about the future.

OPPOSITE

St John, author of the Book of Revelation, hearing the voice of God on Patmos.

THE figure of the prophet in the religions of the Near East was that of go-between or intermediary. The English word 'prophet' is derived from the Greek meaning 'forth-teller' or 'interpreter', and in Akkadian the word *nabu* used for a prophet means 'announcer', while in Hebrew the equivalent is *navi*, meaning 'spokesperson'. These figures connect the physical and metaphysical realms, speaking on behalf of the supernatural. They speak of the future, although not exclusively. Prophets can have what would appear to be supernatural powers, and their advice and counsel is sought, but they are not themselves divine (and their power typically comes from God). This is perhaps typified in the figure of Moses, revered today as a prophet in Judaism, Christianity and Islam, who caused miracles to happen, and who was the intermediary to whom God entrusted the tablets inscribed with the Ten Commandments.

While the prophets of the Bible tend not to deal explicitly in the future – and indeed there is no standard approach to prophecy throughout the Bible – there are many examples in the Bible of future-telling. In the first five books, called the Torah in Judaism, there are frequent prohibitions against consulting mediums and practising divination. In part this was likely a response to the practices of neighbours in ancient Mesopotamia (such as the Babylonians and Assyrians), where future-telling rites and oracles were an integral part of the governance of the region. There is a sense of the Israelites trying to differentiate themselves from the belief systems of surrounding lands.

The later religion of Christianity, meanwhile, sees the Bible as being full of prophecies that point to the coming of Jesus Christ as the Messiah, a long-promised leader and saviour. To Christian eyes, the Old Testament came

ABOVE LEFT

In the Old Testament it is prophesied that the Messiah would come from the family tree of Jesse – here depicted as an actual tree.

ABOVE RIGHT

The Prophet Muhammad and the archangel Jibra'il (Gabriel) ascend through the Heavens.

to be seen more and more as presaging the New Testament, and the figure of Christ was seen as the fulfilment of earlier prophecies. For this reason, the word 'prophet' started to be associated with those specialized in future-telling. This also initiated a tradition of reading the scripture for hidden meanings that could tell the future. This reached its zenith in the Middle Ages with a fascination with discovering 'types' or echoes between the Old and New Testaments and the belief that, to paraphrase St Augustine, the New Testament is concealed in the Old and the Old Testament is revealed in the New. The conviction that Jesus would one day return to Earth (and in all likelihood quite soon) also led to a preoccupation with the future that continues to this day.

The Bible also has examples of apocalyptic literature – the word coming from the Greek *apokalupsis*, meaning 'revelation'. This sort of writing focuses on the end of the world and is often vivid in its imagery. It can be found in the Book of Daniel (written later than other Old Testament books, probably in the second century BCE), which covers a vision of the future of Nebuchadnezzar, king of Babylon, and the prophetical dreams of Daniel that seem to foretell the destruction of the world. However, the book most focused on the future in the Bible is the New Testament Book of Revelation, also known as the Book of the Apocalypse. Attributed to an author known as John of Patmos writing in the first century CE, it details the coming end of the world in spectacular fashion, with a seven-headed dragon, the Four Horsemen of the Apocalypse and the Second Coming of Jesus. It laid the template for all subsequent Christian apocalyptic writings.

The last of the major Abrahamic religions to take shape was Islam, founded following a series of revelations to the Prophet Muhammad in the seventh century CE. Strongly monotheistic, in Islam the role of the prophet evolves yet again into that of guide. In total, twenty-five prophets are named in the Quran, including many figures also revered as prophets in Judaism and Christianity, such as Yusuf (Joseph), Musa (Moses), Suleyman (Solomon) and Isa (Jesus). While Islam condemned future-telling in general as *haram* (forbidden) from early on, over the years it found an accommodation with certain forms of divination that are divinely inspired, such as bibliomancy using the Quran (see p. 240).

RIGHT

The prophet Moses receives the Law on Mount Sinai.

ABOVE AND OPPOSITE

Scenes from the life of Christ as foretold by the sibyls, from a manuscript titled *The Sibyls and Prophets Foretelling Christ the Saviour*, c. 1490.

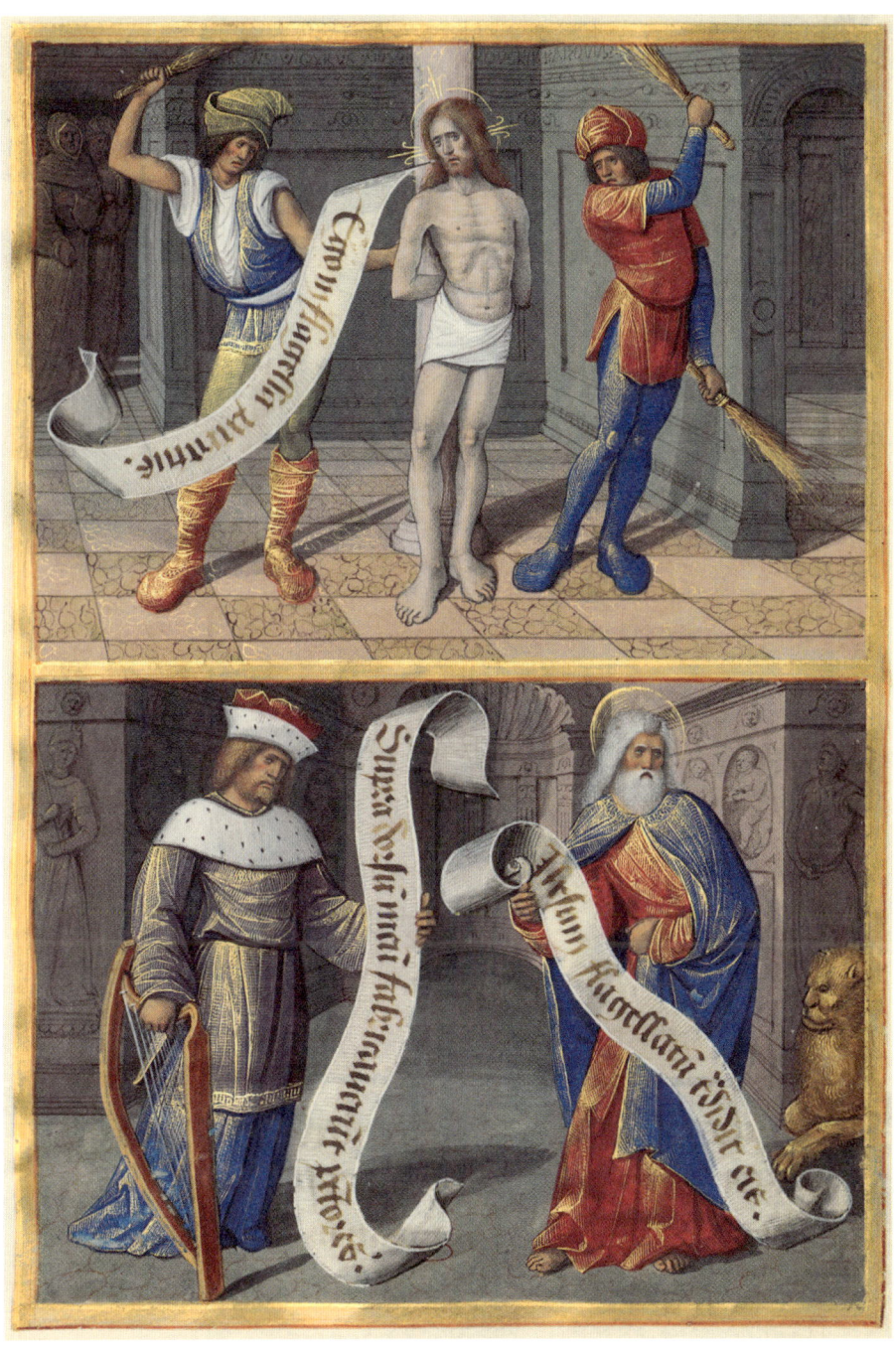

ORIGINS

REVELATION
Active, Passive

CHANNEL
Divine communication, Signs

INTERMEDIARY
Priest, Oracle

CONTEXT
Official

The female ecstatic arose in the temple of Annunitum, saying: 'Zimri-Lim [king of Mari], do not go on campaign! Stay in Mari …'

Cuneiform tablet from the palace of Mari, early second millennium BCE.

THE role of 'prophet' as familiar today in Abrahamic religions has its origin in the polytheistic cultures of Mesopotamia, such as the Akkadians, Sumerians and Babylonians. Written records of prophecies have been found at Mari (in present-day Syria) from the eighteenth century BCE and Nineveh (present-day Iraq) from the seventh century BCE. These records are a mixture of reports of what prophets had said (notably seen in the so-called 'Mari Letters', which document the process as well as the message) and accounts of what prophets did (mostly at the later site of Nineveh, as part of the Library of Ashurbanipal).

The political and the religious were tightly connected in ancient Mesopotamia, with state-sanctioned priests also acting as oracles. There were two classes of priest concerned with divination: *sa'ilu* (askers) and *baru* (observers). In addition, there was a lower class of seer, known as *mahhu*, that would also deal in magic. This last class was precisely what the Bible had in mind when it condemned fortune-telling (see p. 17).

RIGHT

A statue of an attendant god dedicated to the god Nabu – *nabu* ('announcer') is related to the Hebrew *navi*, meaning prophet.

III

LEFT AND OPPOSITE

Tablets from the Library of Ashurbanipal at Nineveh relating to omens and prophecy.

ZOROASTER

REVELATION
Passive

CHANNEL
Divine communication

INTERMEDIARY
Prophet

CONTEXT
Official

> Zoroaster was the first figure to articulate the idea that all humans would suffer an individual judgment after death, being sent either to heaven or to hell.

FOUNDED by the prophet Zoroaster (Zarathustra in the local language today called Avestan), the Persian religion of Zoroastrianism probably dates back to the seventh and sixth centuries BCE and is thought to be the earliest monotheistic religion. Little is known about Zoroaster – in the foundational texts called the *Gathas* he described himself as a 'poet-priest' and 'prophet'.

In the Zoroastrian view, as outlined in the ninth-century CE *Bundahishn*, the end of the world will come when it is hit by a comet called Gochihr (sometimes also referred to as a dragon). This will cause the world to be flooded with molten metal, purifying the sinful while the righteous remain unharmed. There will come a saviour (*Saoshyant*), who will put an end to cruelty, end death and raise the dead. This renewal was called *Frashokereti*, and many of these concepts were later incorporated into other religions. It is likely that Zoroastrian thought influenced the writings on apocalyptic themes found in the Hebrew Bible, in texts such as the Book of Daniel, ultimately informing the apocalyptic thinking of Christianity and Islam too.

OPPOSITE

On the left, two Zoroastrian figures worship at a fire altar – fire represents purity, the coming destruction and rebirth.

ABOVE AND OPPOSITE

A late eighteenth-century Persian manuscript of an earlier Zoroastrian text called the Book of *Arda Viraf*. During a dream-like journey through the afterlife, the narrator witnesses various tortures.

ABRAHAM TO MALACHI

Fifty-five prophets steer the history of Judaism, starting with Abraham in the Book of Genesis and ending with Malachi.

REVELATION
Passive

CHANNEL
Divine communication

INTERMEDIARY
Prophet

CONTEXT
Official

IT was with the emergence of Judaism that the role of the prophet as seer, guide, visionary and interpreter of the divine became fully formed. Moses stands out as the receiver of the Ten Commandments and the person who led the Israelites back to the Promised Land. As recorded in Deuteronomy 18:15, he also introduced the concept of the Messiah, the coming saviour, later assumed by Christians to be Jesus.

Predictions in the Hebrew Bible relate most often to the ultimate victory of Hebrew tribes against other local kingdoms, which was clearly a major concern for the readership at the time it was written. Not only that, but prophecies are frequently conditional on correct behaviour – there are no guarantees as to outcomes. Prophecy could be used against Israel, as when Balaam was sent by King Balak of Moab to curse Israel (though in the end his prophecies are favourable to the Israelites).

Other, older forms of future-telling may be seen in the Hebrew Bible, for example, Ezekiel 21:21 discusses the casting of lots and consultation of entrails. The Bible frequently condemns such acts of divination (especially in the books of Leviticus and Deuteronomy) but does not deny their existence or efficacy. Reference to signs and portents can also be found in Jewish writings of the Second Temple era (516 BCE to 70 CE), although in general Judaism sees that period as being the death of authentic prophecy. The Jewish-Roman historian Josephus, writing in the first century CE, states that the fall of the Temple was preceded by various omens, including a comet and a cow giving birth to a lamb.

RIGHT

Balaam and the Ass, 1626, by Rembrandt. The diviner Balaam had been sent to curse the Israelites, but his donkey refused to carry him any further.

LEFT

Moses on Mount Sinai receiving the Ten Commandments.

ABOVE

Moses chooses seventy elders to help him lead the Israelites. God then bestowed his spirit on them, temporarily giving them power of prophecy.

CHRISTIANITY

REVELATION
Passive

CHANNEL
Divine communication

INTERMEDIARY
Prophet

CONTEXT
Official

> Do not think that I have come to abolish the Law or the Prophets; I have not come to abolish but to fulfil.
>
> Jesus to his disciples, Matthew 5:17.

CHRISTIANITY was a Messianic religion born at a time of upheaval and political unrest. Christians revered the prophets of the Hebrew Bible – especially if they seemed to point the way towards the coming of the Messiah. While Jesus was not seen as a prophet himself, and did not have the ecstatic visions typical of other prophets such as Joseph and Daniel, he predicted his own death and that his disciples would betray him.

There was in the books of the New Testament and early Church a growing concern with false prophets who could lead people astray. As a result, by the second century CE, acts of prophecy and ecstatic revelation were more and more frowned upon, with the focus instead being on the one major New Testament prophecy of the Second Coming of Christ at the end of the world. Inheriting much from the eschatology of Zoroastrianism and Judaism, early Christians lived in anticipation of the end times, which they believed would come in their lifetimes, starting with the apocalypse and leading to the Second Coming. This set in motion a trend that has continued throughout the entire history of Christianity, arguably leading to more prophecies and predictions than any other modern religion.

RIGHT

Angels sounding their trumpets – the seven trumpets each heralded a new phase of the apocalypse.

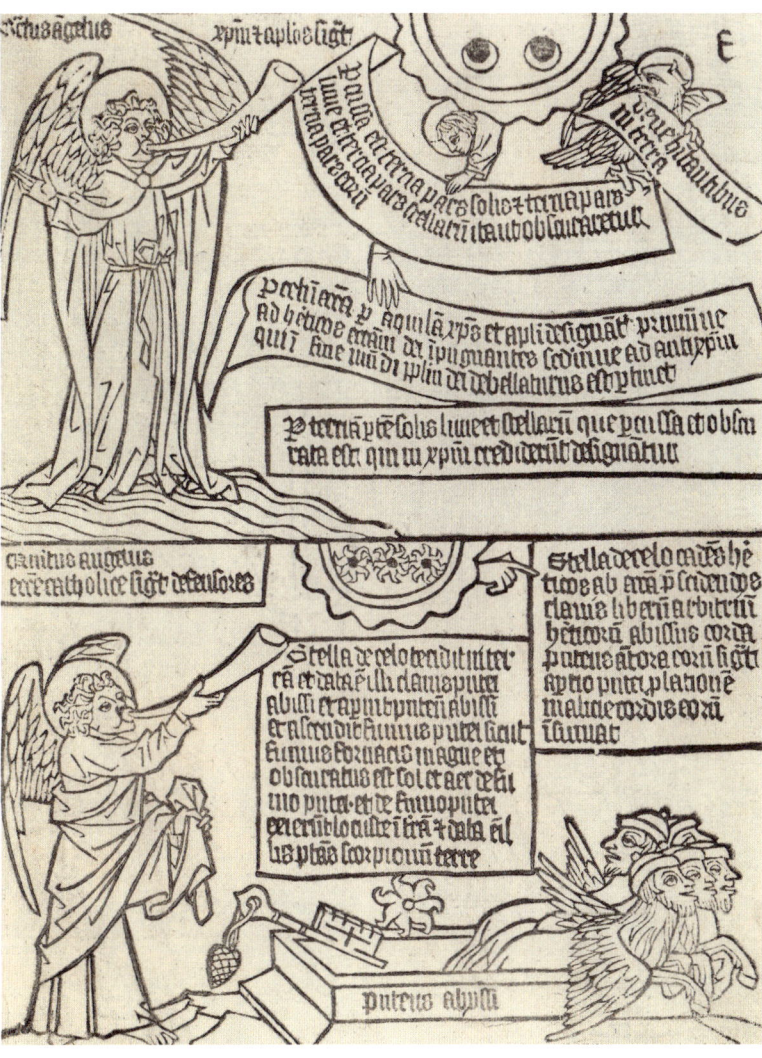

LEFT

The seven-headed beast of the apocalypse is worshipped by all the nations.

OVERLEAF

The Preaching of the Antichrist, a Christ-imitating figure with the Devil whispering in his ear. The coming of the Antichrist would be one of the final stages in the apocalypse and would precede the Second Coming of the real Christ.

ABOVE AND OPPOSITE

Illustrations of the signs of the apocalypse.

Top row, left to right: The Earth's waters sink; sea animals lament to heaven; the sea burns; buildings collapse; the stones fight each other; earthquakes occur.

Bottom row, left to right: The Earth is levelled; humans emerge from hiding places; the dead rise from their graves; the stars fall; all living humans die; the Earth and sky burn.

MONTANUS

REVELATION
Active, Passive

CHANNEL
Divine communication

INTERMEDIARY
Prophet

CONTEXT
Official

Montanism diverged from Christianity in placing particular emphasis on prophecy, vision and ecstasy.

BUILDING on the base of Christianity, Montanism emerged in Anatolia (modern Turkey) in the late second century CE, Montanism was named after its founder and self-declared prophet, Montanus (who, prior to his conversion, may have been a priest of the Greco-Roman god Apollo). Montanus and two key followers, Priscilla and Maximilla, would speak in tongues – a practice in which a person speaks in incomprehensible sounds and words that are supposedly a language not intelligible to the listener. Its adherents referred to the movement as 'New Prophecy', and it was especially influenced by the visions of John of Patmos outlined in the New Testament Book of Revelation. In anticipation of the end of times, many Montanists moved to the towns of Pepuza and Tymion, since they expected the Heavenly Jerusalem that John had decribed in Revelation to descend to Earth there.

The ecstatic and uncontrolled nature of the Montanists' prophecies put them on the fringes of Christianity: in the words of Christian scholar Eusebius, writing in the third century CE, Montanus 'became beside himself, and being suddenly in a sort of frenzy and ecstasy, he raved, and began to babble and utter strange things, prophesying in a manner contrary to the constant custom of the Church' (*Ecclesiastical History*). In fact, the Montanists believed that anyone could be a prophet and have an experience like this. As a result, they were widely seen as false prophets. None of their writings remain, and today they are known mostly through Christian works on heresy.

ABOVE

Tongues of fire descending onto the heads of the Apostles at Pentecost, causing them to speak in tongues – a practice picked up by the Montanists.

MANI

REVELATION
Passive

CHANNEL
Divine communication

INTERMEDIARY
Prophet

CONTEXT
Official

In the third century CE, adherents of Manichaeism believed that a figure known as Mani was the last prophet in a long line of prophets including Jesus, the Buddha and Zoroaster.

ABOVE

Manichaean priests in a ninth- or tenth-century manuscript from modern-day China.

MANI was born in present-day Iraq and grew up exposed to a wide range of beliefs, including Judaeo-Christian Gnosticism, Jainism and Buddhism. He established Manichaeism after receiving a vision, and the religion later spread as far as China. It saw the world as originally divided into light and dark, good and evil, but that the two sides had mixed, resulting in moral decay. The future, according to Mani, would see the restoration of the duality. The role of the prophet in Manichaeism is an important one, with Mani being a communicator with the beyond and revealer of secrets. He wrote seven books, none of which survives in its entirety.

ABOVE

Manichaean priests commemorating the martyrdom of Mani.

THE SEAL OF THE PROPHETS

REVELATION
Passive

CHANNEL
Divine communication

INTERMEDIARY
Prophet

CONTEXT
Official

In one of the Hadiths (accounts of the Prophet's teachings and sayings), Muhammad compares himself to the final missing brick – suggesting a long-held plan that was finally being brought to fruition.

LEFT

The prophet Yunus (Jonah to Christians) rescued by an angel from a fish in a sixteenth-century manuscript from Iran.

ABOVE

The prophet Ayyub (Job) visited by an angel.

THE tenets of Islam are built on a revealed text. The Prophet Muhammad, born in Mecca in around 570 CE, was visited by the angel Gabriel from around 610 CE onwards, and the revelations he received were compiled into a religious text today known as the Quran. Muhammad was the last prophet (the Seal of the Prophets) in a long chain stretching back to the first human being on Earth, Adam (who also appears in the Genesis creation story in the Jewish and Christian traditions).

Prophets in Islam typically either bring good news or warnings. Some prophecies can be found in the Quran and in the Hadiths. For example, the Quran predicts the ultimate victory of the Byzantines ('Romans') against the Persians in Jerusalem and the defeat of the polytheists in Mecca. In keeping with the other monotheistic religions, the Quran is largely opposed to other forms of future-telling such as divination. However, while belief in bad omens is forbidden, belief in good omens is acceptable.

ABOVE AND OPPOSITE

Portraits of the prophets laid out as a genealogical tree, showing (left to right): Daud (David), Sulayman (Solomon), Iskandar, Zakariyya (Zechariah), Yahya (John the Baptist) and Isa (Jesus); Ibrahim (Abraham), Ismail (Ishmael), Ishaq (Isaac) and Yaqub (Jacob); Idris (Enoch) and Nuh (Noah); Ilyas (Elijah), Khidr, Harun (Aaron) and Adhar.

THE BOOK OF MORMON

REVELATION
Passive

CHANNEL
Divine communication

INTERMEDIARY
Prophet

CONTEXT
Official

The religion of Mormonism was founded by Joseph Smith in the United States in the 1820s. Smith and his successors such as Brigham Young were seen as prophets who provided divine guidance to their followers.

JOSEPH Smith was born in a period of religious revival known as the Second Great Awakening to a farming family in New York state. In his early teens he received a series of visions of angels, and, in 1823, he discovered gold plates that had written upon them what is today known as the Book of Mormon. Smith translated the plates from what the book calls 'reformed Egyptian' using 'seer stones' that he referred to as Urim and Thummim (see p. 17). These texts, in addition to ongoing revelation, would determine how the Church of Jesus Christ of Latter-day Saints was organized and led.

Smith made many prophecies, some of which – believers argue – came true. It is claimed that he prophesied a conflict between the Northern and Southern states thirty years before the American Civil War happened. However, several of Smith's prophecies failed to come true, for example: his prediction that his son would translate the golden plates (his son died in infancy); or that a governor of Missouri would be killed (though some have linked Smith to the governor's attempted assassination).

ABOVE

The angel Moroni giving the golden plates to Joseph Smith.

THE BÁB AND BAHA'U'LLAH

REVELATION
Passive

CHANNEL
Divine communication

INTERMEDIARY
Prophet

CONTEXT
Official

Whereas many religions with Abrahamic roots predict a relatively violent end of times, the Baha'i faith predicted a coming golden age of humanity, starting from 1844.

ABOVE LEFT

Baha'u'llah in 1868.

ABOVE RIGHT

A *haykal* (pentagram), symbol of the Baha'i faith, written by the Báb.

THE Baha'i faith aims to unite various pre-existing faiths into a single philosophy. In the 1840s a Persian mystic, called the Báb, declared himself to be the first of two manifestations of God and prophesied the arrival of another divine prophet. This second prophet was Baha'u'llah (born in Tehran in 1817), who accepted his status after receiving a vision in 1844.

For believers, Baha'u'llah was fulfilling prophecies from a range of major religions, including Judaism, Christianity, Islam, Zoroastrianism, Hinduism and Buddhism. Baha'u'llah took to writing prophetical letters – called 'tablets' – to a range of important world leaders including Napoleon III, Queen Victoria and the Pope. These tablets predicted coming wars and presented the Baha'i faith as fulfilling the Old Testament prophet Zechariah's prediction of the rebuilding of the Temple of Jerusalem in the end of times.

IV

Καὶ προχύους φοῖ σύμπαλον ἐκχυθέντων
σὺ Ἰησ νίκης ἡ πλαδ'ας τὰς χεῖρας ὑμοείδως
Καὶ ῥαβδον ἄλλφας ἐνέλλιε τῦ σκηπίρου

IV.

PREDICTIONS & REVELATIONS

WHILE the Mesopotamian and Abrahamic religions fostered the concept of the 'prophet' as a point of connection between humankind and the divine, history shows that prophets are not the only ones privileged to see the future. Clairvoyants, seers and recipients of visions can be found around the world, and at all times, and frequently their fame is global.

OPPOSITE

A page from a compilation
of prophetic and philosophical texts.

THE figures associated with predictions and revelations share common elements. They are often encountered on the edges of society, perhaps due to temperament, disability, religious beliefs or vocation – and this is what allows them to connect with arcane knowledge. They are not always strictly historical: for example, while the sixteenth-century Vietnamese poet Nguyen Binh Khiem undoubtedly existed as a human being and is well documented, the many legends, myths and prophecies that have accumulated around him are likely later fabrications. In other cases, it is questionable whether these people ever existed at all, as with figures such as Mother Shipton, reportedly born in Yorkshire, England, in the late fifteenth century, or the Brahan Seer of seventeenth-century Scotland (who in all likelihood was the fabrication of a nineteenth-century folklorist). This takes nothing away from these figures' importance in the collective psyche, but their supernatural abilities have almost certainly been invented or exaggerated.

One of the oldest traditions of prophetic literature can be found from around the third century BCE onwards in China and grew into a considerable corpus. These oracular texts collectively called *chen* could come from visions and revelations, or from dreams, and were used extensively by Chinese emperors. The most famous example of early Chinese prophetic literature, the *Tui Bei Tu* (a collection of predictions for China's future), emerged in the seventh century CE. While prophecy fell out of favour over time, the tradition continued in works such as the *Shaobing Ge* ('Pancake poem'), which was purportedly written in the fourteenth century by Liu Bowen (though it may have been written much later, maybe even in the nineteenth century). It is believed by some to predict far-off events such as the Sino-Japanese wars of the nineteenth and twentieth centuries.

The fifteenth and sixteenth centuries were a golden age for prophecy and prediction, coinciding with a time of religious and political ferment in Europe. This was particularly true after the development of the moveable-type printing press by Johannes Gutenberg, which led to widely accessible publications aimed at laypeople. These included cheap-to-produce

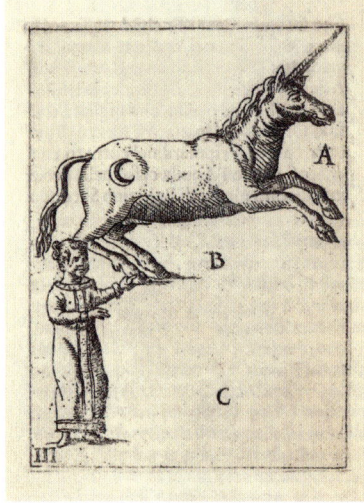

ABOVE, LEFT AND RIGHT

Two enigmatic illustrations likely derived from the *Oracles of Leo the Wise*, a collection of prophecies purportedly by the Byzantine emperor Leo VI. Many of these, however, are *vaticinium ex eventu* – prophecies written after the event they supposedly foretell.

RIGHT

Title page of a prophetic compilation including works by Paracelsus from the late 1540s. The two figures look to the heavens, showing the growing importance of astrology.

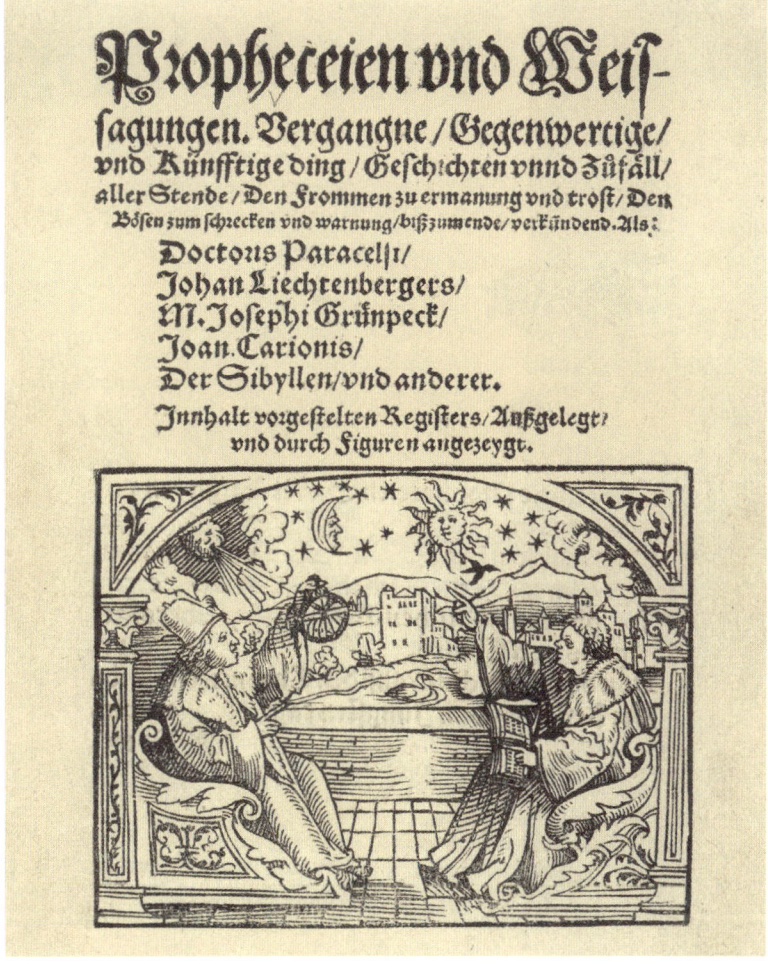

OPPOSITE

An allegorical figure of Pope Gregory XI in a collection of prophetic verses concerning the papacy, fifteenth century.

OVERLEAF

An English broadside ballad telling a tale of two men, who claimed to be over a thousand years old and prophesied the end of the world within nine years, c. 1680.

'broadside ballads' or books such as *Propheceien und Weissagungen*, which brought together various prophecies, including those of figures such as Paracelsus, and a text known as the *Prophecy of the Twelve Sibyls* (which attempted to show that the coming of Christ was foretold by the classical sibyls). Alongside this there was a growing market for *Wunderzeichenbücher* ('books of miracles') filled with omens, prodigies and strange signs.

The most famous example of a seer from that era was the French astrologer Nostradamus. His fame grew considerably in the nineteenth and twentieth centuries, which saw a huge growth in interest in the occult and mysterious, manifested in the vogue for gothic literature, spiritualism and séances and driven in large part by the decline of traditional religion. The popularity of astrology boomed in the twentieth century, especially in the United States where fortune-tellers such as Jeane Dixon became household names. Figures such as Nancy Reagan, wife of US president Ronald Reagan, turned to their favourite clairvoyants. Alongside this, the rise of science fiction led to ever more vivid imaginings of the future, some of which, such as androids, space travel, video communication, and self-driving vehicles, actually came true.

Today prophecy and predictions are a mainstay of books, film and TV. The *Game of Thrones*, *Lord of the Rings* and *Harry Potter* series and the *Star Wars*, *Matrix* and *Dune* films all rely on prophecy as a plot device. With entertainment arguably being the new religion, the attachment to prophecies and omens now lives on on the small screen.

The VVorlds VVonder.

Giving an Account of Two Old Men,

Lately known and seen in the City of *Tholouze* in *France*, who declare themselves to be above a Thousand Years old a peice, and Preach Repentance to the World; telling what shall happen for these Nine Years following, and when the World shall end.

Tune of, *My Bleeding Heart*.

STrange News to England lately came,
  the like I think was never known;
And if it proves a certain truth,
  'twill terror strike to hearts of Stone.

A City great there is in France,
  and Tholouze is it call'd by name;
Two Prophets there was lately found,
  invisibly they thither came.

No Man nor Child could ever tell
  which way these Prophets they came in,
They say that they were sent from God,
  to reprehend the World for Sin.

A Thousand years of Age, and more,
  each of them do declare to be;
Methuselah ne'r liv'd so long,
  as by the Scriptures you may see.

Gods Holy Spirit they declare
  into their Breasts inspired is;
In this our Age a thing so rare, (this.
  I think there's none more strange then

Strange kinds of habit they do wear,
  the like ne'r seen by mortal Eye;
And their deportment is as strange,
  although they Preach continually,

Good Admonition they do give,
  advising all Men to Repent;
They say this is the only cause,
  that they into the World were sent.

Gods Wrath against the Romans they
  do now declare is kindled hot;
And if with speed they dont Repent,
  their Crimes shall never be forgot.

The City of Tholouze, they say,
  to Sodom may compared be,
And in three Months shall be consum'd
  by Flames of Fire undoubtedly.

Except they do their lives amend,
  and quite forsake Iniquity;
Which do the People much amaze,
  for this is their continual cry.

The Magistrates offended were,
  at the strange Doctrine they did Preach;
But they reply'd they came from God,
  the sinful People for to teach.

At length there was an Order made,
  that they should close confined be;
With Jesuits they did discourse
  in several Tongues, most perfectly.

Their Dyet also was most strange,
  on Delicates they never fed;
Their Drink was only Water clear,
  their greatest Banquet was dry Bread.

And then the Magistrates did ask   (came?
  these Prophets strange, from whence they
Their answer was, from Gallilee,
  Galladium was their Cities name.

The Jesuits did then persuade
  the Magistrates, that they should go
To Rome to see his Holiness,
  that he the truth of all might know.

At this they nothing daunted were,
  for they declar'd they knew their doom;
And seemed to be mighty free
  for to go see the Pope at Rome.

But being Fetter'd then with Chains,
  at which they seem'd to make a scoff;
They much amaz'd the People all,
  for with great ease they shook them off.

They Prophesie in Eighty-One,
  there shall be Troubles over all:
In Eighty-Two they do declare,
  the Pope of Rome shall have a Fall.

In Eighty-Three throughout the World,
  they do declare, that Preach they shall:
In Eighty-Four, that Jesus Christ
  shall without doubt be known to all.

In Eighty-Five there shall arise,
  one that shall mighty be with Men:
In Eighty-Six an Earthquake shall
  much terrifie the World agen.

In Eighty-Seven, Africa
  shall quite consumed be by Fire;
In Eighty-Eight, the World amaz'd,
  in Eighty-Nine, the World expire.

FINIS.

Printed for *F. Coles, T. Vere, J. Wright,*
J. Clarke, W. Thackeray, and *T. Passinger.*

TUI BEI TU

REVELATION
Passive

CHANNEL
Divine communication

INTERMEDIARY
Mystic

CONTEXT
Personal

The *Tui Bei Tu* (meaning literally 'back-pushing pictures') is an unusual and famous collection of prophetic literature concerning the future of China.

PREDICTIONS & REVELATIONS

OPPOSITE AND ABOVE

A Qing-dynasty copy of the *Tui Bei Tu*.

THE *Tu Bei Tu* was supposedly written by the Chinese astronomer-astrologers Yuan Tiangang and Li Chunfeng in the seventh century CE, and it is said that the peculiar name comes from when Yuan Tiangang pushed Li Chunfeng's back to encourage him to go to bed, saying: 'We cannot afford to reveal more of heaven's secrets – let's go to sleep.'

The book contains around sixty illustrations with prophecies and poems, most likely derived from the sixty-four hexagrams of the *I Ching* (see p. 256), which is a foundational text for so many Chinese works on astrology and divination. The texts are very cryptic and could be interpreted in multiple ways, in a fashion not dissimilar to the writings of Nostradamus. Over time it has evolved, with parts being added and removed and illustrations gradually changing. Because it is believed to predict the rise and fall of various Chinese dynasties, it has often been politically sensitive.

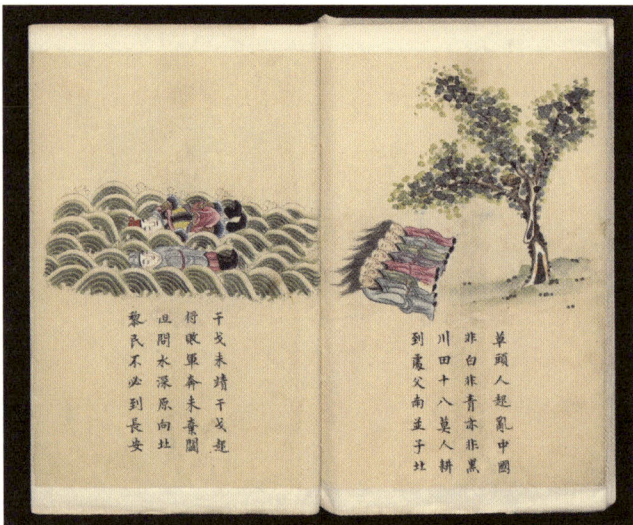

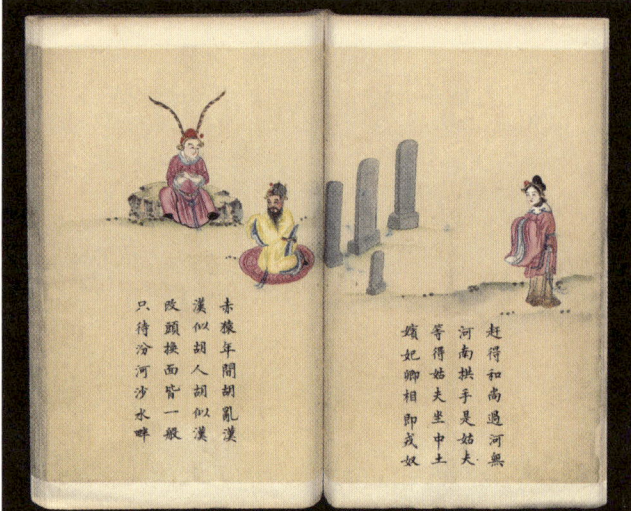

ABOVE AND OPPOSITE

In the *Tui Bei Tu*, each illustration is accompanied by a prophetic verse.

此時卻怕乙頭彼
口稱我是白頭翁
有一武人身帶弓
手邊門裏伏金刀
無事離家入帝宮

日月龍虎水火現
人被山兩神鬼知
十八孩兒興胡戰

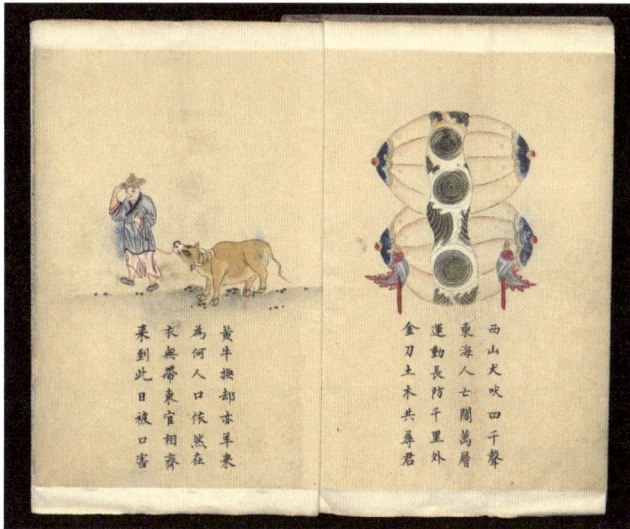

西山犬吠四千聲
東海人亡閙萬層
金刀木共尋君
運動長防千里外

黃牛換卻木羊來
為何人口依然在
長無蕃東宜相養
來到此日被口害

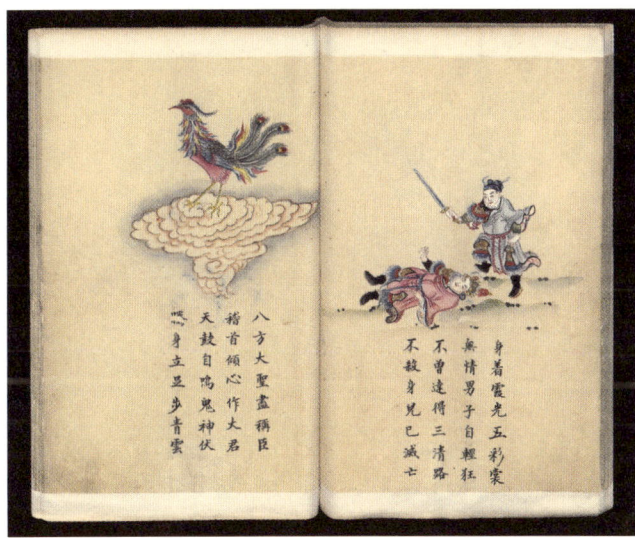

八方大聖盡稱臣
稽首傾心作大君
天鼓自鳴鬼神伏
搖身立旦步青雲

身著霞光五彩裳
無情男子自輕狂
不曾走得三清路
不彼身兒已滅亡

一箇真人受天紀
提拿鑾胡卽位
母子號泣喪英雄
拉火中間方能配

秦川得人何曾生
父于東西受空弓
卻降天使一二人
並時授東一時破

HILDEGARD OF BINGEN

REVELATION
Passive

CHANNEL
Divine communication

INTERMEDIARY
Mystic

CONTEXT
Personal

Also known as the Sibyl of the Rhine, Hildegard of Bingen embarked on four preaching tours in Germany between 1158 and 1170 and attracted large crowds.

LEFT

Hildegard of Bingen receiving divine inspiration, from her work *Scivias*, twelfth century.

PREDICTIONS & REVELATIONS

ABOVE LEFT

Hildegard of Bingen's vision of the human being and the heavenly spheres, *Book of Divine Works*, c. 1230.

ABOVE RIGHT

A vision of 'Wisdom and the Ancient Counsel before the City of God', *Book of Divine Works*, c. 1230.

THE abbess Hildegard of Bingen was a prolific composer, philosopher and scholar during the twelfth century. She is often credited as the founder of the discipline of natural history in Germany, especially through her work *Physica*. However, today she is best known for her visions, which attracted the attention of the Pope and made her famous in her lifetime. Starting when she was three, these visions continued her entire life, and she documented them in three illustrated prophetic books.

While Hildegard's visions weren't solely about the future, she did comment in her book *Scivias* that 'I would relate future things which I saw as if present'. Her visions and prophecies covered the creation of the world and the Second Coming of Christ. They were broadly apocalyptic in nature, building on the Book of Revelation and foretelling the trials and tribulations of the future, including the division of the Church. Her writings were spread across Europe particularly through a compilation of her prophecies known as the *Pentachronon*, or *The Book of Five Times*, and they continued to have influence for the entire medieval period and up to the Reformation in the sixteenth century.

JAYABAYA THE JAVANESE PROPHET KING

REVELATION
Passive

CHANNEL
Divine communication

INTERMEDIARY
Mystic

CONTEXT
Personal

Somewhat unusually, Jayabaya was both a prophet and a king, who ruled the Kediri kingdom in East Java (in what is now Indonesia) from 1135 to 1159.

JAYABAYA supposedly wrote many predictions of the future, some quite specific, such as the invention of planes and automobiles. However, it is also likely that much of what has been attributed to him was written by later authors. There are no surviving editions from before the mid-nineteenth century; however, some of the prophecies clearly echo language from the Mahabharata, which arrived in Indonesia around 1000 CE. Among these are famous passages describing the arrival of a king in a 'time of madness' when society is falling apart.

The prophecies became especially popular in the nineteenth and twentieth centuries, during the colonial occupation of Indonesia by the Dutch. They were seen as foretelling the eventual liberation from colonization with the arrival of the *Ratu Adil* ('just king'). After Indonesia declared independence in 1945, the first president, Sukarno, commissioned a book entitled *The Role of the Jayabaya Prophecies in Our Revolution* (1950), in the preface of which he praised the role of the prophecies in overthrowing the Dutch by giving hope for the future and a strong cultural identity.

PREDICTIONS & REVELATIONS 133

ABOVE LEFT

A twelfth-century Kediri, East Java, sculpture of Vishnu; Jayabaya was believed by some to be an incarnation of Vishnu.

ABOVE RIGHT

A 1932 edition of the book allegedly written by Jayabaya.

NOSTRADAMUS

REVELATION
Passive

CHANNEL
Divine communication

INTERMEDIARY
Mystic

CONTEXT
Personal

> The blood of the just shall be wanting in London,
> Burnt by fire of three and twenty, the Six,
> The ancient Dame shall fall from her high place,
> Of the same Sect many shall be killed.
>
> Century I, Quatrain 51,
> said to predict the Great Fire of London.

MICHEL de Nostredame, better known as Nostradamus, was born in Provence, France, in 1503. He initially aspired to be a physician but abandoned his degree. After a period working as an apothecary (and supposedly inventing a cure for the plague), he undertook a doctorate from which he was expelled, since apothecaries were considered to belong to a forbidden trade. He became interested in the occult and astrology and in 1550 published an almanac, which contained his earliest prophecies, largely focused on weather, war and potential uprisings. These brought him considerable attention from the French nobility, including the queen, Catherine de' Medici, who commissioned him to cast horoscopes for her children. However, surviving horoscopes drawn up by Nostradamus suggest that he had a limited understanding of the principles of astrology, and frequently made miscalculations. In 1555 he published the first edition of the book that would make him world-famous, *Les Prophéties*, which was released in several expanded forms until two years after his death in 1568.

Nostradamus explains in his preface that the work includes prophecies up to the year 3797. It is written in quatrains, four lines of verse, grouped into collections of one hundred quatrains called 'centuries'. Some parts of it are heavily influenced by other compilations, especially various classical sources and the *Mirabilis Liber* compilation of Christian saints' prophecies published in 1522. Nostradamus's quatrains are written mostly in French (though also incorporating some elements of Latin, Greek and Provençal) and are generally cryptic, yet vivid and visceral:

> Slit in the belly, [a creature] shall be born with two heads,
> And four Arms, it shall live some years,
> The day that Aquilare shall celebrate his Festivals,
> Fossan, Thurin, chief Ferrare shall run away.
>
> Century I, Quatrain 58

LEFT

The frontispiece to an early edition of *Les Prophéties*.

BELOW

A fantastical imagining of Catherine de' Medici consulting with Nostradamus on the box of a twentieth-century board game.

This passage combines specific detail with a lot of vivid abstraction, and, though it is impossible to say definitively what is being prophesied here, it reflects a concern with disasters and the potential invasion of Europe by the Ottomans. Some have also suggested that this passage predicts the rise of Napoleon.

It is this vagueness combined with evocative imagery and mystical language that has given Nostradamus's predictions such fame and longevity, as it is relatively easy after any given event to find a verse that could potentially have predicted it. Nostradamus himself claimed to have calculated each prophecy very carefully, and his supporters claim that he predicted the Great Fire of London of 1666, the rise of Adolf Hitler, and the atomic bombs dropped on Japan in 1945. However, such interpretations mostly make sense only in retrospect – there are no clear, unambiguous warnings about the future in Nostradamus's works. Pastiches of his verse have been created to retrofit historical events such as the attack on the World Trade Center in New York in 2001, causing yet more confusion as to what he actually predicted and at the same time boosting his reputation as a seer.

ABOVE

Nostradamus's prophecies inspired the creation of board games such as this, attesting to his long-term appeal.

BELOW

A large part of Nostradamus's fame comes from his important clients – here he reveals secrets to Catherine de' Medici.

NGUYEN BINH KHIEM

REVELATION
Passive

CHANNEL
Divine communication

INTERMEDIARY
Mystic

CONTEXT
Personal

Nguyen Binh Khiem, also known as Trang Trinh, was a poet and prophet active in Vietnam at exactly the same time as Nostradamus.

IN the sixteenth century, Vietnam was embroiled in civil war and unrest and was heavily influenced by neighbouring China, especially in matters of religion. Into this climate was born the scholar Nguyen Binh Khiem, who became an advisor to the king. He was fascinated with the *I Ching*, numerology and Confucian thought, and he was largely reclusive.

He wrote *Sam Trang Trinh* ('The prophecies of Trang Trinh'), a long poem that contains a collection of prophecies and that first appeared in 1564. It includes predictions about Vietnam up to the twentieth century, although as with Nostradamus it is written in a cryptic style. Today it is famous for the line 'Vietnam is being created', which is often considered the first use of the name Vietnam for the country. Various versions exist, and it is hard to pinpoint a definitive original among the later imitations.

OPPOSITE

A 1945 edition of Nguyen Binh Khiem's prophecies.

LUCA GAURICO

REVELATION
Passive

CHANNEL
Celestial

INTERMEDIARY
Mystic

CONTEXT
Personal

Giovanni II Bentivoglio, the ruler of Bologna, was so angered by one of Gaurico's prophecies that he had him tortured.

LEFT

Portrait of Luca Gaurico, *c.* 1628.

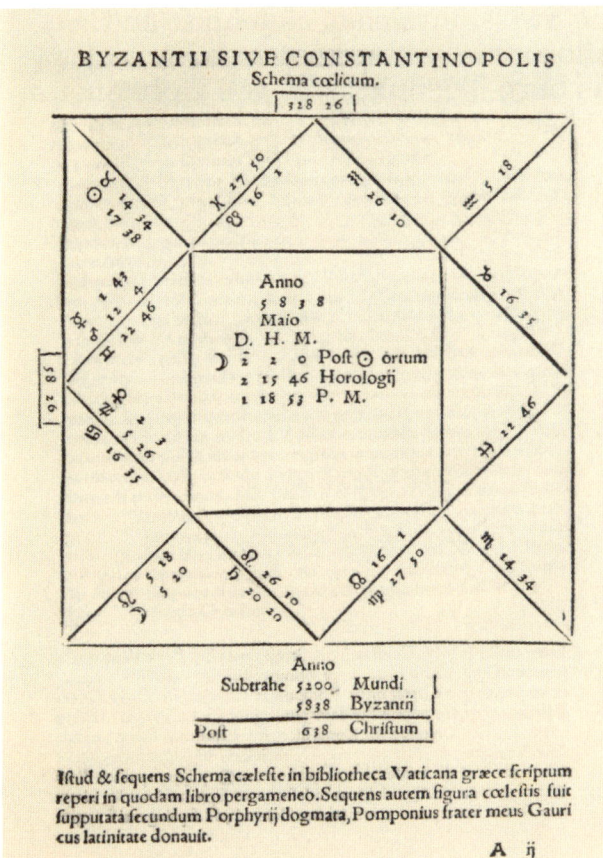
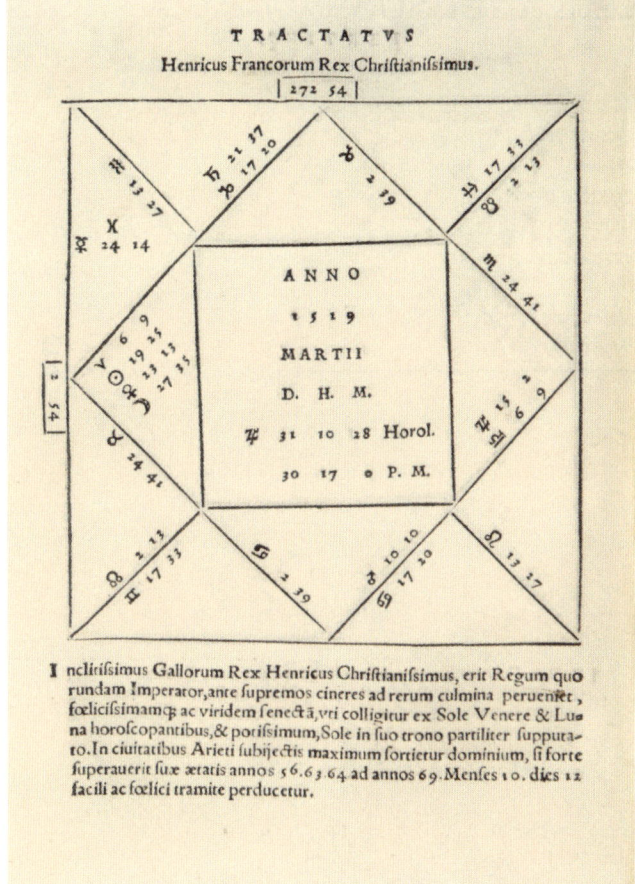

ABOVE LEFT

A celestial chart for the city of Constantinople in Gaurico's *Tractatus astrologicus*.

ABOVE RIGHT

Horoscope for Henry II of France, born March 1519, in the *Tractatus astrologicus*.

BORN in 1475 in Italy, Luca Gaurico was an astrologer and astronomer, and later a bishop in the Catholic Church. He was consulted by Catherine de' Medici (who also sought out Nostradamus) about her children. Instead he predicted the death of her husband, the future King Henry II of France, in a duel. Despite repeated warnings, Henry was killed in a tournament in 1559, just a year after Gaurico's own death in 1558.

Gaurico has also been identified by at least one scholar as the likely author of a 1512 pamphlet that predicted a universal deluge in 1524 (see p. 276). The rival astrologer Girolamo Cardano pointed out several times that Gaurico's predictions had failed to come true, prompting Gaurico to go on the counterattack with his *Tractatus astrologicus* of 1552 in which he drew attention to Cardano's own failings.

PARACELSUS

REVELATION
Passive

CHANNEL
Celestial

INTERMEDIARY
Mystic

CONTEXT
Personal

The Swiss physician, alchemist and philosopher better known as Paracelsus was born Theophrastus von Hohenheim in 1493.

PARACELSUS was a habitual traveller, had a rebellious nature and on occasion publicly burned books that he disagreed with. He placed a premium on practical experience but also incorporated astrology into his medical practice, creating talismans to combat disease and tying the gathering of medicinal herbs to specific times and dates.

Paracelsus's most accomplished work on prophecy was his *Prophecy for the Next Twenty-Four Years*, published in Augsburg in 1536. Covering the period up to 1560 and spanning Europe, the cryptic and mystical texts are accompanied by thirty-two fascinating and strange illustrations that mostly deal with eschatology (death, judgment, final destiny). He anticipated the end of days to come around 1560, though did include a disclaimer that one can never really know.

OPPOSITE

Paracelsus at work, surrounded by alchemical and astrological equipment.

THEOPHRASTUS PARACELSUS

ABOVE AND OPPOSITE

Paracelsus's extremely cryptic prognostications were accompanied by equally cryptic and allegorical figures, as in this 1560 edition.

MOTHER SHIPTON

REVELATION
Passive

CHANNEL
Divine communication

INTERMEDIARY
Mystic

CONTEXT
Personal

It is believed that Mother Shipton's Cave is the oldest tourist attraction in England, open to visitors since 1630, attesting to the early interest in her story.

LEFT

Mother Shipton in the company of the prophet Merlin, a sybil and Cardinal Wolsey on the frontispiece to *Shiptons Prophesie*, 1650.

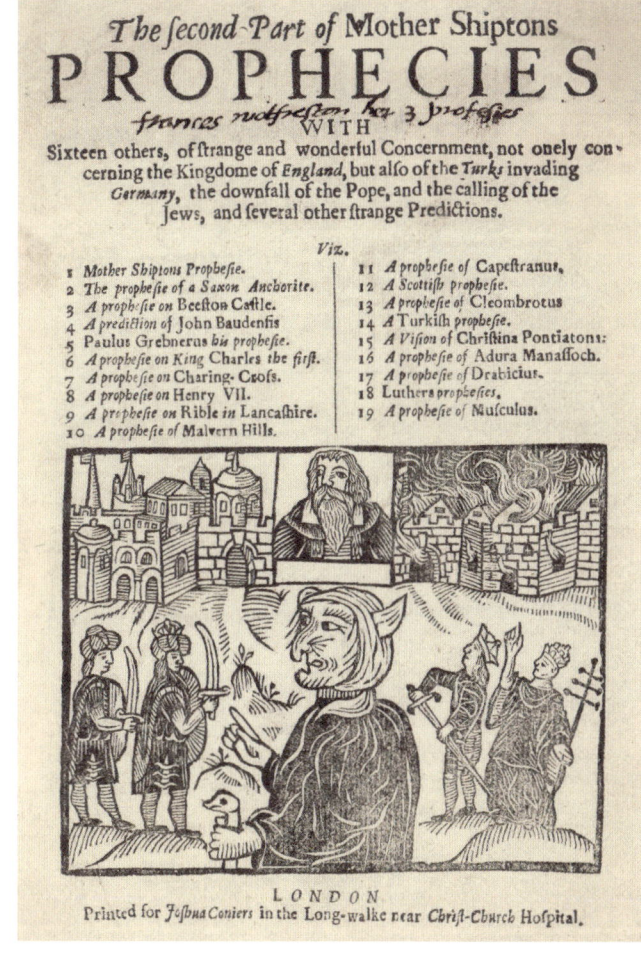

ABOVE LEFT

Mother Shipton depicted as a witch with her spirit 'familiar'.

ABOVE RIGHT

A seventeenth-century pamphlet giving details of prophecies attributed to Mother Shipton.

SUPPOSEDLY born in a cave in Knaresborough, England, in around 1488, the figure of Ursula Sontheil would morph over time into the semi-legendary figure of Mother Shipton. Described in some accounts as 'deformed and ugly' (reflecting a fixation on physical appearance which rarely seems to apply to male prophets and oracles), she studied botany and acquired a reputation as a witch with prophetic powers. Mother Shipton is most interesting for what she came to represent in the public imagination. The first mentions of her come from several decades after her death in 1561, and a pamphlet from 1641 credits her with predicting Henry VIII's dissolution of the monasteries and the downfall of his former advisor Cardinal Wolsey. Later, in 1666, the diarist Samuel Pepys mentions that the royal family had discussed her prediction of the Great Fire of London.

However, many of her prophecies are of doubtful origin. For example, her most famous prediction – 'The world to an end shall come; in eighteen hundred and eighty-one' – first appeared in a book titled *The Life, Prophecies and Death of the Famous Mother Shipton* in 1862, three hundred years after her death. This curiously specific revelation was later revealed to have been a hoax, added by the publishers to drive up sales. However, this did not stop later editions updating it to 1981 and then 1991 – leading to yet more press interest in the late 1970s.

EDGAR CAYCE

REVELATION
Passive

CHANNEL
Divine communication

INTERMEDIARY
Mystic

CONTEXT
Personal

Edgar Cayce became known as the 'sleeping prophet', since his visions came to him in trances. By the time of his death in 1945, Cayce had given 14,500 'readings', which he claimed not to be able to remember afterwards.

THE early history of Edgar Cayce closely mirrors those of the American religious visionaries of the nineteenth century. Like Joseph Smith, founder of the Latter-day Saint movement (see p. 118), Cayce had an angelic visitation when he was young; Cayce also received revelations while in a trance. Born in Kentucky, in 1877, in the 1910s he began as a 'medical clairvoyant', claiming to be able to diagnose and heal people (including himself) through supernatural means.

Cayce's predictions focused on a huge coming destruction. In the 1930s he predicted that 1936 would bring huge devastation and an earthquake that would destroy San Francisco – which did not happen. Then in 1936 he had a dream in which he had been born again in 2100 and witnessed the destruction of Los Angeles and New York. He predicted many more such 'earth changes' occurring between 1958 and 1998 that would have worldwide impact, including the changing of the Earth's axis, and the re-emergence of Atlantis. In 1935 he was charged with practising medicine without a licence.

LEFT AND BELOW

Edgar Cayce was a prolific clairvoyant, and his theories became highly influential on New Age thinking.

JEANE DIXON

REVELATION
Passive

CHANNEL
Divine communication

INTERMEDIARY
Mystic

CONTEXT
Personal

The tendency to highlight successful predictions and ignoring unsuccessful ones has been termed the Jeane Dixon Effect.

BORN as Lydia Emma Pinckert in Wisconsin in 1904, Jeane Dixon became one of the best-known American psychics of the twentieth century. Over the years, she met with President Richard Nixon, and was consulted as an astrologer by Nancy Reagan, wife of President Ronald Reagan. She also claimed to have been consulted by President Franklin D. Roosevelt. The prediction that made her famous was that of the assassination of President John F. Kennedy. In 1956 she claimed that the 1960 election would be 'won by a Democrat' who would 'be assassinated or die in office'. President Kennedy was killed by an assassin in 1963.

However, in 1960 she had also predicted that Kennedy *wouldn't* win the election, so she had clearly tried to cover all possibilities. In fact, she made many predictions that did not come true (for example, that World War III would start in 1958), and as a result some have accused her and her followers of selectively foregrounding correct predictions. She died in 1997, with her last words reported as being 'I knew this would happen.'

OPPOSITE

Among Jeane Dixon's many predictions was that a cure for cancer would be found in 1967.

RIGHT

Dixon made regular appearances in print and on screen.

BABA VANGA

REVELATION
Passive

CHANNEL
Divine communication

INTERMEDIARY
Mystic

CONTEXT
Personal

The Bulgarian mystic Baba Vanga was born in 1911 and lost her sight in an accident when she was twelve years old. During World War II she became famous for her predictions.

WHILE the Bulgarian government tried to suppress Baba Vanga by limiting her public appearances (fearing that her predictions might undermine the state), it has also been suggested that various government ministers also consulted her. Each day hundreds of people would turn up at her home to ask her about their futures.

She was somewhat unusual in that she assigned each of her predictions a specific year when they would occur – up to the year 5079 – and they are surprisingly precise. She died in 1996, but even today her predictions are closely scrutinized by people around the world and regularly reprinted. However, her popularity has led to the emergence of a sub-industry dedicated to creating 'Baba Vanga' prophecies. This has made it increasingly difficult to distinguish which prophecies actually come from her, and which have been invented retrospectively. In addition, it has been suggested that some prophecies attributed to her have been faked as propaganda tools to bolster political viewpoints, especially during conflicts.

PREDICTIONS & REVELATIONS

ABOVE

The blind Baba Vanga, whose fame has only continued to grow after her death.

V.

DREAMS

DREAMS hold a special place in revelation and prophecy in almost every culture and at every time. As a near-universal experience, and one that delves deep into the human unconscious, dreams often bring up strange imagery that seems to demand interpretation. Dreams have been seen as warnings, as visions of the future, of messages from spirits or gods, and as insights into the inner workings of the universe. For this reason, dreams, visions and the future are inextricably linked.

OPPOSITE

Prince Shreyamsa dreams of the coming of a spiritual teacher in a Jain series of *Five Auspicious Events*, 1670–80.

DREAMS that seem to predict the future are referred to by psychologists as 'precognitive dreams' or 'prophetic dreams', but those in the business of oneiromancy (dream interpretation) have often debated how to tell a prophetic dream from a regular one. So while some dreams may have content that is self-explanatory or obviously about the future, the majority of prophetic dreams require some sort of interpretation. Historically, oneiromancy is most often performed by priests or specialist diviners. For example, the biblical prophet Daniel established his credentials by interpreting a dream of Nebuchadnezzar II, the king of Babylon, in which he saw a giant statue made up of different metals (including a head made of gold and feet of clay and iron). Daniel interpreted this as representing different coming empires, resulting in an enduring Kingdom of God.

While this was a reactive form of divination (interpreting a dream that had already been had), in ancient Egypt people would sleep in temples and proactively try to have dreams that priests would later interpret. Later, these temples would influence the ancient Greek sanctuaries of Asclepius, which sick people would visit to receive curative dreams in their sleep. In the Celtic cultures of northern Europe, druids would put people to sleep, chant over their sleeping bodies, and then interpret their dreams afterwards.

In Hindu philosophy, dreams can be categorized into *su-swapna* (those with positive omens) and *duh-swapna* (those with negative omens). In the *Agni Purana*, one of a large collection of encyclopaedic Indian texts, dreams are classified in this way, and actions are given to counteract negative dream omens. The *Linga Purana* meanwhile lists some curiously specific dream portents: 'If one dreams of going towards the southern direction in a chariot to which monkeys and bears are yoked, and sings and dances in the meantime, it should be known that death is imminent.'

The ancient Greeks were particularly interested in the interpretation of dreams. However, their understanding of the nature of dreams evolved over time. So while in the works of Homer dreams are inspired directly by the gods (in the *Iliad* Zeus sends Agamemnon a false dream), Aristotle, writing

ABOVE

In a variation on the story of Joseph/Yusuf known from the Bible and Quran, Zuleykha dreams of Yusuf, who will become her husband.

OPPOSITE

The dream of St Ursula, in which an angel brings news of Ursula's martyrdom.

ABOVE

Daniel interprets Nebuchadnezzar's dream of the giant statue in an illustrated manuscript of *Dante's Divine Comedy*, c. 1450.

in the fourth century BCE, endeavoured to take a more scientific approach. He asserted that sometimes dreams are simply the result of the sensory impressions of our days (while conceding that some dreams still have a divine origin). Aristotle wrote two works on dreams, including *On Prophesying by Dreams*, in which he concluded that, since everyone dreams (even people who are unimportant), 'most [prophetic] dreams are ... to be classed as mere coincidences'.

While Aristotle may have been dismissive of most dreams, today we are more familiar with the idea of Sigmund Freud, founder of psychoanalysis, that dreams can be manifestations of our unconscious mind. However, while Freud was sceptical about the possibility of dreams that tell the future, his contemporary Carl Jung was fascinated by dreams that tapped into a collective unconscious and precognitive dreams. He argued that dreams could offer genuine warnings about certain situations before they happen, stemming from the idea that most crises have a long, but unconscious, incubation period – dreams simply brought the warning signs to the surface.

ABOVE

An Indian manuscript of the fourteen auspicious dreams of Queen Trishala, an important figure in Jainism, showing some of the things she dreamt of: the moon, the sun, a jar full of water and a pile of jewels, among other things.

MESOPOTAMIAN DREAM INTERPRETATION

REVELATION
Passive

CHANNEL
Divine communication

INTERMEDIARY
Any

CONTEXT
Personal

The earliest examples of dream interpretation date from the third millennium BCE in Mesopotamia in poems such as *The Dream of Dumuzid* and *The Epic of Gilgamesh*.

In the Sumerian epic poem *The Dream of Dumuzid*, the deity Dumuzid tells his sister Geshtinanna about a strange dream in which an owl seizes a lamb, his shepherd's stick is taken from him and his drinking cup falls down, among many other occurrences. She, as the goddess of dream divination, tells him 'your dream is not favourable' – and later Dumuzid is taken to the Underworld by demons.

The Gilgamesh Dream Tablet, dating to *c*. 1500 BCE, on which parts of the poem are preserved, records Gilgamesh recounting some of his prophetic dreams to his mother Ninsun, who interprets them as heralding the arrival of a companion (shortly before he meets the character of Enkidu). Later, before battling the monstrous Humbaba, Gilgamesh experiences five terrifying dreams of a fire-breathing thunderbird and collapsing mountains. His companion Enkidu interprets these as positive omens, and indeed Gilgamesh does go on to kill Humbaba.

The Chaldeans of Mesopotamia were later seen as skilful interpreters of dreams. For example, in the biblical Book of Daniel when Nebuchadnezzar II has troubling dreams, he sends for 'Chaldeans', meaning astrologers. They fail to interpret the dream, however, and are put to death, giving the prophet Daniel the opportunity to interpret them correctly (see p. 156).

RIGHT

A Late Babylonian manual used by a professional dream interpreter to instruct their clients.

LEFT

The Mesopotamian goddess Nanshe had the ability to send messages about the future, as well as to interpret dreams.

EGYPTIAN DREAM BOOKS

REVELATION
Active, Passive

CHANNEL
Divine communication

INTERMEDIARY
Any

CONTEXT
Societal, Personal

Chemical analysis of residue found in a mug in the form of the god Bes suggests that the ancient Egyptians may have administered hallucinogens to induce prophetic visions.

LEFT

The Dream Stele of Thutmose IV.

THE Egyptians set huge store by dreams and generally saw them as prophetic. Manuals for dream interpretation have survived, such as the one in the British Museum written around 1220 BCE, that categorize dreams into good and bad omens.

Dreams were seen as important in relaying the will of the gods and were often used to legitimize power. 'Instructions of Amenemhat' is a poem, frequently copied and widely disseminated, that seems to show the appearance of the murdered Amenemhat I to his son Senusret I in a dream as a way of eulogizing the dead king.

One of the most famous examples of a revelatory dream in ancient Egypt is that captured in the Dream Stele or Sphinx Stele. Erected between the front legs of the Great Sphinx of Giza, it tells the story of Thutmose, who fell asleep in the shadow of the Sphinx, which at that time was partially buried under sand. In the dream he is told by a god that if he clears the sand around the Sphinx, he will be rewarded by becoming pharaoh – which he did in approximately 1400 BCE as Thutmose IV, after which he promptly erected the stele.

ABOVE

A sleeping Egyptian figurine, *c.* 1550–1295 BCE.

RIGHT

A papyrus, *c.* 1220 BCE, which contains a manual for dream interpretation.

BUDDHISM AND DREAMING

REVELATION
Passive

CHANNEL
Divine communication

INTERMEDIARY
Any

CONTEXT
Personal

The night before his enlightenment, the Buddha received five dreams – the Five Great Dreams of Prophecies – including one in which his pillow was formed by the Himalayas (or Mount Meru in some accounts) that told of his coming Buddhahood and omniscience.

LEFT AND OPPOSITE

Two depictions of the dream of Queen Maya, showing the conception of the future Buddha in the form of an elephant which entered her side.

DREAMS are central to the story of the Buddha. According to Buddhist tradition, Maya, queen of Shakya, dreamt of a white elephant with six tusks entering her side. When she woke, her husband sent for a priest, who interpreted the dream as meaning she had conceived and would give birth to a great man. The child, Siddhartha Gautama, would go on to become the Buddha.

The *Milindapanha* collection of writings from around 100 BCE–200 CE claims that among the causes of dreams are supernatural forces, past experiences and future events – only the last kind, the author says, are important. In the *Jataka* collection of tales about the Buddha's previous lives there is the story of how the Buddha helped interpret the sixteen nightmares of King Pasenadi, which featured a horse with two heads, animals drinking from a polluted lake and a large rock floating in water, among others. He explained that they all concerned the future, specifically what happens in times of unjust rule: wild bulls breaking into a courtyard foreshadows the chaos of weak leadership, while a dream of fast-growing trees symbolizes coming change and turbulence.

DREAMS IN THE BIBLE

REVELATION
Passive

CHANNEL
Divine communication

INTERMEDIARY
Prophet

CONTEXT
Personal

Hear my words: When there are prophets among you, I the Lord make myself known to them in visions; I speak to them in dreams.

Numbers 12:6.

LEFT

The dream of the Magi relief from Chartres Cathedral, France.

ABOVE LEFT

Joseph dreams of sheaves of wheat bowing down to him, predicting his future ascendance.

ABOVE RIGHT

St Joseph, the father of Jesus, had four dreams instructing him to take Mary as his wife, to escape to Egypt, to return to Israel, and to settle in Nazareth.

DREAMS are frequently used in the Bible to communicate messages, particularly to prophets. They occur considerably more in the Old Testament than in the New Testament, marking an interesting shift from God revealing himself through dreams to revealing himself through the acts and words of Jesus. The best-known dreams in the Old Testament are probably those of the Egyptian pharaoh that are decoded by Joseph. The pharaoh dreams of seven emaciated cows eating seven fat cows, and Joseph explains that there will be seven years of plenty, followed by seven years of famine. The pharaoh, impressed, put Joseph in charge of managing grain stores, and through careful management Egypt survives the seven years of famine.

In the New Testament (Matthew 2:1-12), the Three Magi, having paid homage to the infant Jesus, were warned in a dream not to return to the local ruler, Herod, since he was looking for the child, whom he saw as a potential rival. And Joseph, Jesus's (earthly) father, was also warned in a dream by an angel to escape with his family to Egypt. In fact, it is Joseph who receives most of the dreams in the New Testament, helping him play a key role in safeguarding his son.

ARTEMIDORUS'S ONEIROCRITICA

REVELATION
Passive

CHANNEL
Divine communication

INTERMEDIARY
Any

CONTEXT
Personal

The most complete surviving work on dreams from the Greek and Roman world is *Oneirocritica* by Artemidorus, written in the second to early third century CE.

LEFT

Artemidorus came from Ephesus, a city associated with magic. In this painting, St Paul has a pile of books of magic burned in the same city.

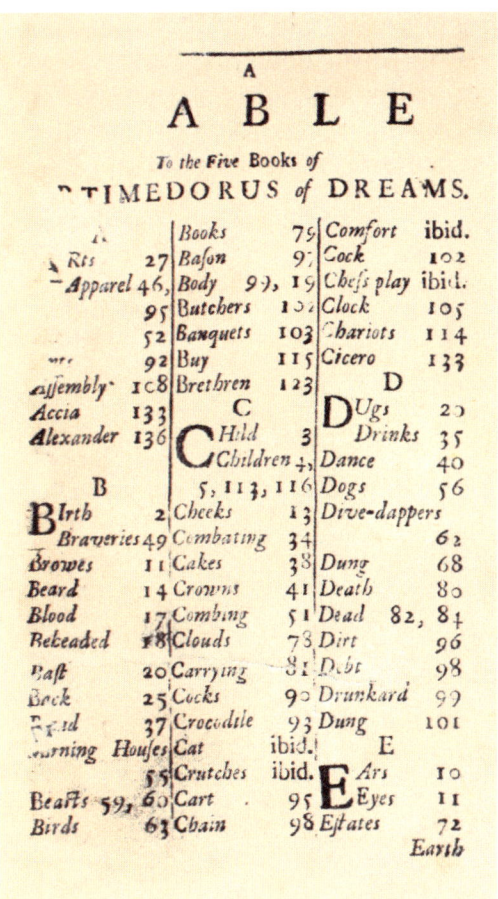
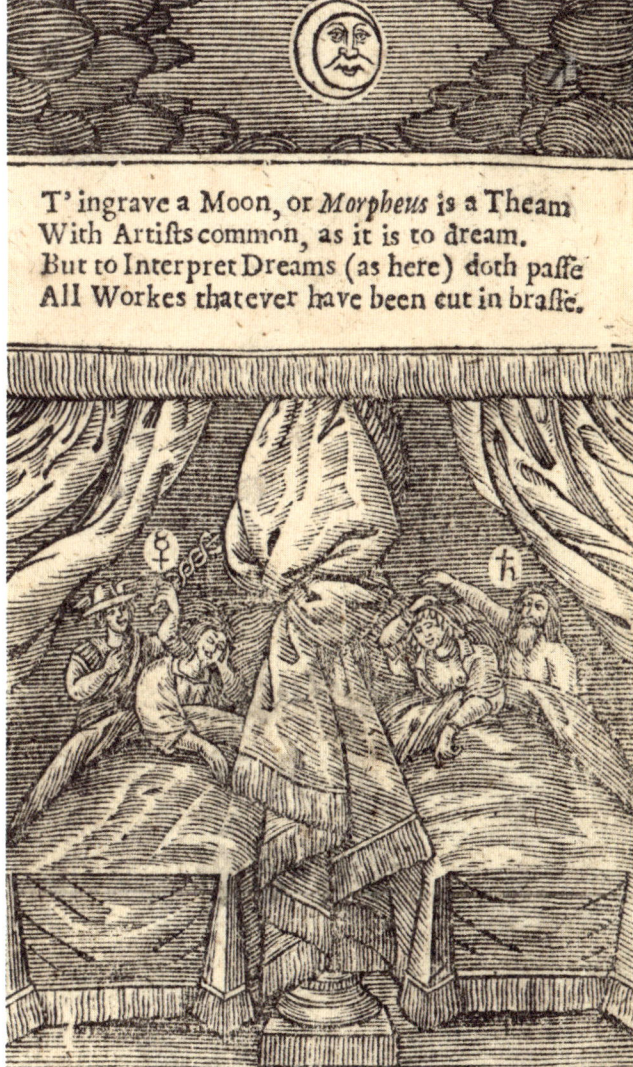

ABOVE

Seventeenth- and eighteenth-century English translations of his work attest to Artemidorus's long-lasting influence.

ARTEMIDORUS was a professional diviner and dream interpreter operating within an established tradition, and he cites many earlier sources such as Aristander of Telmessos, the favourite seer of Alexander the Great. His work is largely a practical guide to dream interpretation, with some additional content addressed to the author's son on the practicalities and techniques involved.

In the book he distinguishes between predictive dreams (*oneiroi*) and non-predictive dreams (*enhypnia*). The latter kind, to his mind, required little skill to interpret – they were simply reflections of day-to-day worries.

As the title of his work suggests, Artemidorus was more interested in dreams that carried a future meaning. He is clear that dreams are rarely sent by the gods, mostly just those that take place during incubation in a temple.

A sign of his enduring fame is that many centuries later Shakespeare used the name 'Artemidorus' for the figure who warns Caesar of his coming assassination in *Julius Caesar*. Even later admirers of Artemidorus's work included Sigmund Freud, who in a footnote in *The Interpretation of Dreams* said that it was Greco-Roman world's most comprehensive study of dream interpretation.

SYNESIUS ON DREAMS

REVELATION
Passive

CHANNEL
Divine communication

INTERMEDIARY
Any

CONTEXT
Personal

On Dreams is a philosophical work, designed to help understand the mechanism of dreaming as a divinatory practice, though it also offers practical tips on how to keep a 'dream book'.

BORN in around 373 CE in the Greek colony of Cyrene, modern-day Libya, Synesius travelled all around the Mediterranean. He visited Athens, Constantinople (now Istanbul) and Alexandria, coming into contact with many philosophical and religious movements. He was even made a bishop in Ptolemais, in modern-day Libya. A philosopher and thinker, he became interested in alchemy, but it is his *On Dreams*, which he wrote for his children, that is one of his most famous books today.

Synesius believed that while everyone dreams, only a few can have access to profoundly meaningful dreams: 'man through divination attains to much more than belongs to our human nature. For the mass of mankind can know only the present,' (*On Dreams*). However, the divine can reveal itself to anyone – men, women and children – though Synesius acknowledges that interpreting revelations can be hard since the gods like to keep some things concealed.

OPPOSITE

A statue of the Greek god Hypnos (Sleep).

RIGHT

A sixteenth-century depiction of Synesius.

THE GREAT BOOK OF INTERPRETATION OF DREAMS

REVELATION
Passive

CHANNEL
Divine communication

INTERMEDIARY
Any

CONTEXT
Personal

At its core this is a collection of Islamic thinking on how to interpret dreams – effectively a dream dictionary covering a staggering range of topics, each with an interpretation.

THIS compilation has long been attributed to the seventh-century scholar Ibn Sirin of Basra, who is seen as the earliest student of dream interpretation in the Islamic world. In reality, the book was likely compiled much later, potentially in the fifteenth century. Many later writers, such as the Syrian scholar Abd al-Ghani al-Nabulsi (1641–1731) in his *Book of Dreams*, drew on and added to the text. For any given dream a specific explanation is provided, for example: a dream of a dead person sleeping indicates that the person is happy in the afterlife. It has been in wide circulation since the nineteenth century and remains popular today.

Some of this thinking also made it into Western traditions, largely through the Byzantine *Oneirocriticon* written in Greek between 843 and 1075 by a writer calling himself Achmet ibn Sirin (meaning 'son of Sirin', a name used frequently by Byzantine authors of dream books to indicate intellectual roots in the work of Ibn Sirin of Basra). This very important work also drew on earlier Greco-Roman traditions. It was translated from Greek into Latin by Leo Tuscus, an interpreter for the Byzantine emperor, in 1176 and thereby made its way into the Western world of the Renaissance through subsequent French and Italian editions. Also in the twelfth century, the Constantinople-based Italian priest Pascalis Romanus compiled the *Liber thesauri occulti*, a book on dream interpretation that drew on both Achmet's *Oneirocriticon* and on Artemidorus, thus bringing together two traditions.

OPPOSITE

Pages from Ibn al-Muqri's summary of Ibn Sirin's *Interpretation of Dreams*. Ibn Sirin gives particular attention to dreams of a religious nature.

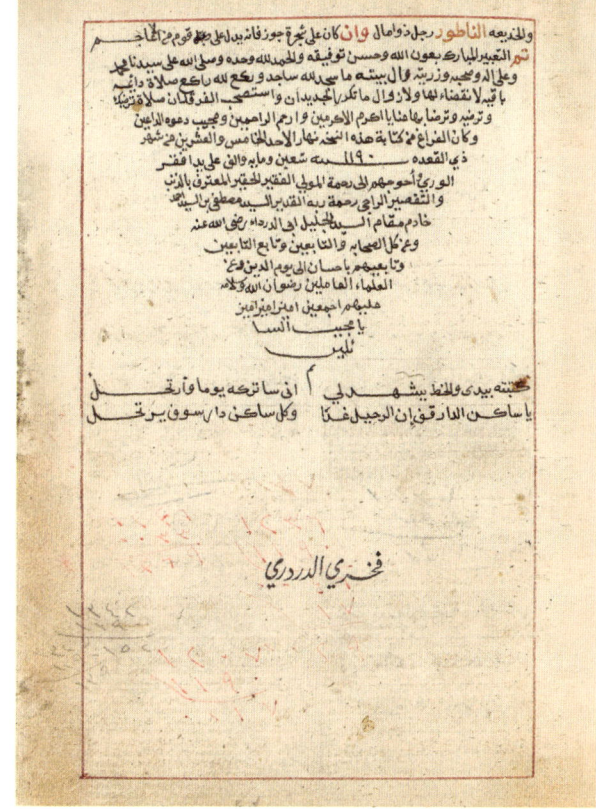

NATIVE AMERICAN DREAMS

REVELATION
Active, Passive

CHANNEL
Divine communication

INTERMEDIARY
Any

CONTEXT
Personal

Dreams and visions are important among several Native American cultures, where they are generally believed to be messages, sent by dream spirits, often with prophetic content.

LEFT

A Sioux drawing capturing a dream about a black tail deer, c. 1890. Those who dreamt of specific animals repeatedly were believed to have greater power.

RIGHT AND BELOW RIGHT

Two drawings by the artist Black Hawk showing dreams or visions of himself riding a Buffalo Eagle, both 1881.

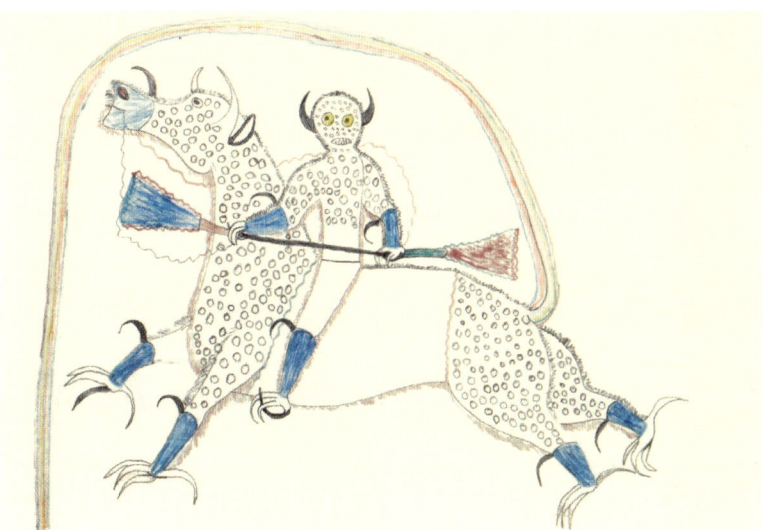

FOR the Maricopa people of modern-day Arizona, the same word – *cara'g* – is used for 'spirit' and 'dream'. In many Native American cultures, members will fast and isolate themselves to provoke 'vision quests' as an important rite of passage. In 1876 the famous Hunkpapa Lakota leader Sitting Bull performed a Sun Dance ritual, a combination of prolonged dancing and self-mortification that resulted in him passing out. When he awoke, he claimed he had had a vision of the enemy soldiers upside-down with their feet pointing at the sky that foretold the coming victory of the Lakota – this victory then happened at the Battle of the Little Bighorn.

Plenty Coups, a famous chief of the Crow people of the region around present-day Montana, was well known for his dreams and visions of the future. In one of his prophetic visions, he saw all but one of the trees in a forest blown over. This was interpreted as representing the downfall of all Native American nations bar his own. The Anishinaabe of the Great Lakes region believe that the physical world and the world of dreams are inextricably linked, and that dreams are a vehicle for passing important knowledge to humanity.

ABOVE

A depiction by Short Bull of the annual Lakota Sun Dance, *c.* 1893.

DREAMS

MAORI DREAMS

REVELATION
Passive

CHANNEL
Divine communication

INTERMEDIARY
Any

CONTEXT
Personal

Moemoea (dreams) are central to the cultures of the Maori people of New Zealand/Aotearoa. Often, they are seen as a vehicle for the communication of *atua* (gods) or spirits, with little or no separation between the material and immaterial worlds.

PROPHECIES and warnings within dreams are considered very real among the Maori. *Tohunga* (experts) are critical to helping understand dreams (done by *tohunga moemoea*) and other divinatory signs about the future (done by *tohunga matakite*).

In his 1898 book *Omens and Superstitious beliefs of the Maori*, the ethnographer Elsdon Best set out good and bad dream omens that he had amassed through first-hand interviews with Maori. It is a good omen to have a dream about embracing a woman, but a bad omen to dream of being in a house with two doorways. Raniera Ellison, writing in *te reo* (the Maori language) in the late nineteenth century, captured in his diaries many dream meanings, including 'If a moon is seen in the dream, the dream denotes prosperity'.

ABOVE

Many of the works of contemporary Maori artist Nigel Borell reference the concept of *moemoea*. *Talking to the Moon*, 2023.

VI.

ASTROLOGY

ASTROLOGY is divination of the future through the study of the stars, sun, moon and planets. All astrological traditions – and there are many around the world – assert that the positions and attitudes of these bodies reflect a higher order of things, have a meaningful influence on our lives and can give us insights into the future.

OPPOSITE

An astrological volvelle – a rotating paper disc – used to calculate the position of the moon relative to the signs of the zodiac, mid-sixteenth century.

OF all the many forms of divination, astrology is perhaps the best known and most widespread. A 2022 poll in the United States suggested that more than one quarter of people in that country believe in it, while a 2020 study showed that 83 per cent of people in India will ensure that important events fall on the dates indicated as auspicious by their horoscope. The stars have been, and remain, highly influential in our decision-making.

At its core, astrology exemplifies the maxim, 'As above, so below' (which is in fact, a modern paraphrase of a text attributed to the legendary figure of Hermes Trismegistus). It identifies a causal link between what happens in the celestial and terrestrial realms.

The earliest examples of astrology as a discipline can be found in ancient Mesopotamia in the second millennium BCE. The Akkadian and Babylonian cultures were already close observers of celestial omens such as comets and the waxing and waning of the moon, and it is clear that astronomy, the study of stars and planets and their movements, had already been in existence in many cultures for millennia before that. From around 500 BCE onwards, astrology started to become a more popular form of divination, and by the second century CE it had already taken the form that is familiar in many parts of the world today: horoscopic astrology. Horoscopic astrology is a form of astrology that looks at the relationship of astral bodies to each other at a specific moment in time – for example, the moment of an individual's birth.

Despite sharing some similarities (i.e. the use of horoscopes) and being aware of each other's existence and occasionally borrowing from each other, there are, however, distinct astrological traditions – principally Hellenistic, Vedic (Indian) and Chinese. These take quite different approaches: some start from the movements of the sun, and others the moon. Sometimes these different strains of astrology have merged to create new approaches, for example, the influence of China and India combined to create Tibetan astrology, while the systems found in Japan and Vietnam built on those of China but add unique elements.

Where does the power in astrology come from? Fundamentally, the idea that the planets and stars have different 'wavelengths' and

ABOVE LEFT

An illustration of the 'Dendera zodiac', showing constellations as signs of the zodiac, from the ceiling of the Temple of Hathor at Dendera, Egypt – the most complete surviving image of the ancient skies.

ABOVE RIGHT

Personifications of the planets on their trajectories, including an armoured Mars and a nude Venus, c. 1479.

'energies' that can influence humans and other celestial bodies. Over time, however, the system grew more and more complex. In China the five phases (Water, Earth, Fire, Metal and Wood) and the forces of yin and yang are also invoked in astrology. In the West each of the four classical elements (Earth, Water, Fire and Air) is associated with three of the twelve zodiac signs, again implying a bridge between the supernatural and physical realms.

In the face of increasingly complex thinking, one of the reasons for the enduring appeal of astrology is its proximity to astronomy (the study of celestial objects). For much of history there was little distinction between the two; in medieval Europe the word *astronomia* was used to describe both branches. The science of astronomy was always seen as a legitimate, essential and important discipline – one that allowed for correct orientation and timekeeping and that has clear (if complex) rules. The Byzantine historian Nicephorus Gregoras believed that astrology could also be useful due to these mathematical foundations. It is grounded in the physical, observable world. Today, however, especially after the Western Enlightenment of the eighteenth century and the emergence of modern scientific method, astrology tends to be seen as lacking scientific rigour, while at the same time being embraced by millions for the sense of control and predictability it can bring in an ever more complex world.

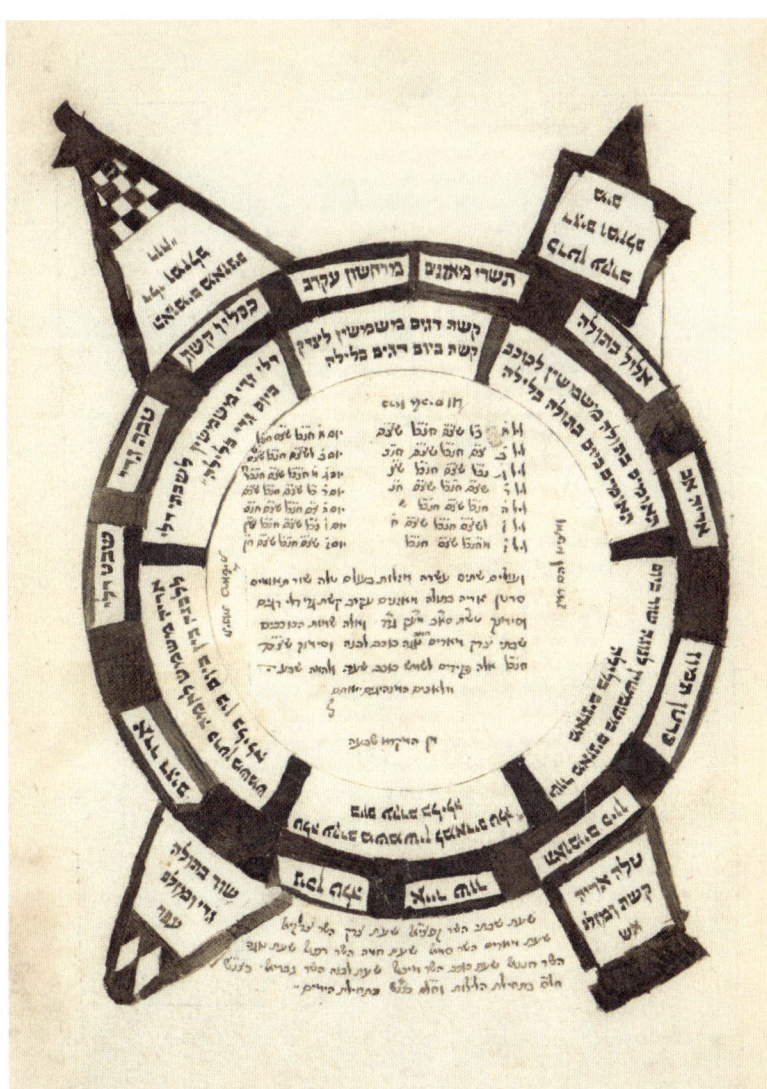

RIGHT

An astrological calendar, divided into the twelve signs of the zodiac, from a Kabbalistic manuscript.

ABOVE

A Thai astrological manuscript with animals of the Chinese zodiac and their avatars.

THE ORIGINS OF ASTROLOGY

REVELATION
Active

CHANNEL
Celestial

INTERMEDIARY
Any

CONTEXT
Official, Societal

If Venus enters into the sun, the king's son will kill his father.

Cuneiform inscription, second millennium BCE.

LEFT

An Old Babylonian plaque with a crescent symbolizing the Mesopotamian moon god Sin on top of two bulls.

RIGHT

A Babylonian calendar of the zodiac sign Leo, early second century BCE. The planet Jupiter is represented by a star, and next to it are the constellations of Hydra and Leo.

BELOW RIGHT

A Babylonian astrological tablet from the fourth to second centuries BCE, showing seven stars and a figure of a 'man in the moon'.

ASTRONOMICAL observations of the position and movements of celestial bodies had existed in Egypt since the fifth millennium BCE; the pyramids, built from the third millennium BCE onwards, were carefully orientated to the North Star. In China, star names have been found etched into oracle bones dating from 1300 BCE. The Warren Field site in Scotland is believed to be home to the oldest lunisolar calendar in the world, from 8000 BCE. Evidence for the application of such astronomical observations to divining the future – *astrology* – however, first emerged in Mesopotamia among the Babylonians. This is not to say that it emerged exclusively in Mesopotamia – there would have existed other indigenous astrological traditions around the world, even if evidence for them is scant. For example, the sun and moon have been seen as gods in many cultures (for example, in ancient Egypt and Greece, and among the Aztecs), so it is reasonable for these cultures to have tried to divine meaning in their movements.

The predecessors of the Babylonians, the Akkadians, had already established causal relationships between the stars and earthly events and believed that every star was a god. The Babylonians connected each of the five planets that they had observed to a god: Jupiter with Marduk, Venus with Ishtar and so forth. The zodiac (from the Greek for 'circle of animals'), referring to the twelve astrological signs associated with the belt of stars around the Earth, was introduced in Mesopotamia around the middle of the fifth century BCE. The zodiac signs were also correlated to the months, bringing time into the equation.

ASTROLOGY & ASTRONOMY

REVELATION
Active

CHANNEL
Celestial

INTERMEDIARY
Any

CONTEXT
Official, Societal

It is only since the Western Enlightenment and scientific advances of the eighteenth century that astronomy and astrology have diverged meaningfully, with astrology being treated increasingly as superstition.

Both astrology and astronomy deal with that which can be observed beyond the Earth's atmosphere: planets, stars and other celestial bodies and phenomena. For most of history there was little or no distinction between the two disciplines, although the astrological part would have been considered more important than the astronomical part, due to its practical value in governance and predictions. In ancient China, Babylon, Japan, Greece and Rome the same practitioners would have dealt with both disciplines.

Where they differ is in the meaning extracted from the observations. While astronomy describes the universe in an attempt to understand and extrapolate rules about how it works, astrology seeks to discover how it might affect those on Earth. Astrology wants to link the totality of the universe in a chain of being that projects far into the future, where the dependable yet hard to fathom movements of the sun, moon and planets can be revealed as guides as to what will happen. However, since the seventeenth century, growing scepticism and huge steps forwards in the understanding of the universe have left astrology more and more detached from the scientific community.

OPPOSITE

A volvelle used to calculate the relative positions of the sun and moon.

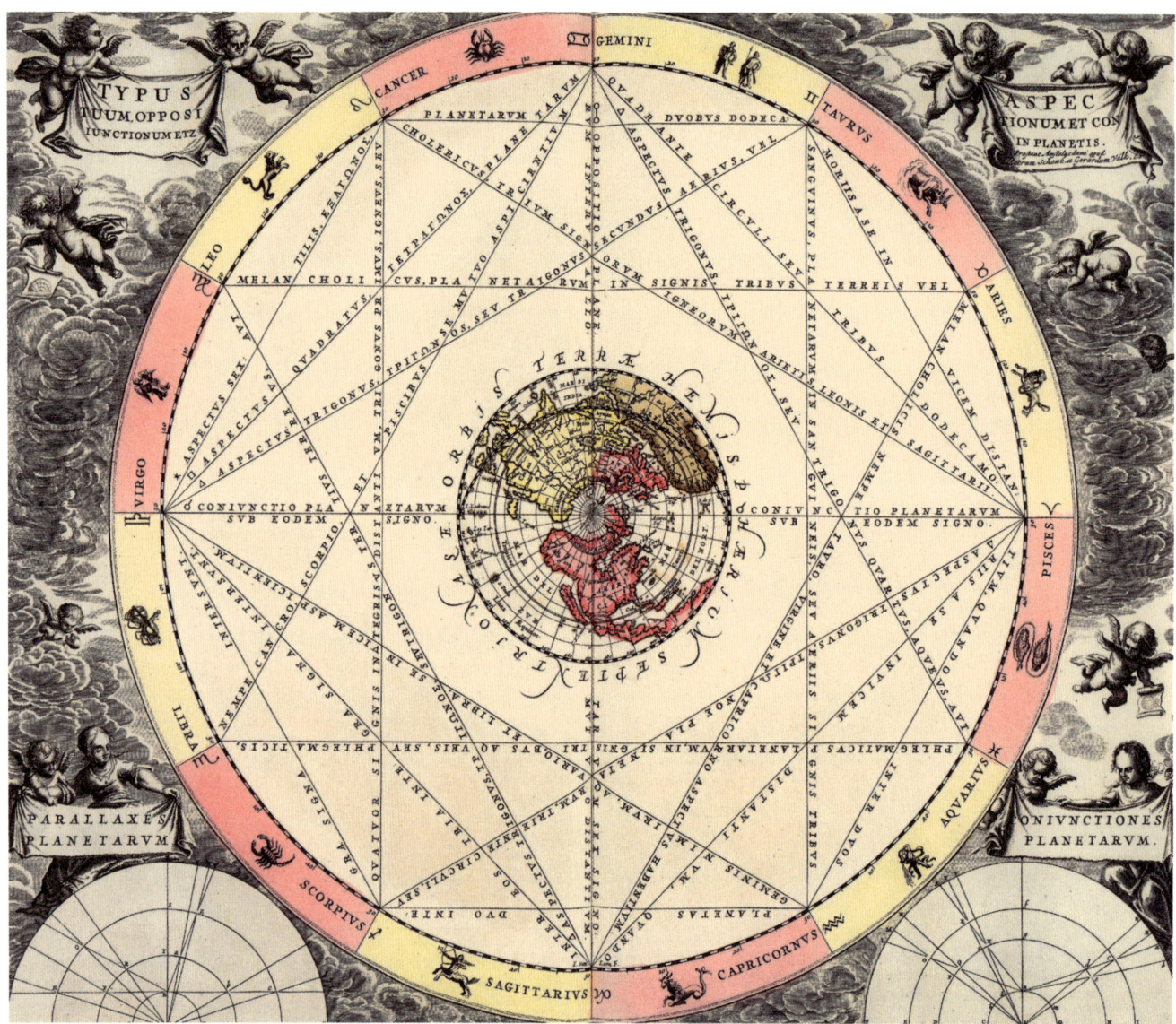

Plates from *Harmonia Macrocosmica* by Andreas Cellarius, first published in 1660.

ABOVE

A map of the northern hemisphere, in which California is still depicted as an island. That the zodiac signs are prominently included demonstrates the continued importance of astrology.

OPPOSITE

The 'Planisphere of Aratus' shows a Ptolemaic view of the universe, with the Earth at its centre.

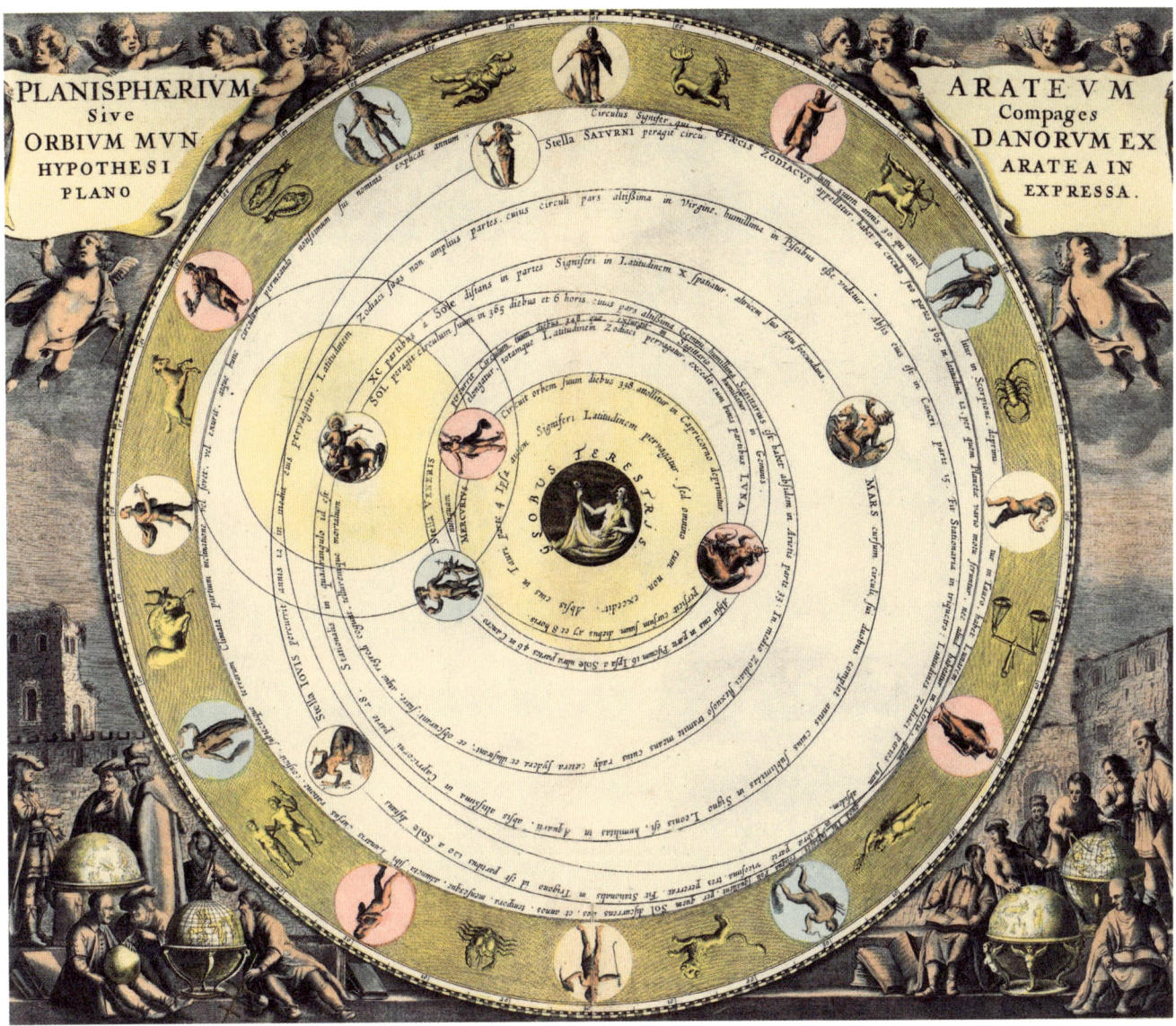

ABOVE

Calendar entry for June in the *Très Riches Heures du Duc de Berry*, a fifteenth-century book of hours. The stars were even more meaningful in the past, closely tied to the seasons, work and the land.

THE BASICS OF ASTROLOGY

There are a few vital concepts that are found in most astrological traditions, though with some variations.

First, there is a fundamental belief that what happens in the celestial realm and what happens on Earth are inextricably linked. And a corresponding belief that, with the right level of observation and understanding of extraterrestrial phenomena, it is possible to predict the future.

✠

Second, that the planets, stars, sun and moon each have an impact on us, and that the time we are born – and the relative positions of these entities at that moment – has considerable influence on who we are, how we are and how we lead our lives.

✠

Third, that there are generic attributes that can be applied to all people. In Western and Hellenistic astrology these attributes are built on the concept of the sun, or zodiac, sign. Zodiac signs refer to the constellations that are most visible within the ecliptic (the region of the sky most visible from Earth), and what's critical is where the sun or moon appear in those signs, as well as the relative position of the planets. In Chinese astrology they are built on the lunar year sign, as well as month, day and hour. Hindu or Vedic astrology prioritizes the lunar house, or the region of the ecliptic in which the moon appears.

✠

And fourth, that these celestially revealed truths can be accessed by drawing up a chart, or horoscope, which requires a degree of expertise and insight to divine.

ABOVE AND OPPOSITE

The personifications of the planets alongside the zodiac signs they are associated with (above) and the aspects of life that they have influence over (below). Mars, for example, presides over scenes of war.

HOROSCOPES

REVELATION
Active

CHANNEL
Celestial

INTERMEDIARY
Any

CONTEXT
Official, Societal

Coming from the Greek meaning 'hour marker', a horoscope is a chart that shows the position of the sun, moon and other planets and stars at a specific point in time.

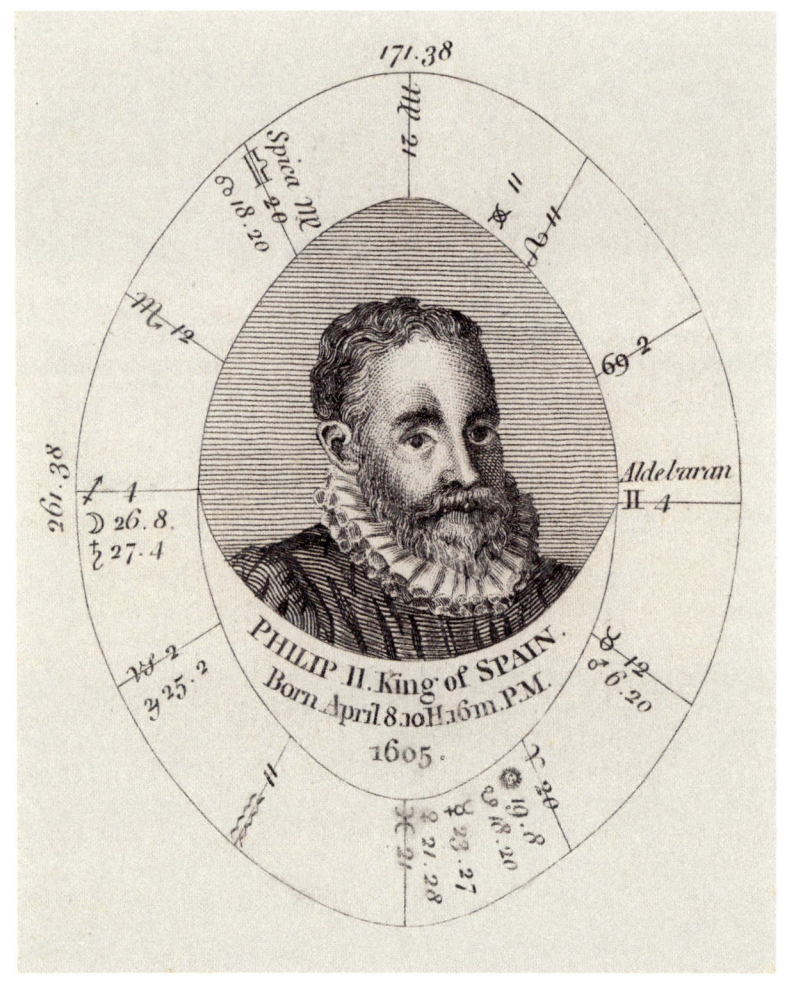

LEFT

A horoscope for Philip II of Spain.

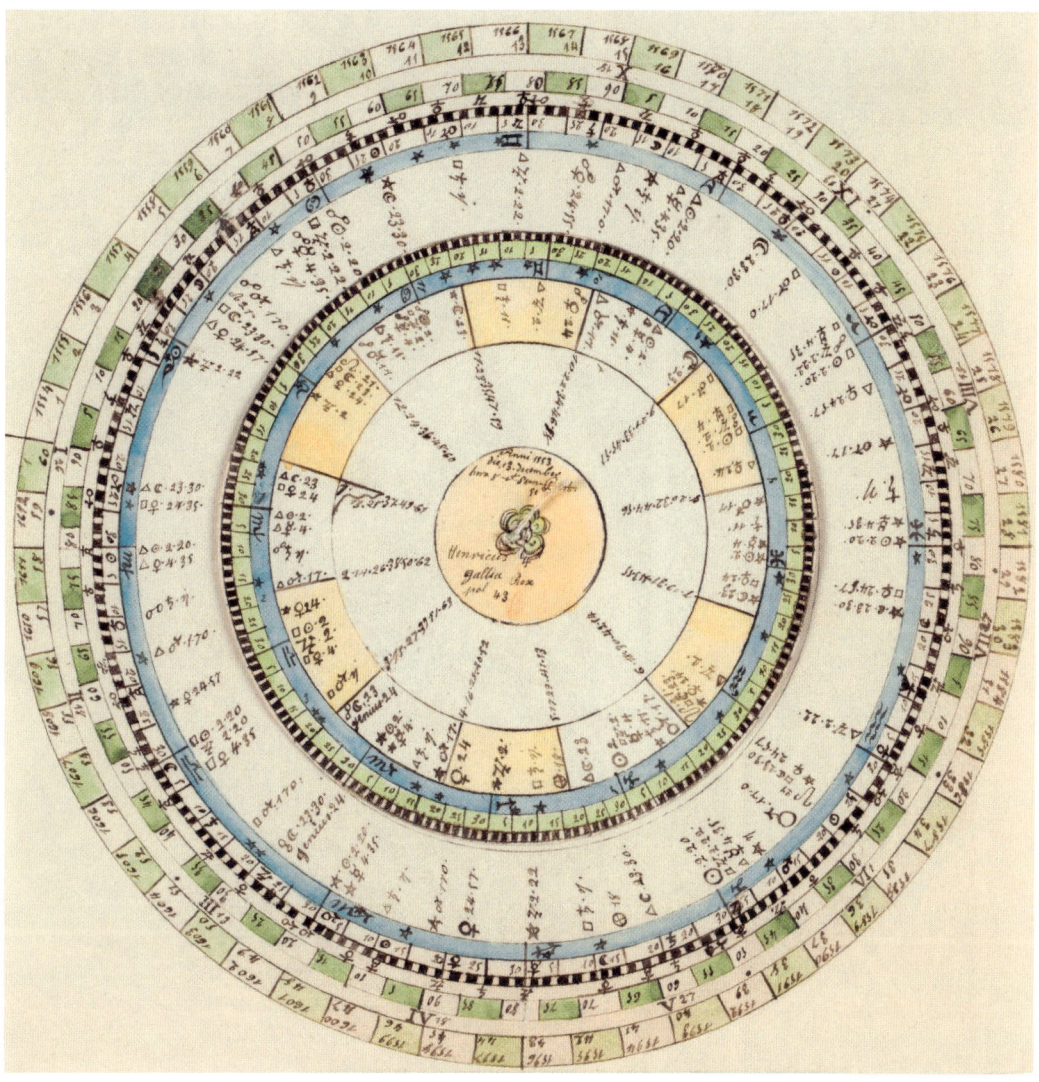

ABOVE

A horoscope for Henry IV of France.

OVERLEAF

The birth horoscope of Iskandar, grandson of Timur, drawn up in 1411 in Iran.

To extract meaning from astrology, normally a horoscope is drawn up to reflect the skies at a specific time. And that time is most often the moment of birth of the person for whom the horoscope is being calculated. Two people with identical birthdays and places of birth will have identical horoscopes – a fact that led the sceptical St Augustine to ask why twins can have such different personalities (*The City of God*, Book 5, parts 1 and 2). However, horoscopes can also be drawn up for specific events, such as weddings.

Western astrological charts focus on sun signs, houses and planets – the ascendant (where the sun rises) is regarded as important. With this information, a life horoscope can be drawn up in which the birth sign can be looked at in the context of the relative locations of celestial bodies at any moment in time. In Hindu traditions, natal horoscopes called *kundali* can be instrumental in informing major life decisions, such as determining matches between couples. As in the West, it is effectively a snapshot of the stars and planets at the time of birth, with ascendants marked.

Chinese horoscopes focus less on the skies at the moment of birth, and more on when in the twelve-year lunar calendar the birthday falls (often also called a zodiac sign, since each year is associated with an animal). Horoscopes in this tradition are more about the year ahead rather than the day or week.

ASTROLOGY IN INDIA

REVELATION
Active

CHANNEL
Celestial

INTERMEDIARY
Any

CONTEXT
Societal

Central to Indian astrology, as in Hellenistic astrology, is the idea of connection between the microcosm and the macrocosm – something that is intrinsic to Hinduism itself.

THE Vedic astrology (after the body of Hindu religious texts known as the Vedas), or *jyotisha*, that developed in India likely post-dates the genesis of the Vedas themselves between around 1500 and 500 BCE. The Vedas do discuss the tracking of the movements of the moon and sun, which were important in helping pick auspicious moments for rituals, but the leap from astronomical observations to astrology mostly likely was catalysed by the arrival of collections of omens from Mesopotamia, facilitated by well-established trade routes between the two regions.

The method of casting a horoscope in Vedic astrology is not dissimilar from that used in Hellenistic astrology, but whereas the Hellenistic approach focuses on sun signs, the twenty-seven or twenty-eight *nakshatras* (lunar mansions) are of more importance in Hindu astrology. There are twelve *bhavas* (houses) in the Vedic chart, with each house corresponding to a particular facet of an individual's make-up. The first house, Lagna, represents the self; the seventh house represents relationships; and the tenth house, career. However, the houses and signs do not map precisely to those of Hellenistic astrology, since Vedic astrology uses the sidereal zodiac rather than the tropical zodiac.

RIGHT

A section of an eighteenth-century Sanskrit horoscope roll, measuring over 11 m (36 ft), showing gods, planets and zodiac signs.

ABOVE

Nine celestial bodies, as depicted on a lintel from the eighth century CE. From left to right: the sun, the moon, Mercury, Venus, Mars, Jupiter, Saturn, Rahu (the eclipse) and a serpent-tailed comet.

ASTROLOGY

ABOVE AND OPPOSITE

Taurus and Sagittarius, from an Indian manuscript, *c.* 1810.

HELLENISTIC ASTROLOGY

REVELATION
Active

CHANNEL
Celestial

INTERMEDIARY
Any

CONTEXT
Societal

Hellenistic astrology as known today originated in Hellenized Egypt in the second or first centuries BCE and was inspired largely by Babylonian astrology, with Egyptian influences.

LEFT

The zodiac as represented in a ninth-century CE edition of Ptolemy's astronomical tables.

RIGHT

Aion, the Greco-Roman personification of eternity, standing in the centre of the zodiac wheel.

ASTROLOGY in more primitive forms had already existed in Greece and Italy, but with the fourth-century BCE campaigns of Alexander the Great in Egypt and Persia, the Greeks came into contact with much more complex thinking. This spread throughout the Greek and Roman empires, blending with Egyptian temple practices and the older schools of Greek philosophy, such as the Aristotelian tradition, which saw a connection between the heavens and human affairs, and Stoicism, which viewed the universe as deterministic. It represents the first formalization of the science of astrology into a single system that we might recognize today. Not only that, but it introduced the concept of horoscopes and most importantly democratized astrology, making it something that anyone could do as opposed to something that was principally used by ruling classes and that required a highly trained priest.

The Romans, in particular during the imperial period, embraced new developments in astrology. In the first century CE, the emperor Tiberius regularly consulted an astrologer (he was particularly close to the Greek Egyptian Thrasyllus of Mendes, who also predicted that Caligula would succeed Tiberius). At the same time Marcus Manilius wrote a five-volume treatise, the *Astronomica*, which introduced the concept of 'houses' (the subdivision of the sky into twelve equal sections within a twenty-four-hour day, each with its own meaning). The most famous Greek astrologer was Ptolemy, whose *Tetrabiblos* ('Four books'), written in the second century CE in Roman-ruled Alexandria, continued to be consulted for many centuries. With the rise of Christianity, astrology gradually fell from favour – the early Church Fathers such as St Augustine saw it as incompatible with Christianity – and so it disappeared from Europe for several centuries. However, Hellenistic astrology continued to be studied in the Middle East and Persia, and it was via Arabic that the *Tetrabiblos* was eventually translated into Latin, and thereby introduced to medieval Europe, in 1138.

ASTROLOGY IN EAST ASIA

REVELATION
Active

CHANNEL
Celestial

INTERMEDIARY
Any

CONTEXT
Official, Societal

Chinese astrology emerged in the first millennium BCE, fusing a long tradition of observing the planets and stars with existing philosophical concepts such as yin-yang and the five phases. From there it spread to Japan, Korea, Vietnam and Thailand.

LEFT

A nineteenth-century Thai fortune-telling diagram, with the Chinese zodiac animals on the inner ring.

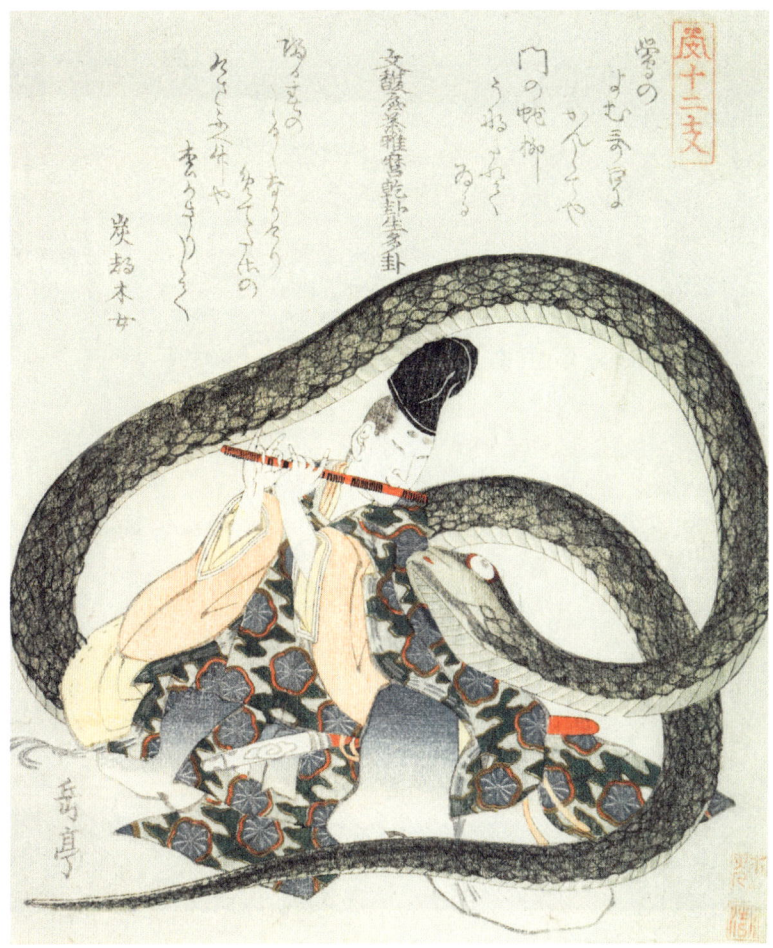

ABOVE

Two of the twelve animals of the East Asian zodiac; on the left a Ming-era tile with the Ox, and on the right a nineteenth-century Japanese print with the Snake.

THE study of astrology in China rose to prominence in the early centuries CE. This aligned with the introduction of the Mandate of Heaven, the idea that Chinese emperors were ordained by the heavens and that celestial phenomena indicated whether things were going well or not.

To simplify a rather complex and interconnected range of approaches, there are two main astrological systems: *ziwei doushu* ('purple star astrology'), which is based on stars, and the *bazi* (Four Pillars of Destiny) system, which is based on the solar calendar – both of which were practised in the Imperial court. Both tie in very closely to the *I Ching* and other forms of divination in China, particularly in the concept of *wuxing* ('the five phases'), each of which are associated with a particular planet and a particular element (Fire, Earth, Water, Wood, Metal), as well as yin-yang.

The Chinese zodiac has twelve animals, which became standardized during the Han dynasty (206 BCE–220 CE). However, unlike the Hellenistic zodiac, the animals are associated with years, not months. Each animal has characteristics associated with them, and they are arranged into a sixty-year cycle (more or less the time it takes for Jupiter to complete a turn around the sun – twelve Earth years – multiplied by five). Each of those five sets is associated with one of the elements mentioned above. There are, however, also a set of animals for the month, day and hour that you were born – these help create a more accurate horoscope.

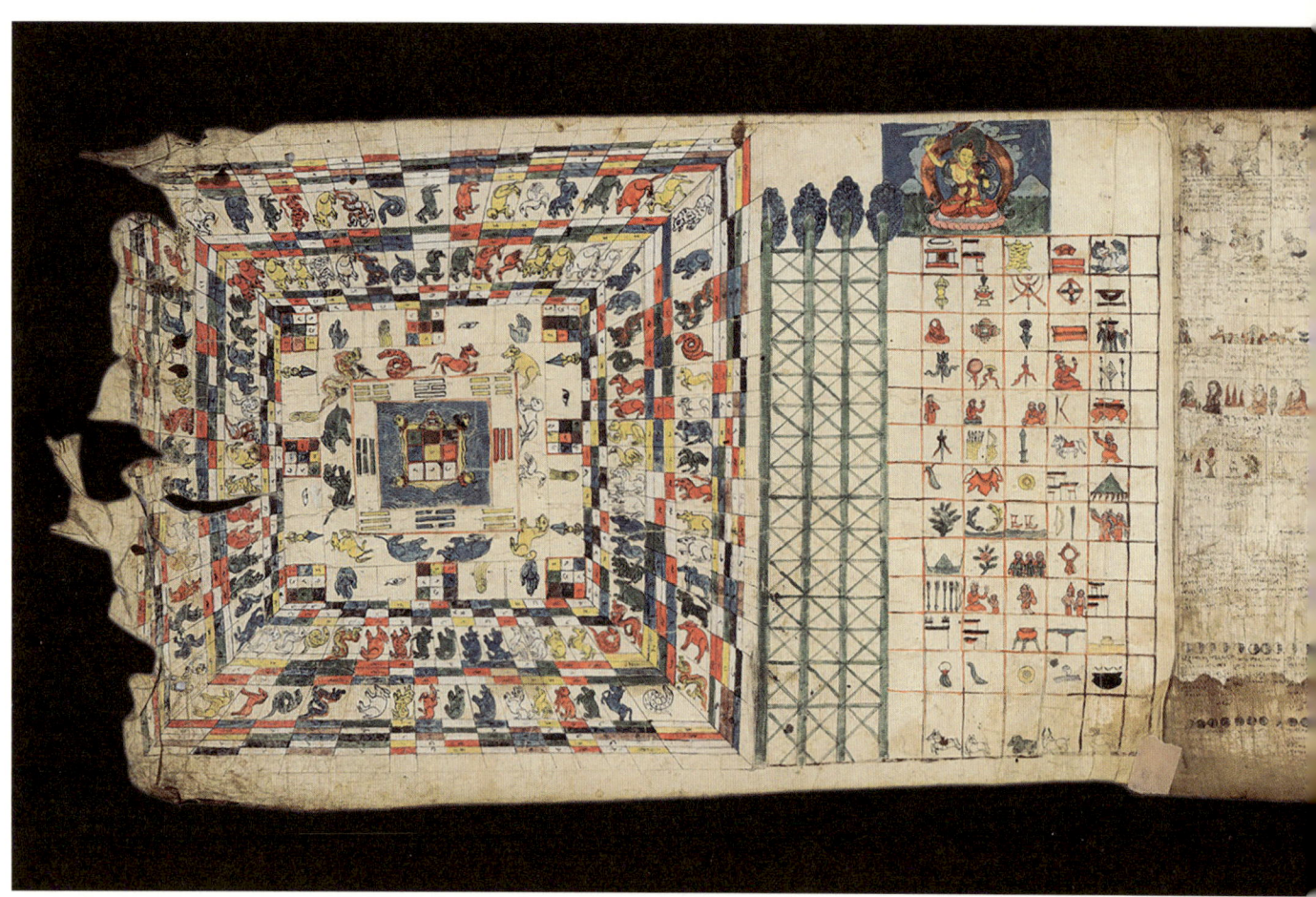

ABOVE

This astrological and numerological handscroll from Tibet would have been used to choose auspicious days for events.

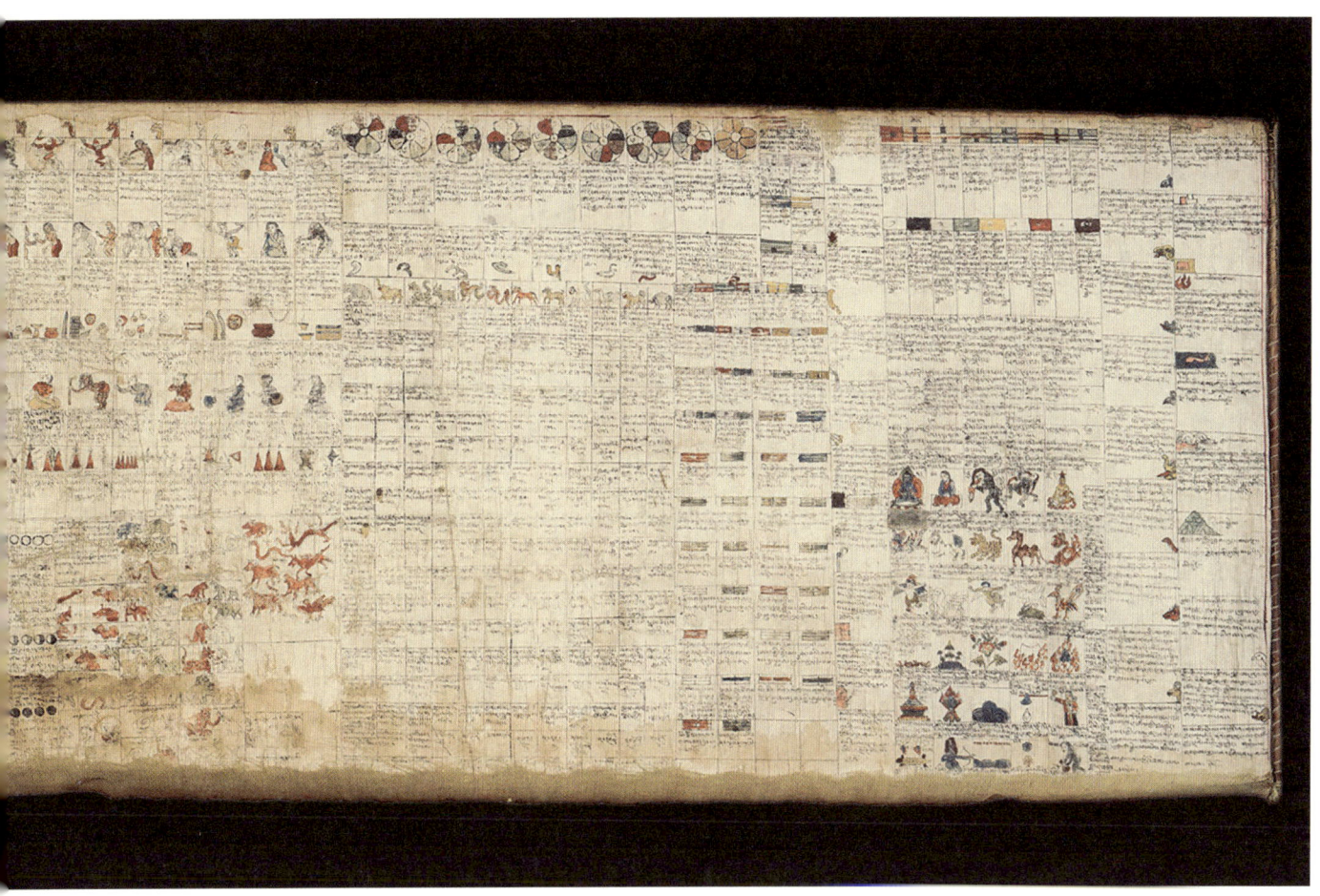

ASTROLOGY IN ISLAM

REVELATION
Active

CHANNEL
Celestial

INTERMEDIARY
Any

CONTEXT
Societal

Despite the Quran forbidding divination, a good grasp of astronomy was essential for knowing where the Kaaba was and what time of day it was – both of which were essential for prayers.

LEFT

A drawing of the zodiac as part of a design for a water clock by al-Jazari, c. 1354.

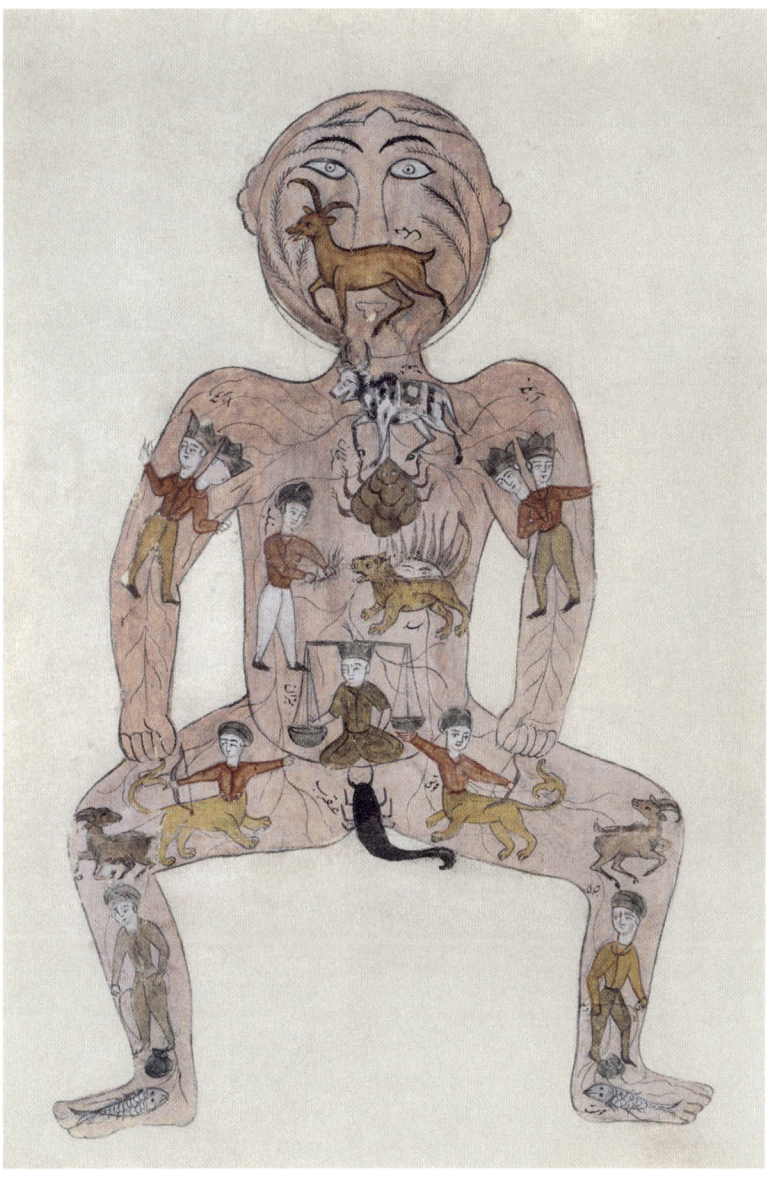

RIGHT

The 'zodiac man', from Persia, relates the signs to different body parts, showing the close perceived relationship between humans and the stars.

IN countries across North Africa, the Middle East and Central Asia from the seventh century CE onwards, astrology has historically been the most popular form of future-telling. The early Islamic world embraced all forms of celestial study and its first observatory was established in Baghdad under the Abbasid Caliphate in the ninth century CE, and at the same time large volumes of secular works by Greek authors were being translated into Arabic.

Scholars of that time wrote important works that would later influence European medieval thought, with the foremost scholar being the Persian Abu Ma'shar al-Balkhi (known as Albumasar in Western contexts), who wrote the *Great Introduction to the Science of Astrology* in the ninth century, influenced by Ptolemy. Another well-known astrologer under the Abbasids was Sahl ibn Bishr, who translated Ptolemy's *Almagest*. Particularly popular was 'electional' or 'event' astrology, which allowed rulers to make optimal decisions about when to start new ventures – for example, the time of founding the new Abbasid capital of Baghdad by al-Mansur was taken by the famous astrologers Nawbakht and Mashallah ibn Athari.

ABOVE AND OPPOSITE

The drama of the zodiac constellations as depicted in a seventeenth-century edition of the *Wonders of Creation* of al-Qazwini.

ABOVE AND OPPOSITE

Two leaves from a fourteenth-century manuscript of Abu Ma'shar's *Kitab al-Mawalid* ('Book of nativities'). It features personifications of the planets and phases of the moon as well as zodiacal signs.

ABOVE AND OPPOSITE

The planets with the constellations they 'rule' in a fourteenth-century Arabic manuscript (above) and a sixteenth-century Ottoman manuscript (below).

From left to right: Mars in Scorpio; Mercury in Gemini; Mercury in Virgo; the moon in Cancer; the sun in Leo; Venus in Libra.

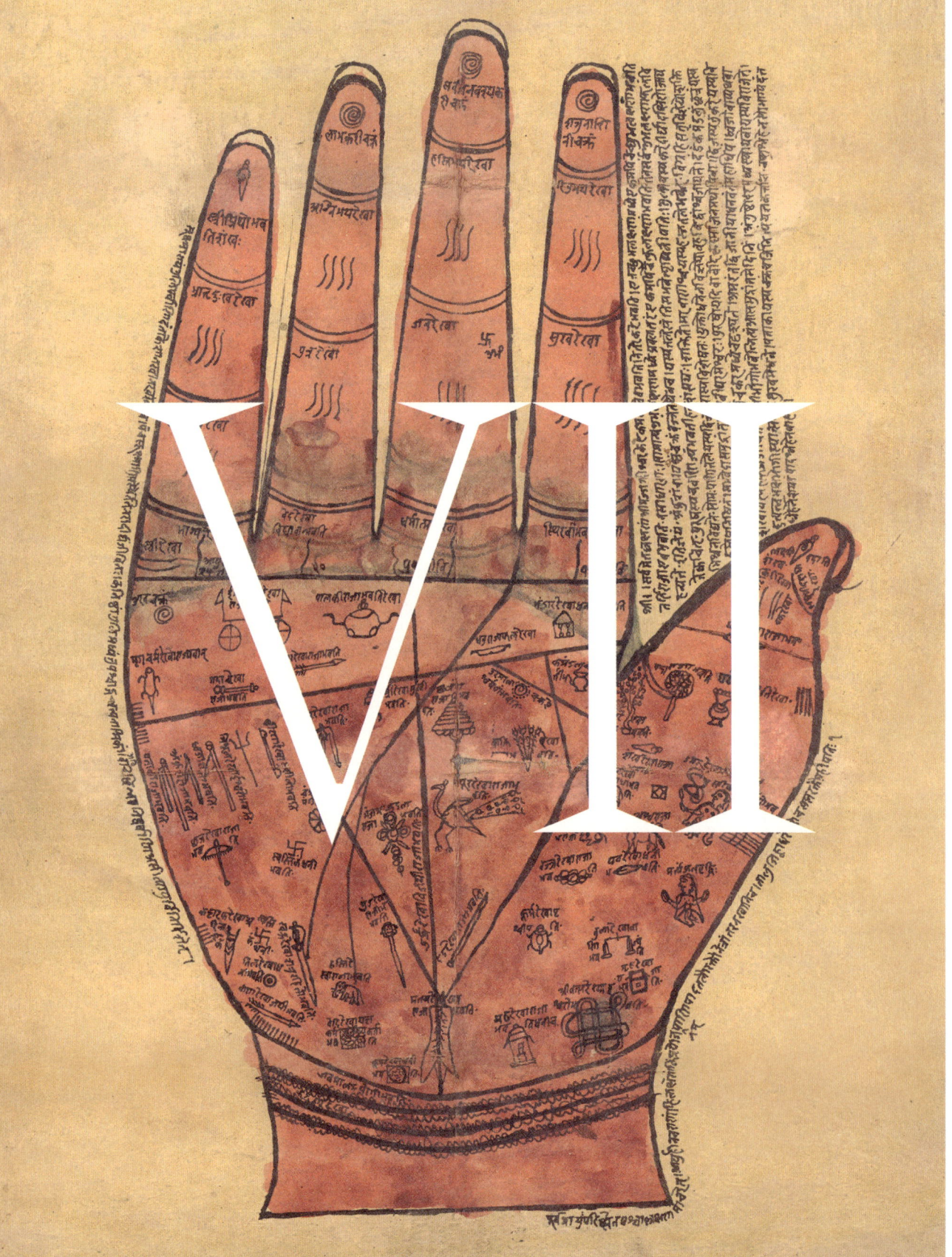

VII.

DIVINATION & FORTUNE-TELLING

DIVINATION covers a wide range of practices, all of which allow a brief glimpse of the supernatural realm. However, most forms of divination do not provide immediately obvious answers and therefore require skill in ritual and interpretation. There are innumerable forms of divination covering things such as smoke (capnomancy), books (bibliomancy) and mirrors (catoptromancy). Perhaps the best-known forms of divination are casting lots (cleromancy), the reading of animal behaviour (such as ornithomancy) or entrails (haruspicy) and astrology. All of these forms date back at least three thousand years.

OPPOSITE

An eighteenth-century Sanskrit palm-reading manual.

CLEROMANCY is perhaps the oldest and simplest form of divination and refers to the drawing of lots: to physically cast some material and interpret the patterns it forms when it falls. The substances cast can be very ordinary, for example salt (halomancy), beans (favomancy) or dust (abacomancy), or a little more special such as the *sozhi* (cowrie shells) found in South India. Sometimes human-made objects are thrown: chains made of brass, seeds and wood (in *Ifá* divination), 'moon blocks' (crescent-shaped pieces of wood used in the *Poe* divination found in China and Taiwan), dice (astragalomancy), or tablets made of wood or bone (known as *hakata* in Zimbabwe). After casting, the process of interpretation can be simple or complex. *I Ching* divination can start with the casting of coins, and the pattern they fall in is then interpreted in a highly formalized way by consulting the *I Ching* texts.

Another common and ancient form of divination is through animals, which reflects the importance that animals had in the development of early human society through hunting and farming. In some cases, this divination involved observing the behaviour and movement of animals in the wild – as did the augurs of ancient Rome, who interpreted the flight of birds (see p. 30). In other cases, it involved captive animals making some sort of choice, consciously or not. Ninth-century CE compilations of the *Shardulakarnavadana* Buddhist treatise on astrology and omens feature various forms of animal divination, including how to interpret the howls of jackals. On the behaviour of crows, it asserts, 'If a crow sets down on a man's head and tears away at his ear, it indicates his death within seven nights'. In Cameroon and Nigeria, a form of divination called *Nggàm*, in which the movements of spiders and crabs are observed and interpreted, is still practised by some peoples. From very early on – certainly the second millennium BCE – we also find the burning of animal bones. In China from the late Shang period onwards (c. 1250–1050 BCE), ox shoulder blades and turtle plastrons and were burned until they cracked, and then the cracks were interpreted. Other scapulimancy techniques can be found across East Asia (influenced by China) and among certain

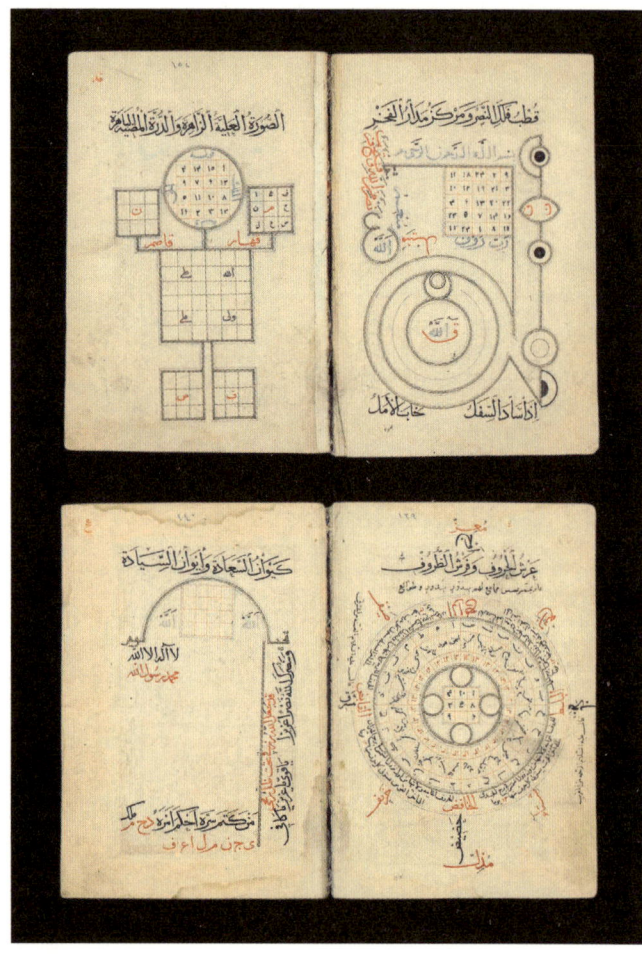

ABOVE

Diagrams from a late fifteenth-century Ottoman work on divination, *The Key to Comprehensive Prognostication*.

BELOW

Hakata made of bone used for casting and telling the future, Zimbabwe.

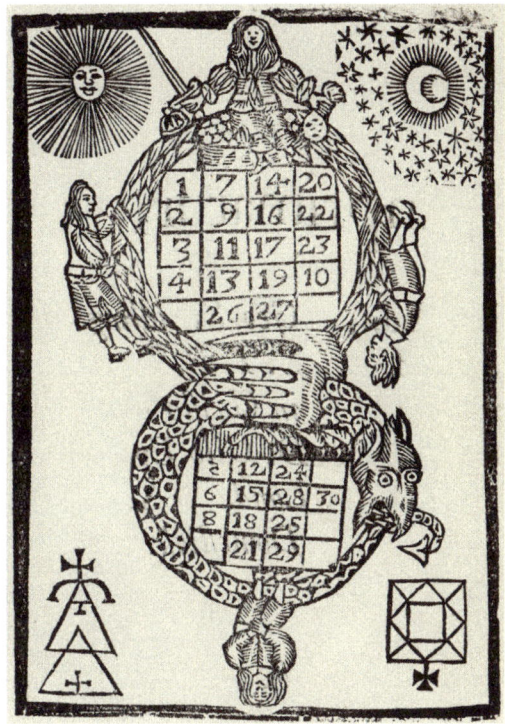

ABOVE LEFT

Two wheels of fortune from an English book published in 1663; the top represents good luck, the bottom bad luck.

ABOVE RIGHT

The Crystal Ball, John William Waterhouse, 1902.

OVERLEAF

People consult a palmistry chart in Tokyo.

indigenous peoples such as the Mistassini Cree and the Naskapi Innu in modern-day Canada.

Closely related to divination is fortune-telling. Whereas divination is frequently part of a religion or wider philosophical framework, fortune-telling is typically more of a folk belief. Rituals associated with fortune-telling include tea-leaf reading, which was said to originate in China, and coffee-ground reading, originating in Turkey. Both are forms of tasseography, or reading the sediment in a cup, and became increasingly popular in Europe from the seventeenth century onwards. The device most associated with fortune-telling in popular imagination, the crystal ball, was first mentioned in the first century CE, and a crystal ball was buried with the Merovingian king Childeric I in the fifth century in Tournai in present-day Belgium. A later, famous user of crystal ball scrying was John Dee, and by the twentieth century it had come into widespread use. The way it distorts reality and conjures up strange optical effects leaves ample space for interpretation.

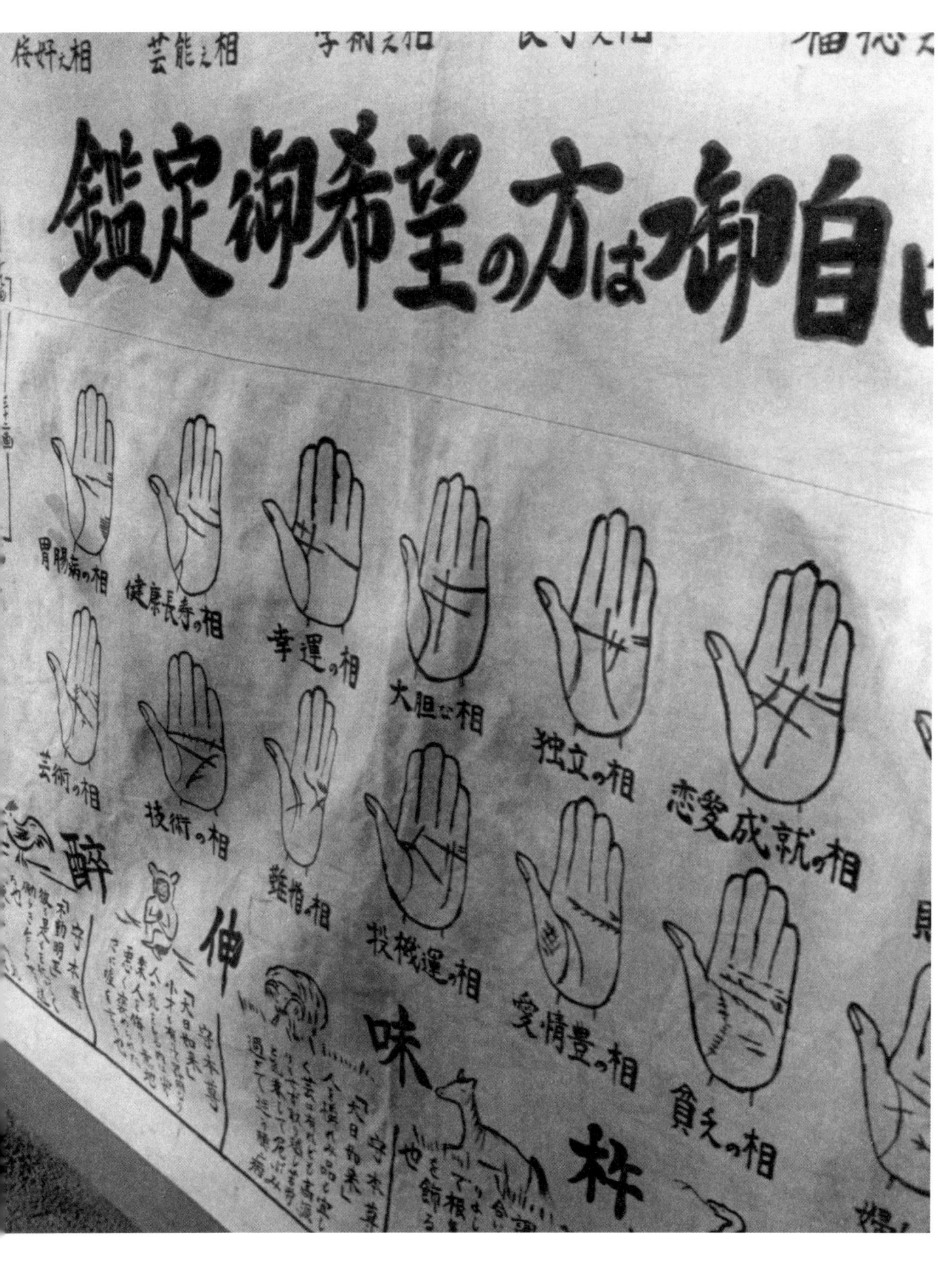

ABOVE AND OPPOSITE

Pages from a 'lottery book', used to divine from Christian texts, Strasbourg, 1539. At the centre of the right-hand page is a volvelle (moveable paper disc).

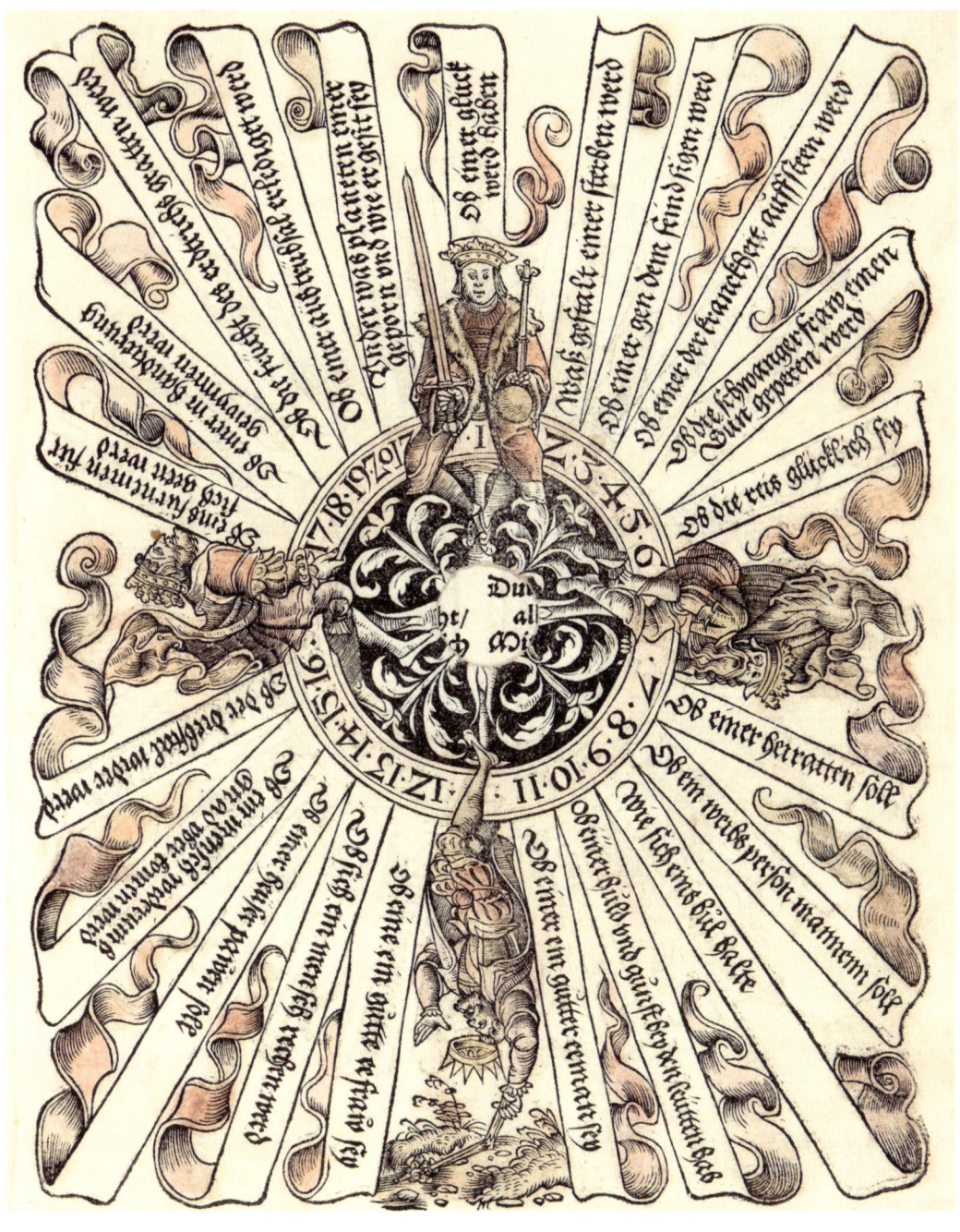

DICE

REVELATION
Active

CHANNEL
Tool

INTERMEDIARY
Any

CONTEXT
Societal, Personal

The precursors of today's six-sided dice were the ankle bones of sheep and goats, called *astragaloi* or, colloquially, 'knucklebones', which often had numbers inscribed on each side.

In ancient Greece dice were typically inscribed with 1, 3, 4 and 6, with opposing sides adding up to seven. They were used in gaming, but also for divination, normally by throwing four or five and then adding the numbers that fell face up. The sum would then indicate which of the numbered oracles to look up in a public inscription. These 'dice oracle' inscriptions are often found by city gates; an example can be found among the ruins of Termessos (near modern-day Antalya, Turkey).

Later on, six-sided dice were produced, but also twenty-sided versions inscribed with the first twenty letters of the Greek alphabet, each of which corresponded to an oracle in a list. Results could include oracles such as 'You have divine helpers on this path', or 'To fight with the waves is difficult; endure, friend' (as seen in an inscription from ancient Lycia, now Turkey).

The Shona people of modern-day Zimbabwe use a form of two-sided dice or tablets called *hakata* to divine the future, whether to help make decisions or get a prognosis on illness. They are thrown and the inscribed upwards-facing sides are interpreted. In Tibet the dice-based *Mo* divination system is used by everyone, including the Dalai Lama. Two dice are cast, leading to one of thirty-six possible outcomes which are then consulted in a text.

It is thought that the *Irk Bitig* (*Book of Omens*), an ancient Turkic manuscript of omens from the ninth century CE found in Dunhuang, western China, was used to interpret the result of throwing four-sided dice. Three dice were cast and then the resulting numbers looked up in the text for an omen and prognosis. The omens are somewhat oblique, for example, a result of 1-1-2 is associated with the ill omen of a woman dropping a mirror in a lake, while 2-4-1 refers to a favourable omen of a tent.

DIVINATION & FORTUNE-TELLING 229

ABOVE LEFT

A twenty-sided die (icosahedron) inscribed with Greek letters.

ABOVE RIGHT

Bone divination tablets (*hakata*) from the Zambezi river area, East Africa.

RIGHT

The Turkic *Irk Bitig* book of omens; the groups of red circles represent the combinations of dice throws to be interpreted.

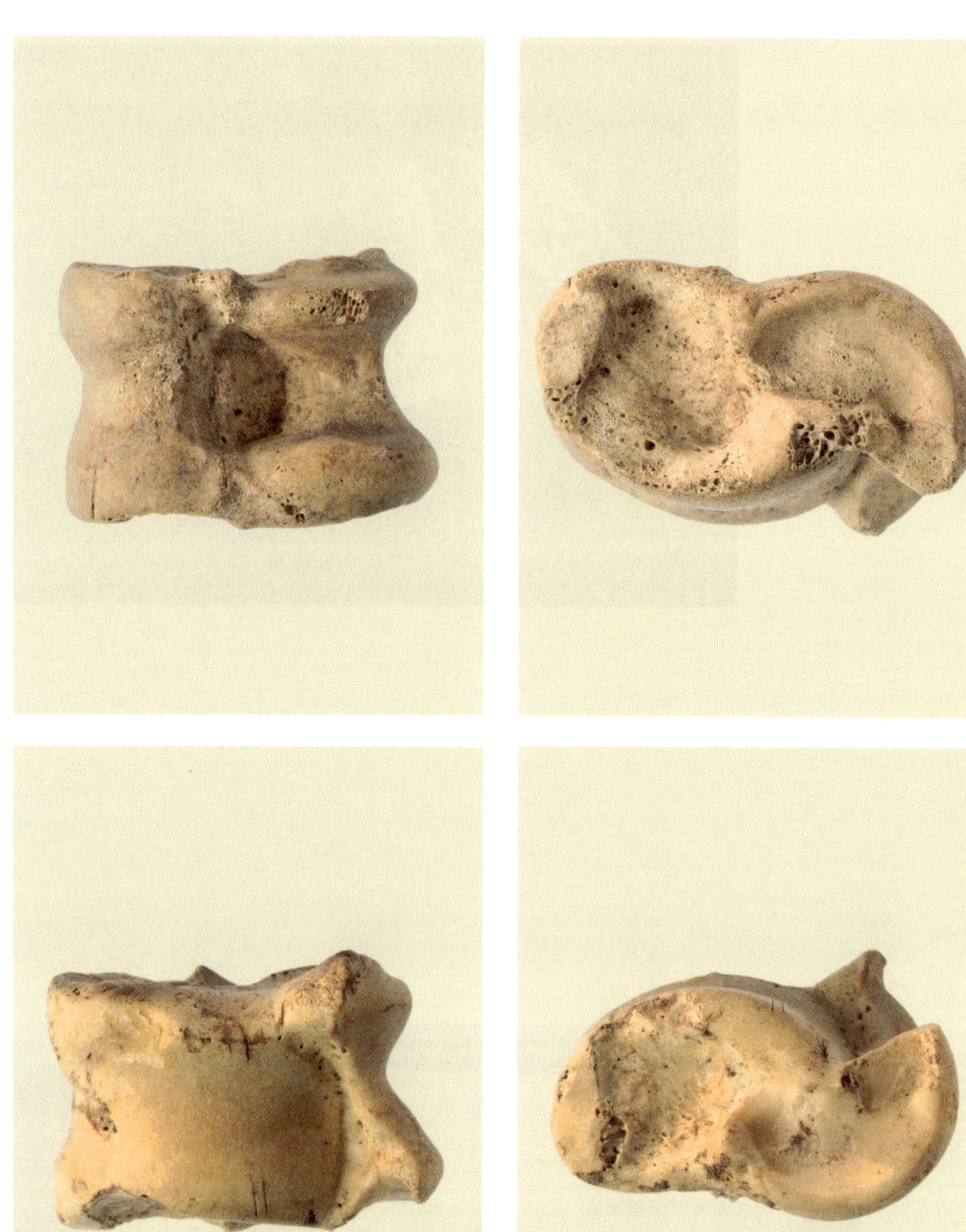

ABOVE AND OPPOSITE

Astragaloi, or 'knucklebones', used in games and in divination. Unlike modern dice, they have just four sides.

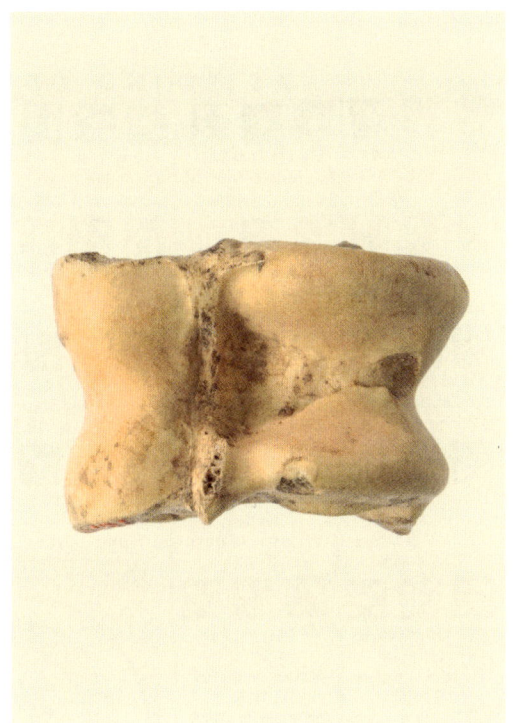

ABOVE

A page showing possible outcomes of dice from a 'book of fortune', 1547.

ABOVE

The combination of dice would direct readers to further pages that would reveal their fortune.

SCRYING

REVELATION
Active

CHANNEL
Tool

INTERMEDIARY
Any

CONTEXT
Personal

Scrying is the practice of peering into a reflective surface to find signs of the future. The material used can include a mirror, glass, crystal, oil or water. The distorted images and reflections produced are then interpreted.

LEFT

A depiction of catoptromancy from a compendium of magical arts, c. 1775.

ABOVE LEFT

A crystal ball, with Greek inscription, found in Denmark.

ABOVE RIGHT

A mirror from around 1200 decorated with a pair of sphinxes.

SCRYING is a highly subjective and frequently mystical affair, lacking the rigour suggested by the standardized, and often elaborate, processes of some other forms of divination. The technique is ancient – the first mirrors were likely created in Anatolia, modern-day Turkey, around eight thousand years ago, and both mirrors and crystal balls were mentioned by the ancient Romans, where mirror divination (today called catoptromancy) was performed by *specularii*. The Greek writer Pausanias in his *Description of Greece* from the second century CE described a divination process whereby a mirror was dipped into water to determine whether a patient would live or die.

Mirrors were also particularly important in Mesoamerica. For the Maya, their mosaic mirrors were symbols of authority and used for seeing the future. Cuauhtemoc, the last Aztec emperor between 1520 and 1521, had a vision in a mirror of the Aztec people, which he interpreted as concerning their coming defeat at the hands of the Spanish. An Aztec mirror of polished obsidian was likely used by the English astrologer and occultist John Dee, who practised in the late sixteenth century. It was probably brought to Europe in the 1520s and is today in the British Museum.

One early surviving crystal ball with a Greek magical inscription was found in a late fourth-century CE grave in Årslev, Denmark. A small crystal ball made of beryl was discovered in the tomb of Merovingian king Childeric I (c. 457–481 CE), and the assumption is that it was used in scrying. Similar crystal balls have been found in other Frankish and Saxon graves of the same time (around the fifth to seventh centuries CE), with a large number found in women's tombs in Kent, England.

HARUSPICES

REVELATION
Active

CHANNEL
Tool

INTERMEDIARY
Priest

CONTEXT
Official

The practice of examining a liver for signs of the future likely comes from ancient Mesopotamia, where models of livers indicating the meaning of unusual markings have been found.

LEFT

An Old Babylonian model of a sheep's liver, divided into sections inscribed with the meanings of a blemish in that section.

OPPOSITE

A sacrificed animal's entrails are interpreted by Roman *haruspices*.

WHILE augurs could divine the future from observing the behaviour of animals, others, known as *haruspices*, found the future in animals' entrails, particularly the liver since it was seen as one of the best reflectors of health in an animal. It was among the Etruscans of ancient Italy that haruspicy became particularly important. A foundational figure in Etruscan mythology, Tages, was said to have written on haruspicy (in the *Libri Tagetici*, which were referred to by later Roman authors). The practice was then inherited by the Romans, and although it never became part of the state religion as it had been for the Etruscans, many emperors took it seriously. Claudius (r. 41–54 CE) tried to revive it through legislation.

Animal sacrifice for omens was practised elsewhere. For example, the Inca (reaching their greatest extent 1438–1533 across modern-day Peru and neighbouring countries) sacrificed llamas, and while they were still alive the organs were inspected. On some occasions the lungs of sacrificed llamas were extracted and inflated so that priests could examine and interpret the patterns of veins. In the words of the Spanish chronicler of 'idolatry' Rodrigo Hernández Príncipe, writing in 1622, 'They regarded it as a most happy omen if the lungs came out still quivering.'

BELOW

A *haruspex* examines the entrails of a recently sacrificed bull in a relief from Trajan's Forum, Rome.

DIVINATION & FORTUNE-TELLING

RIGHT

An Etruscan bronze statuette depicting a *haruspex*, from the fourth century BCE.

BIBLIOMANCY

REVELATION
Active

CHANNEL
Tool

INTERMEDIARY
Any

CONTEXT
Societal

In the practice of bibliomancy, a book is opened randomly and whatever text is found is interpreted in the light of the future.

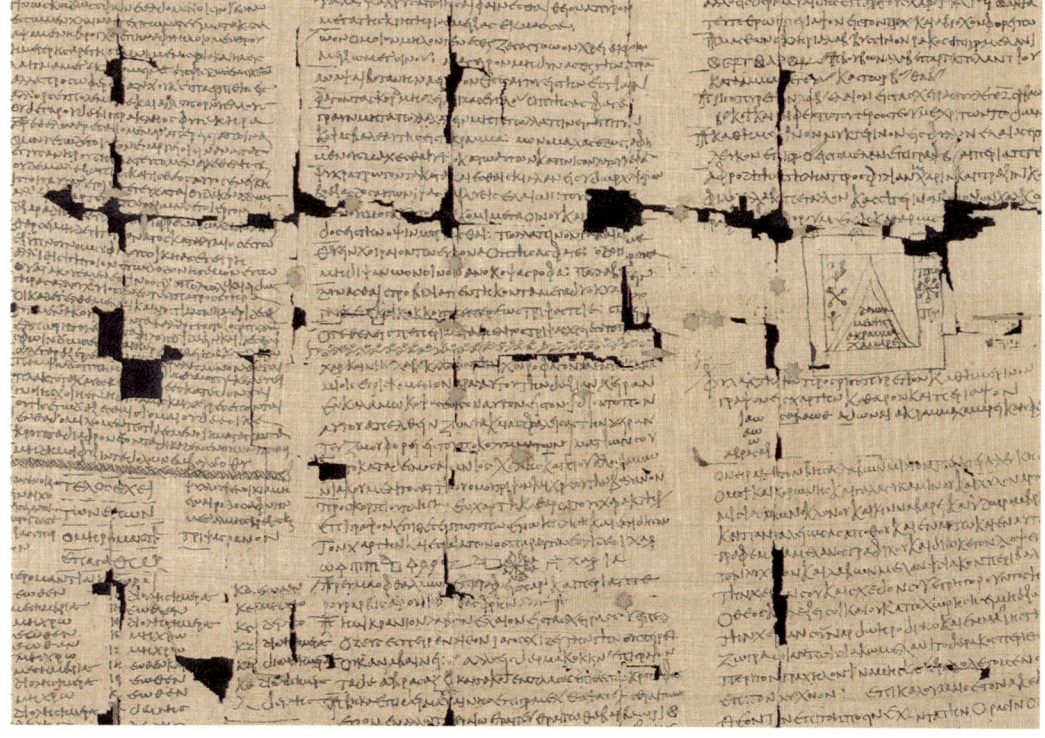

LEFT

The *Homeromanteion* ('Homer oracle') pointed users towards a Homeric verse that would shed light on their future.

DIVINATION & FORTUNE-TELLING

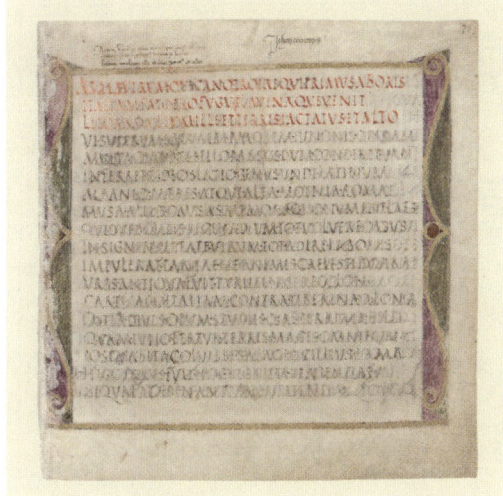

ABOVE LEFT

The opening lines of the *Aeneid* from a fifth-century CE edition of Vergil. The poet's works were used in a form of bibliomancy known as the *Sortes Vergilianae*.

ABOVE RIGHT

A page from one of the few surviving complete Falnamas. Opposite each miniature is a text that explains whether the scene bodes well or not.

BIBLIOMANCY could be undertaken by priests or by laypeople (so long as they could read). Various books have been used: a collection of the poems of Hafez known as *The Divan*, from fourteenth-century Iran; the Bible; and the Quran. If consulting the Bible for this purpose it was common to use the Book of Psalms, since it was already used for guidance. For the Romans it was the works of Vergil that were most often used in the *Sortes Vergilianae* ('Vergilian lots'). The emperors Hadrian and Claudius Gothicus used the *Aeneid*, opening it at a random point and taking guidance from whatever they found. In the case of Hadrian, he chose the section 6.808, which he saw as predicting his adoption by Trajan – which did actually happen.

At the gathering of bishops known as the Council of Vannes in 465 CE, bibliomancy was strictly prohibited. Among the canons published afterwards was one to '[excommunicate] those of the clergy who meddle in divinations, and superstitiously pretend to foretell the future by chance readings of Holy Scripture'. However, the practice continued as evidenced by annotations made in around 550–650 CE to the early fifth-century Greek-Latin *Codex Bezae*.

In India and Iran during the fifteenth to eighteenth centuries, the use of Falnamas (from the Persian word for 'books of omens') became popular. This could refer to divination tables included at the end of the Quran, which could be used to interpret the result of a page being opened at random, or else to specially commissioned manuscripts with spectacular illustrations used in the same way.

ABOVE AND OPPOSITE

Illustrations from an eighteenth-century copy of the *Divan* of Hafez, which was commonly used for bibliomancy.

OVERLEAF

A seventeenth-century Iranian table of divination used in bibliomancy.

SACRED LOTS

REVELATION
Active

CHANNEL
Tool

INTERMEDIARY
Any

CONTEXT
Societal, Personal

The casting of lots appears in many religions as a way of making decisions. Typically starting with a question, the process would gradually eliminate options until there was only one left.

THE casting of lots appears in the Old Testament of the Bible, for example when Joshua cast lots in front of God to assign land to different tribes (Joshua 18:6–10). In Chinese-speaking countries we find *kau chim*, which are bamboo sticks shaken from a container to give a number that relates to a poem that gives a response.

In Japan, *omikuji* ('sacred lots'), which can be bought from temples, are used in a similar way. Generally printed on paper, they offer one hundred possible verses which range from 'great blessing' to 'great misfortune'. The verses themselves are ascribed sometimes to the Bodhisattva Avalokiteshvara (Kannon), or else to the tenth-century monk Ryogen. *Omikuji* are obtained by selecting a metal stick from a bamboo cylinder, which gives the number of a drawer – the paper slip is in that drawer. If the reading is unfavourable, it can be tied to a pine tree, since the word for pine (*matsu*) is very similar for the verb 'to wait', the implication being that the bad fortune will wait by the pine tree and therefore detach itself from the recipient.

RIGHT

In Japan, unfavourable prognoses are tied to a tree so that the bad luck isn't attached to the recipient.

BELOW

A Chinese fortune-teller with a tube to his right likely containing *kau chim*. To the left is a bowl holding a turtle shell.

OVERLEAF

Votive plaques called *ema* left at a shrine in Japan. Often decorated on one side with astrological signs, on the other side visitors write their wishes for the future. Underneath *omikuji* are tied to a line.

TAROT

REVELATION
Active

CHANNEL
Tool

INTERMEDIARY
Any

CONTEXT
Personal

Tarot cards are one of the newer forms of divination. The playing cards originated in Italy in the mid-fifteenth century, but it wasn't until the mid-eighteenth century that they were used in cartomancy.

PERHAPS the person most instrumental in popularizing the Tarot deck for divinatory use was the French Protestant pastor Antoine Court de Gébelin, who published an article on its allegedly ancient and occult origins in 1781. He claimed that the deck contained the wisdom of the ancient Egyptian Book of Thoth – largely influenced by the recent discoveries by French archaeologists and contemporary fascination with Egyptology. In 1783, Jean-Baptiste Alliette published *Manière de se récréer avec le jeu de cartes nommées tarots* under the name Etteilla, which popularized the occult use of Tarot.

Today the Tarot deck consists of seventy-eight cards, which include into twenty-two Major Arcana ('greater secrets') cards and fifty-six Minor Arcana ('lesser secrets') split into four suits (Wands, Cups, Pentacles, Swords) of fourteen cards each. There are many ways to read the cards, by selecting them from the deck and arranging them. There are several popular editions of the Tarot deck, with the most common being the Rider–Waite–Smith deck that was first published in 1909 – it is estimated that over 100 million copies have been sold worldwide to date.

RIGHT

'Judgment' from the Cary–Yale Tarot deck, c. 1442–47, one of the oldest surviving sets.

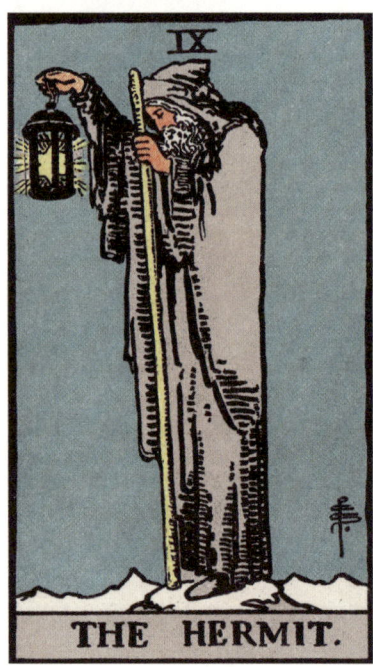

ABOVE AND OPPOSITE, TOP ROW

Photographic prints for *Mountain Dream Tarot* by Bea Nettles, 1970–75.

ABOVE AND OPPOSITE, BOTTOM ROW

The same cards from the Rider–Waite–Smith deck, first published in 1909.

PALMISTRY

The practice of reading a palm covers the totality of the hand and analyses its lines and marks to assess present and future health, wealth, luck and relationships.

REVELATION
Active

CHANNEL
Tool

INTERMEDIARY
Any

CONTEXT
Personal

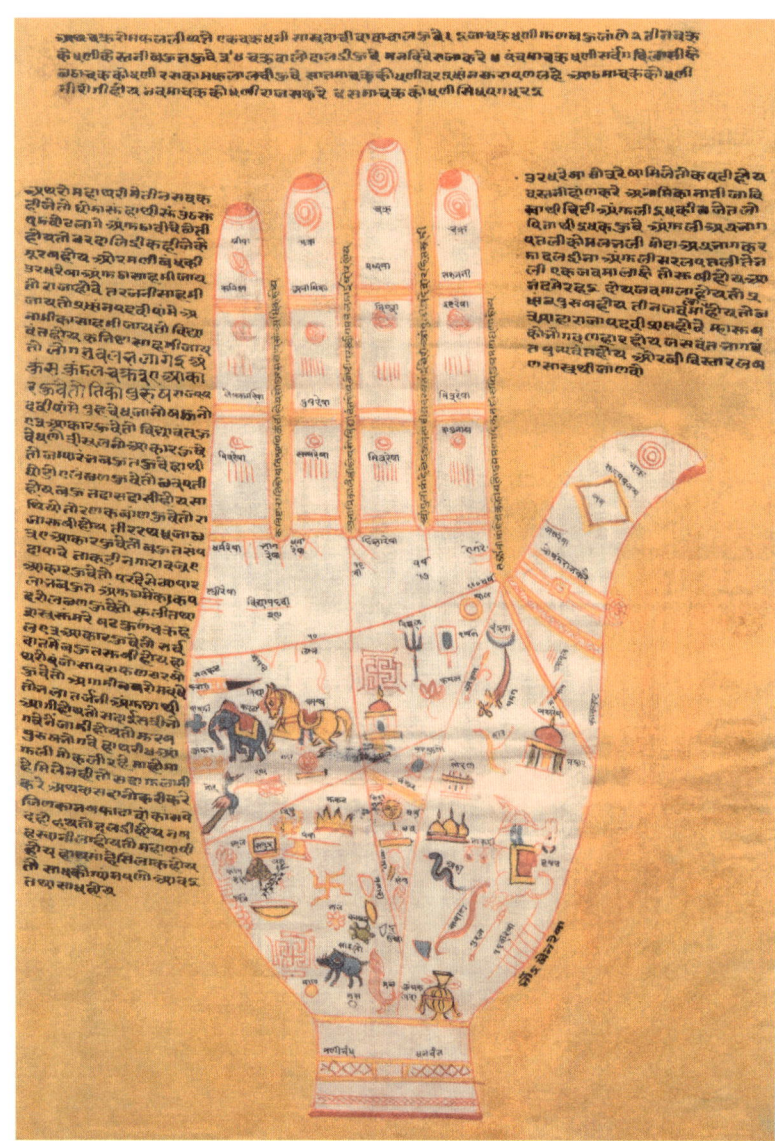

LEFT

A nineteenth-century Vedic palmistry diagram from India.

RIGHT

An eighteenth-century edition of *Wisdom of the Hand*. In Kabbalistic thinking, a person's soul is etched into their body – notably in the lines of their palms.

BELOW RIGHT

Diagram from a fifteenth-century German treatise on chiromancy and geomancy.

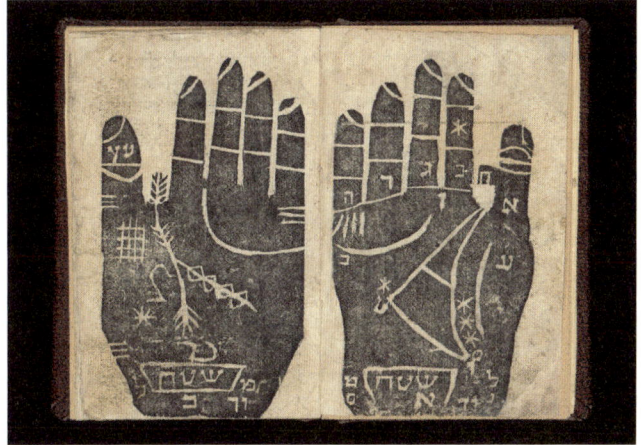

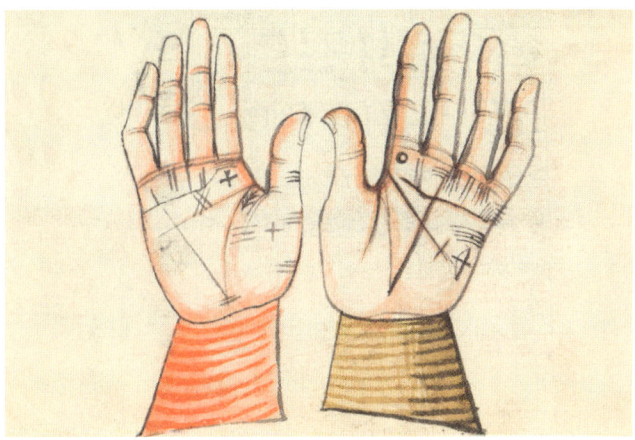

PALMISTRY, also called chiromancy, goes back millennia, possibly to ancient India of the first millennium BCE. Valmiki, the traditional author of the *Ramayana*, also allegedly wrote *The Teachings of Valmiki Maharishi on Male Palmistry*. The study of palms seems to have spread from India to China, Persia and beyond.

It was said that the Greek philosopher Aristotle became fascinated with palmistry after discovering a treatise on the subject on the altar of Hermes in Egypt and that he then sent the treatise to Alexander the Great. Aristotle certainly wrote on palm-reading in his *History of Animals*, in which he suggested that the lines that cross our palm indicate how long we are likely to live – this has since become a commonplace in palmistry. During the Renaissance, palmistry was denounced as one of seven divinatory arts forbidden by the Church. At the same time, more and more books were published on the topic, particularly in the north of Europe where the Catholic Church had less influence.

In Europe the practice of palm-reading became associated with the Roma, who had originally come from India. In part this association reflects a concern among the Romani people with spiritual practices (*drabarimos*), and in part because it was a convenient way of earning a living in non-Romani societies. From the late nineteenth century many chirological societies were established as part of a wider contemporary interest in the occult, and several famous palm-readers emerged. Foremost was the Irish palm-reader known as Cheiro (William John Warner), who read the fortunes of the rich and famous such as Oscar Wilde, Nellie Melba, Mata Hari and Edward, Prince of Wales. Mark Twain wrote in Cheiro's visitor's book: 'Cheiro has exposed my character to me with humiliating accuracy. I ought not to confess this accuracy, still I am moved to do so.'

I CHING

REVELATION
Active

CHANNEL
Tool

INTERMEDIARY
Any

CONTEXT
Societal

The *I Ching*, or *Book of Changes*, likely dates to the Western Zhou period *c.* 1046–771 BCE). Over time it became one of the Five Classics of Confucian thought.

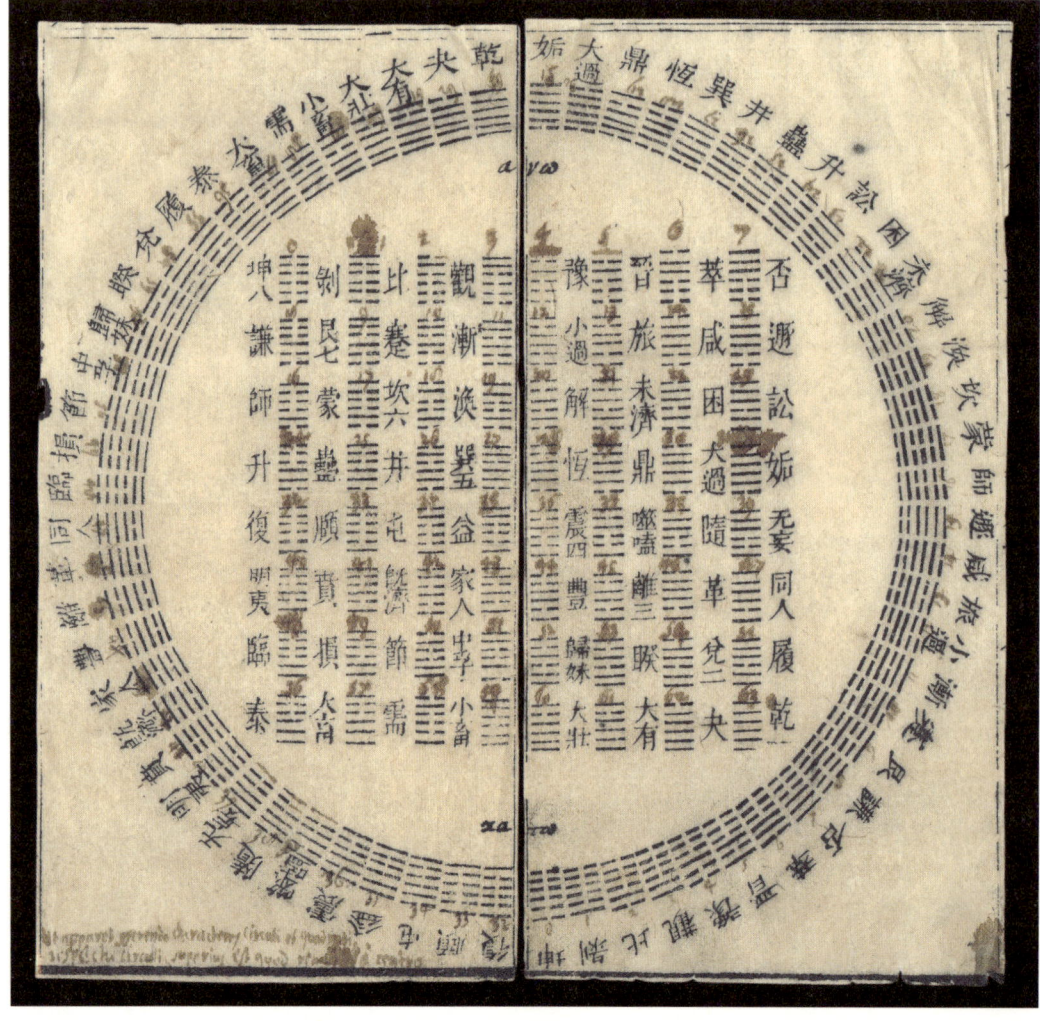

LEFT

The hexagrams of the *I Ching* in a document belonging to the German mathematician Gottfried Wilhelm Leibniz.

EVEN today the *I Ching* retains huge cultural influence in East Asia. From the nineteenth century onwards, it also became popular in the West, reaching peak influence in the 1950s and 1960s alongside a wider interest in Eastern philosophy.

To use the *I Ching*, first a question is formulated (though generally the *I Ching* does not work well with yes/no questions, since the texts require interpretation). Then the casting process is started – this is slow and deliberative. Originally yarrow stalks were used to generate the lines of a hexagram. The lines could be 'solid' (representing yang) or 'broken' (representing yin), and 'old' (changing) or 'young' (unchanging). Three lines were stacked on top of each other from bottom to top to make up a 'trigram' (interestingly, the South Korean flag today incorporates some of the same trigrams found in the *I Ching*, wa testament to how influential this thinking has been). Two stacked trigrams make up a hexagram, and there are sixty-four potential hexagrams, each with its own particular (and often cryptic) meaning that can be looked up in the *I Ching* book itself. So, to take a concrete example, a question such as 'Should I change my job?' would ultimately lead to one of sixty-four answers.

RIGHT

A modern Japanese interpretation of *I Ching* divination by Kitawaki Noboru, 1941.

OVERLEAF

A fortune-teller in Japan holds a bundle of yarrow stalks with which to perform *I Ching* divination, *c.* 1914.

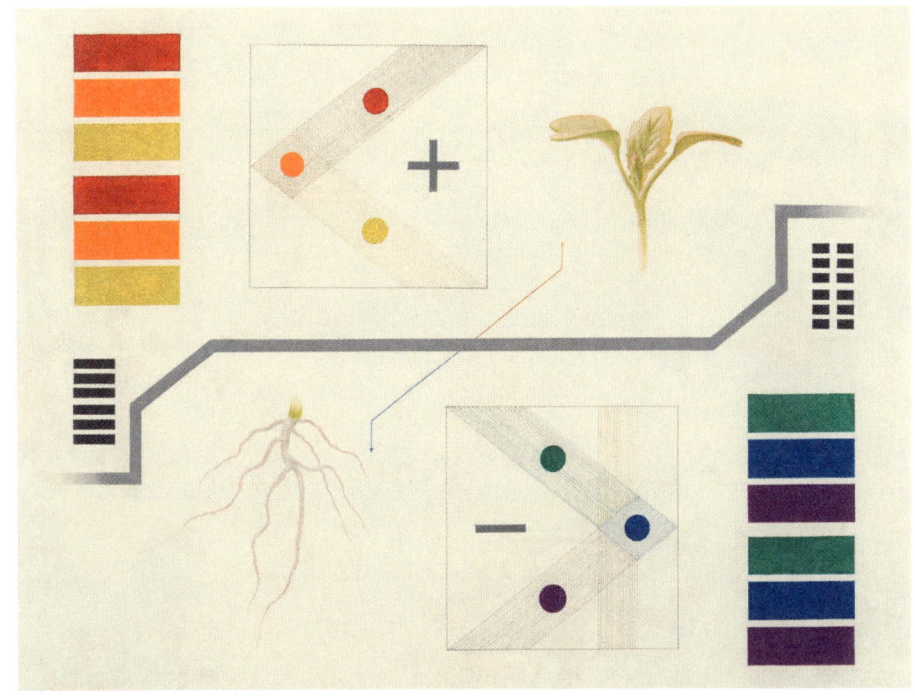

SCAPULIMANCY & PLASTROMANCY

REVELATION
Active

CHANNEL
Tool

INTERMEDIARY
Any

CONTEXT
Societal

The scapulae (shoulder blades) of oxen, cattle and deer are large, relatively flat and when exposed to heat, crack in a distinctive way – all qualities that led to their usefulness in divination.

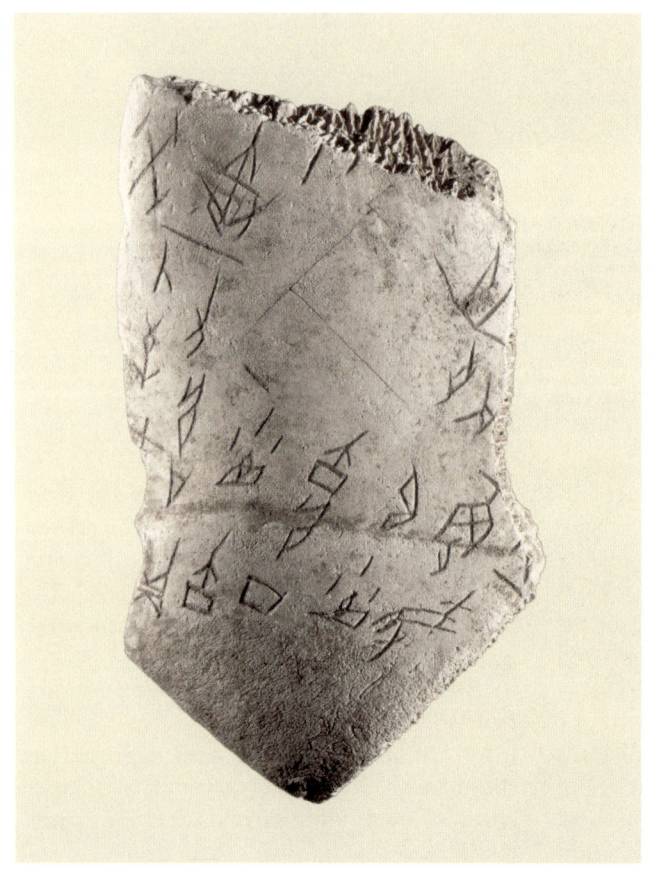

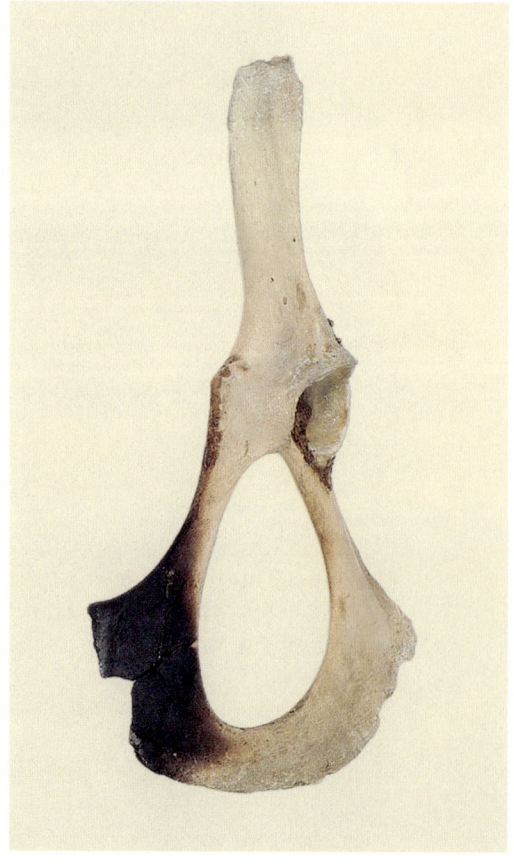

RIGHT

An inscribed Shang-dynasty turtle plastron from China.

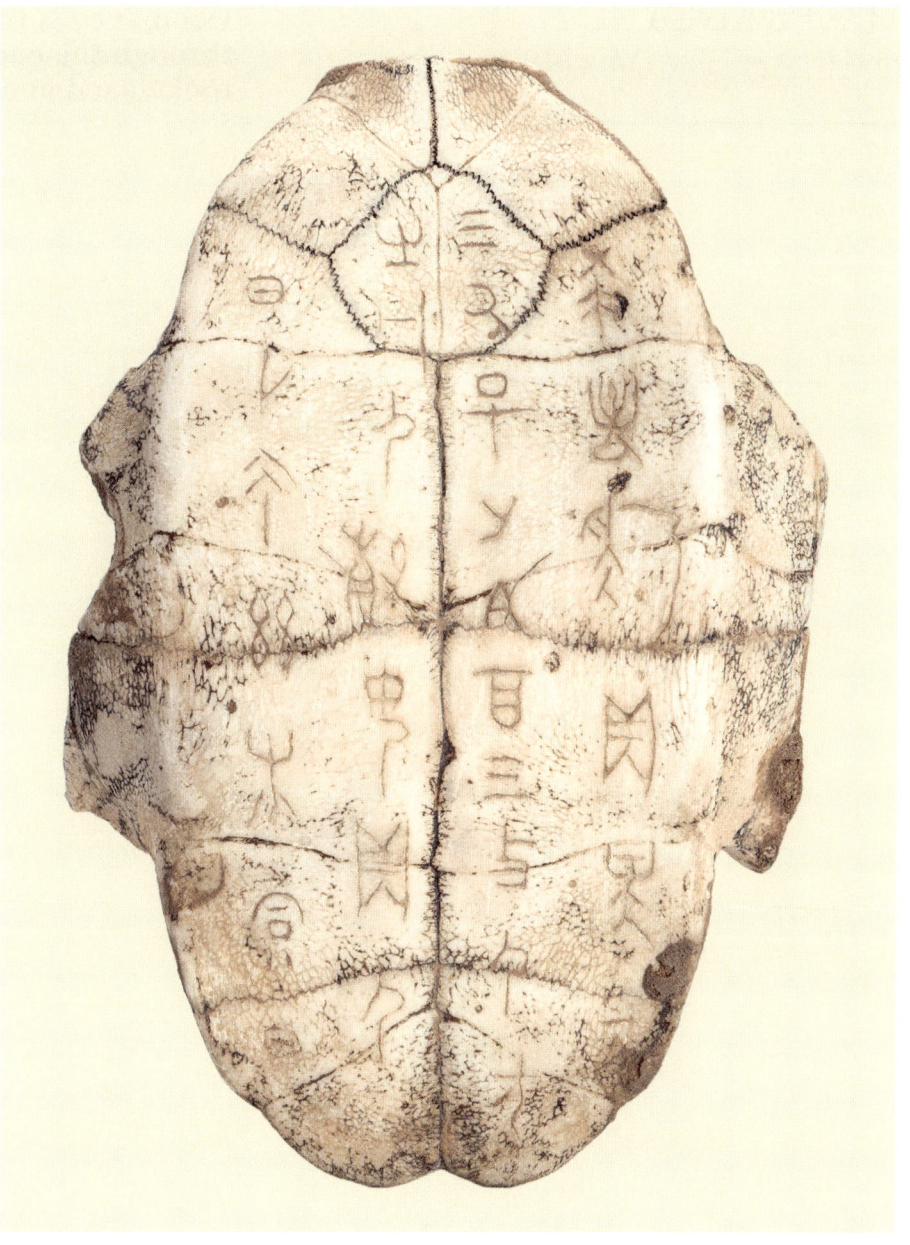

OPPOSITE, LEFT

A Shang-dynasty oracle bone.

OPPOSITE, RIGHT

A bone from a beaver burned for divination among the Innu people of modern-day Canada, c. 1924.

LARGE numbers of bones from around the thirteenth century BCE have been found in China that show evidence of having been used in divination rituals.

In ancient China, the scapula would be prepared by having all the flesh removed and then being drilled into, to encourage cracking. A question or situation would be inscribed into it, and then it was burned in a fire. Scapula bones crack when burned, and the length, depth and placement of these cracks would then be interpreted in light of the question. The response to the divination was then also sometimes inscribed on the same bone. The undersides of turtle shells (known as the plastron) were also used. They have been found in Mongolia, Siberia, Tibet and Korea.

Another practice can be found among Native American tribes such as the Naskapi Innu, where a caribou scapula represented the hunting plains. Held over the fire, marks would appear, indicating where animals could be found.

GEOMANCY

Geomancy is the process of divination through the earth and its markings, rocks, sand and plants.

REVELATION
Active

CHANNEL
Tool

INTERMEDIARY
Any

CONTEXT
Societal

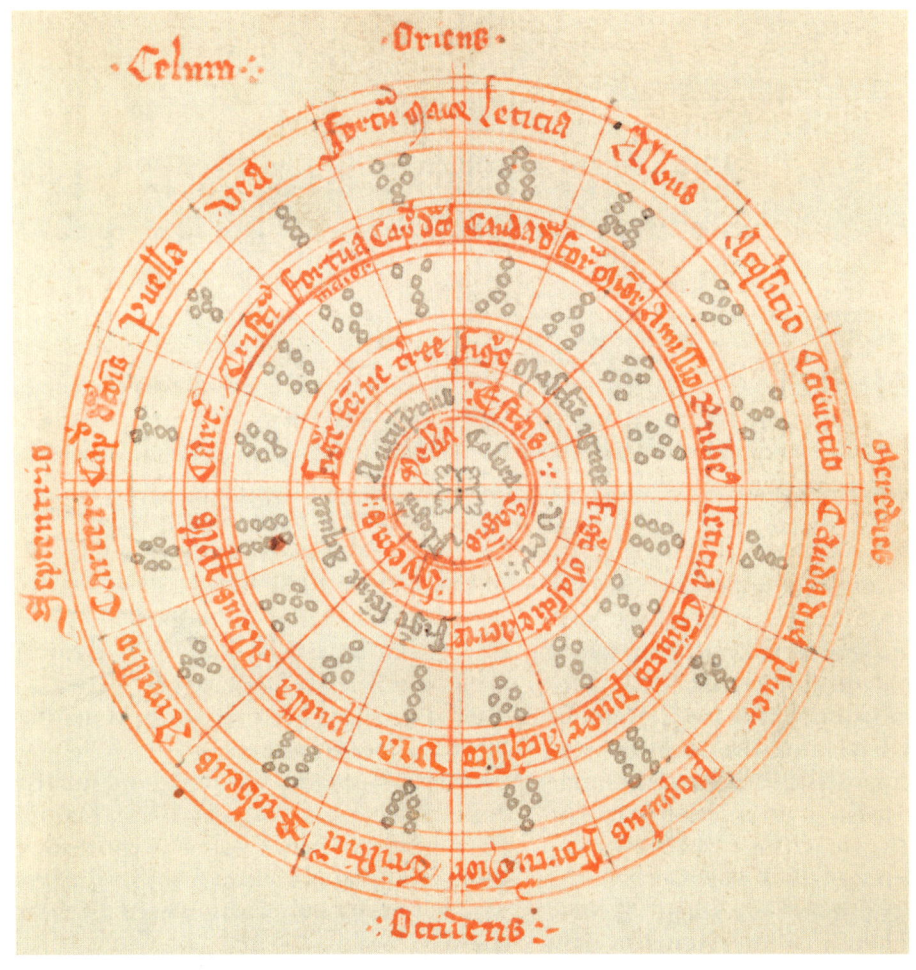

LEFT

Geomantic diagram from an early fifteenth-century treatise on geomancy, alchemy and astrology. Note the different patterns of dots which represent the different geomantic figures.

RIGHT

Geomantic divination tables being drawn in the earth in Mali.

OVERLEAF

Pages from an eighteenth-century Persian copy of a work called *Hidayat al-raml* ('Instructions on sand divination'), originally written for the Mughal emperor Akbar.

IN Arabic, geomancy is known as *'ilm al-raml* (the 'science of the sand'), which most likely originated in North Africa and is considered one of the most elaborate divination practices. One begins by holding a question in mind while casting sand, or creating dots in the sand, and then turning the results into patterns or 'figures' (typically by determining whether each column of dots was odd or even in number). These patterns are then grouped into a 'tableau' for interpretation, resulting in a 'judge' figure that answers the question originally posed – there are sixteen potential answers. It entered medieval Europe in the twelfth century CE when many Arabic and Hebrew manuscripts began to be translated into Latin by scholars such as Hugh of Santalla and Gerard of Cremona. Later it became another of the 'seven forbidden arts' in Europe, alongside nigromancy (black magic), hydromancy, aeromancy, pyromancy, chiromancy and scapulimancy.

Today geomancy survives in various forms across Africa, notably in the *Sikidy* of Madagascar, the *Ifá* of Nigeria and the *Gara* of Chad, which all rely on chance to form patterns and figures that have prescribed meanings. In Iran 'geomantic dice' are still used (that allow the figures to be created faster), while a related divination technique, called *Kumalak*, is found in Central Asia and uses forty-one pieces of dried sheep dung, which are arranged into patterns that again can be interpreted in light of the question posed.

شود مثال رحمت بود و نقطه آب بیرون از چهار رم به هفتم منتهی شود مثال ظلمت بود از طول بعرض رفته
بود و مغفرت از عرض بطول آمده باشد و در ملهای تمام آنست

مثال نور ست	مثال رحمت ست

مثال مغفرت ست	مثال ظلمت ست

نقطه آتش احد ست و نقطه باد عشرات ست و نقطه آب مآت ست و نقطه خاک
الوف ست و چون حروف میست و هشت گانه با بتها بخش کنند الف که حرف حادثه آتش الیان سد و یی
که مرتبه عشرات ست باد ه همزه سد و ق که مرتبه مآت ست ب بیاض سد و ع که مرتبه الوفت
بنخاک ایکس رسد و این را بنهایات اصلی کو یند و آمد ه کلی این ست ی ه ق ه ع یعنی
ابقع و از این ابنهایات طریق حاصل شد و نقاط در مرکز خود باشند مثال رو شنتر از این ست که نمود ه شد
خوب
دریاب

و حرکت خانه سیّوم و شکل طریق ؞ و میان دو کس تولد ؞ اجتماع از نقطه هوا در خانه آب که آن آبادی کفته
علی دیدیم و این صورت آمده و رسل این است ؞ که دویم نار سیّوم
میزانی است باد ؞ ضرب کردیم ؞ اجتماع صورت به این طریق
که اصل است در وشن شرح دکر آنکه جمره پنجم صاحب خانه سیوم است بدآنکه کلی
که آمده اصل نیز کونند و نقطه باد ؞ نصرة الخارج بطریق سیوم منتهی شده ؞ نقی الخصور
ست ؞ طریق باد و ؞ خانه با ض است ؞ ضرب کردیم ؞ اجتماع صورت بست تا واضح با بس
دلالت کند بر حال کسی بلکه میان دو کس و در آن خانه ؞ طریق بود و در خانه آب ؞ اجتماع صورت
اجتماع میان دو کس بل شد و در خانه حرکت است و بیز طریق اسنجاست پس حرکتی نیز بالا و چون قاعده
و در جمیع نقاطکه چون نقطه مرکزی فرود آید آن شکل بالا با خانه خانه و دائره ابدع ضرب باید نمود و حکم باید کرد پس
طریق را باد ؞ نصرة الخارج که حسا بیت خانه بیست ضرب نمودیم ؞ نصرة الداخل حاصل شد پس دلیل است آمد
کسی از جای بلکه جمع جنبیدن چرا که نتیجه ؞ نصرة الداخل آب آمد است و حرکت خانه سیوم و شکل طریق و میان
دو کس تولد ؞ اجتماع کرد از نقطه بر باد و خانه آب که آن آبادی کفته ایم و ذکور شده و رسل این است که
نموده می شود ؞ و چون مقرر است که هر نقطه به هر شکل که منتهی شود و آن شکل را
بدائره ضرب باید نمود و احکام وضیر انسی و ضیر از آن شکل و آز آن شکل با
کفت و دائره ابدع این است ؞
و دلائل این البسیار است و حسا مفاتیح همین مسائل را آنرا و که یونا نیده و بیان
نموده و آن رکن شمال الرمل است و خواب افشا مدائن شالی و حسا فا و کا قول شجره میفرماید که نقطه آتش نور است و نقطه
هوا رحمت است و نقطه آب مغفرت ست و نقطه خاک ظلمت و حمله بر طول عرض بیدآمی شود و احاد و عشرا
و مات و الوف که میزان او طریق ست و در ر بازده هم عدد در آرد به آنکه از طول به آنها ست و از عرض نهایت
و چون آتش از بین آن به چهارم آید و از انجا به پنجم منتهی شود و شمال بنور بود و نقطه باد از چهارم که به ششم منتهی

VIII.

WHEN PROPHECY FAILS

By its very nature, future-telling is not immediately verifiable – but history inevitably catches up to record its failures. So what happens when predictions fail to come true? This section explores the most notable failed predictions around the world, and the punishments meted out to future-tellers who fell from favour or who turned out to be less reliable over the years.

OPPOSITE

An illustration of Christ's teaching to 'beware of false prophets', from the Mömpelgard altarpiece, *c.* 1538.

FUTURE-TELLING is inherently risky, and when things do not materialize the way they were predicted to, many reasons can be given: lack of belief from the enquirer, lack of appropriate conditions, or a failure in the divination ritual. Records show that these were all familiar excuses in ancient Mesopotamia, and to counter them diviners there would perform rituals before the divination act to ensure that the gods were on their side (especially when they had an important client such as a king). This meant that whatever the outcome was, it was the will of the gods – a sort of insurance policy.

From the beginning, the credulous were keeping an eye out for 'false prophets' (those who pretend to future-tell, or who were intent on leading people astray). In Matthew 7:15 Christ warns his followers of them, and they are referred to in earlier books of the Bible, such as Jeremiah 28 which discusses the false prophet Hananiah. The Bible also questions whether the will of God is even knowable. Matthew 24:36 prophesies the Second Coming of Christ, but states that 'about that day and hour no one knows, neither the angels of heaven, nor the Son, but only the Father'. That didn't help manage expectations for Christ's earliest followers, however – the scholarly consensus today is that the earliest Christians fully expected it to happen in their lifetimes (which is to say, in the first and second centuries CE).

The cycle of predictions of an imminent salvation followed by disappointment continues to this day – one of the best-known recent examples was the US preacher Harold Camping, who predicted the Rapture would happen in 2011. However, it arguably peaked in Europe in the late fifteenth and early sixteenth centuries. The Italian painter Botticelli was convinced that he was already living in

ABOVE LEFT

Botticelli's *Mystic Nativity*, 1500, has an inscription referring to the 'troubles of Italy', which the artist associated with the end of the world described in the Book of Revelation.

ABOVE RIGHT

Botticelli was a follower of Girolamo Savonarola, who was executed in 1498 having confessed to making false prophecies.

the Great Tribulation (the period of unrest and chaos preceding the Second Coming), as can be seen in the inscription in his work *Mystic Nativity*. This was not uncommon at the time, since it was a period of social and religious upheaval, with the first major challenges to the Roman Catholic Church across Europe in the form of the Protestant Reformation. Botticelli was likely influenced by the firebrand preacher Girolamo Savonarola, who had seized control of the imagination of Florence in the 1490s, making prophecies about the city and the coming end of the world. Eventually arrested for heresy and tortured, Savonarola confessed to having invented his prophecies (he later recanted his confession) and was finally hanged and burned. The sixteenth century retained a strong expectation that the end was coming, most obviously in the commotion of the Great Conjunction of 1524, which was also observed in China.

Members of the Anabaptist movement in northern and central Europe believed that the end of the world would come in 1533–34 (1,500 years from the death of Christ) and a wave of religious fundamentalism led to attempts by the Anabapists to create a theocracy in the city of Münster, with one of the leaders, Jan Matthys, believing that Münster was the 'New Jerusalem'. While the rebellion was soon crushed, it led panicked authorities to crack down on future-telling and self-appointed 'prophets'.

Even today fortune-telling is illegal in some countries, including Tajikistan, Saudi Arabia and Nigeria, some states in Australia (where it is considered fraud), and some cities in the United States, including New York and Baltimore. In many other countries it potentially falls under anti-fraud laws – for example, in the UK the Fraudulent Mediums Act 1951 was repealed and replaced in 2008 by stronger consumer protection laws.

There will always be those happy to profit from the credulous. What's curious, however, is that even after so many prophecies have been shown to be fake, or utterly mistaken, the appetite for new prophecies seems to continue unabated. It seems that humans always want to believe that the future can be understood and controlled.

RIGHT

Soldiers attack Anabaptists in Amsterdam, 1535.

FALSE PROPHETS

REVELATION
Passive

CHANNEL
Divine communication

INTERMEDIARY
Prophet, Mystic

CONTEXT
Societal, Personal

Those involved in divination have routinely been persecuted, sometimes for dabbling in what can be perceived as 'magic', but sometimes because of the inaccuracy of their forecasts.

LEFT

St Paul blinds the false prophet called Elymas or Bar-Jesus.

WHEN PROPHECY FAILS

ABOVE

An illustration of Matthew 7:15 in which Christ denounces false prophets.

ABOVE

Soothsayers and false prophets are punished in the eighth circle of Hell in Dante's *Inferno*.

The Roman emperor Augustus banned astrology in 11 CE – specifically astrological enquiries into politics and the possible deaths of political figures. In the second and third centuries CE, the emperor Septimius Severus persecuted astrologers and prophets and had some people who consulted them put to death – even though Severus himself had regularly consulted astrologers (and may even have been a competent astrologer himself). Astrology was eventually banned completely in the Roman Empire in the fourth century, and Constantine was also claimed to have executed those interpreting omens and those using the oracle of Bes in Abydos, Egypt.

Islam is opposed to most forms of divination, with the Quran stating in Surah 5:3 that it is forbidden to use divining arrows, though it is sometimes tolerant of astrology and divination coming from the Quran itself (see p. 240). While the Bible in general condemns divination but promotes prophecy, it also warns to be wary of 'false prophets' – as Deuteronomy 18:20 stipulates, 'but any prophet who presumes to speak in my name a word that I have not commanded … that prophet shall die'.

In Greek mythology we find the opposite: a figure who has been given a genuine divine gift of prophecy, but who is cursed never to be believed. Cassandra warned the Trojans about accepting the Wooden Horse from the Greeks, but went unheeded, leading to the Trojans' defeat.

EARLY CHRISTIAN MILLENNIALISM

REVELATION
Active

CHANNEL
Divine communication

INTERMEDIARY
Prophet

CONTEXT
Official

After the death and Ascension of Jesus, his followers were convinced that he would return and that when the Kingdom of God arrived, it would last for a thousand years, giving rise to the term 'millennialism'.

PASSAGES in the gospels of Matthew, Mark and Luke spoken by Jesus, known as the Olivet discourse, are usually interpreted as indicating that Christ's return to Earth would occur in their own generation. Paul, writing in the mid-first century CE, warned followers not to marry, because Christ would be returning soon. There are very few records of what those earliest followers felt when this did not happen, but it has been speculated that the failure of Jesus to return led to significant turmoil. In Paul's epistles to the Thessalonians he reassures them that Christ is indeed coming, though it is unknown when: 'the day of the Lord will come like a thief in the night' (1 Thessalonians 5:2). Debate ensued as to what Jesus's words in the Olivet discourse could actually mean; some still took it very literally.

Among the early sects who believed strongly in the imminent return of Christ were the Montanists (see p. 110). However, by the sixth century CE the movement had disappeared after sustained persecution.

The failure of Christ to return led to speculation as to whether he might actually come again after the thousand years (postmillennial) rather than before (premillennial). In around 1200, the Italian theologian Joachim of Fiore would propose a new way of looking at the prophecy of Christ's return, postulating a three-era version of history, covering the age of the Father (the Old Testament), the Son (the New Testament) and the Holy Spirit (the coming utopia). This would influence all later Christian and related apocalyptic literature, cementing the concept of a golden age to come.

OPPOSITE

Joachim of Fiore's depiction of the seven-headed dragon of the apocalypse, a representation of the historical and spiritual enemies of the Christian Church.

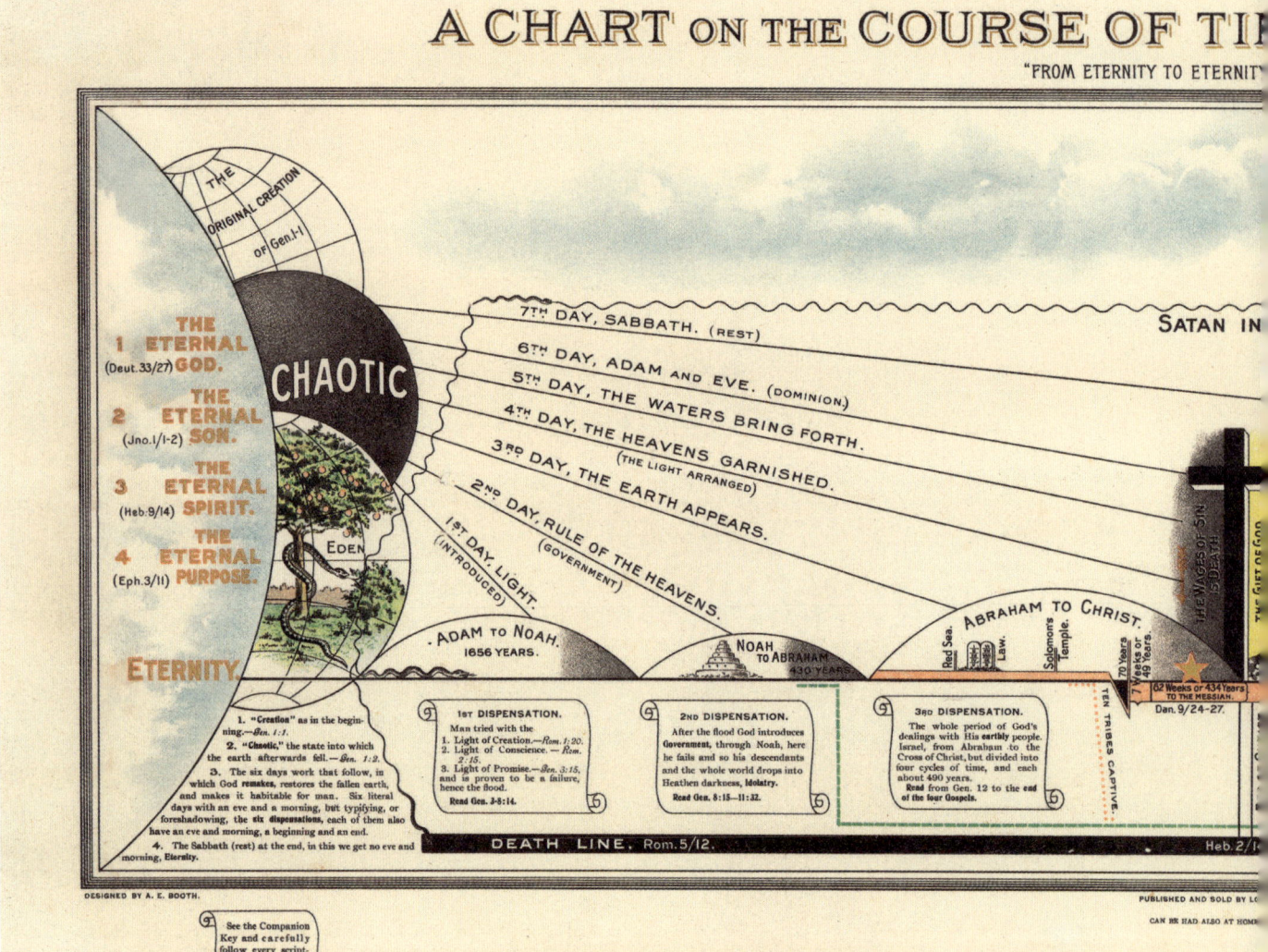

ABOVE

A. E. Booth's 'Chart of the Ages', first published in 1896, offers a clear timeline of the future. Here the Second Coming is shown at the beginning of the thousand-year Kingdom of Heaven – a 'premillennial' view.

FROM ETERNITY TO ETERNITY.

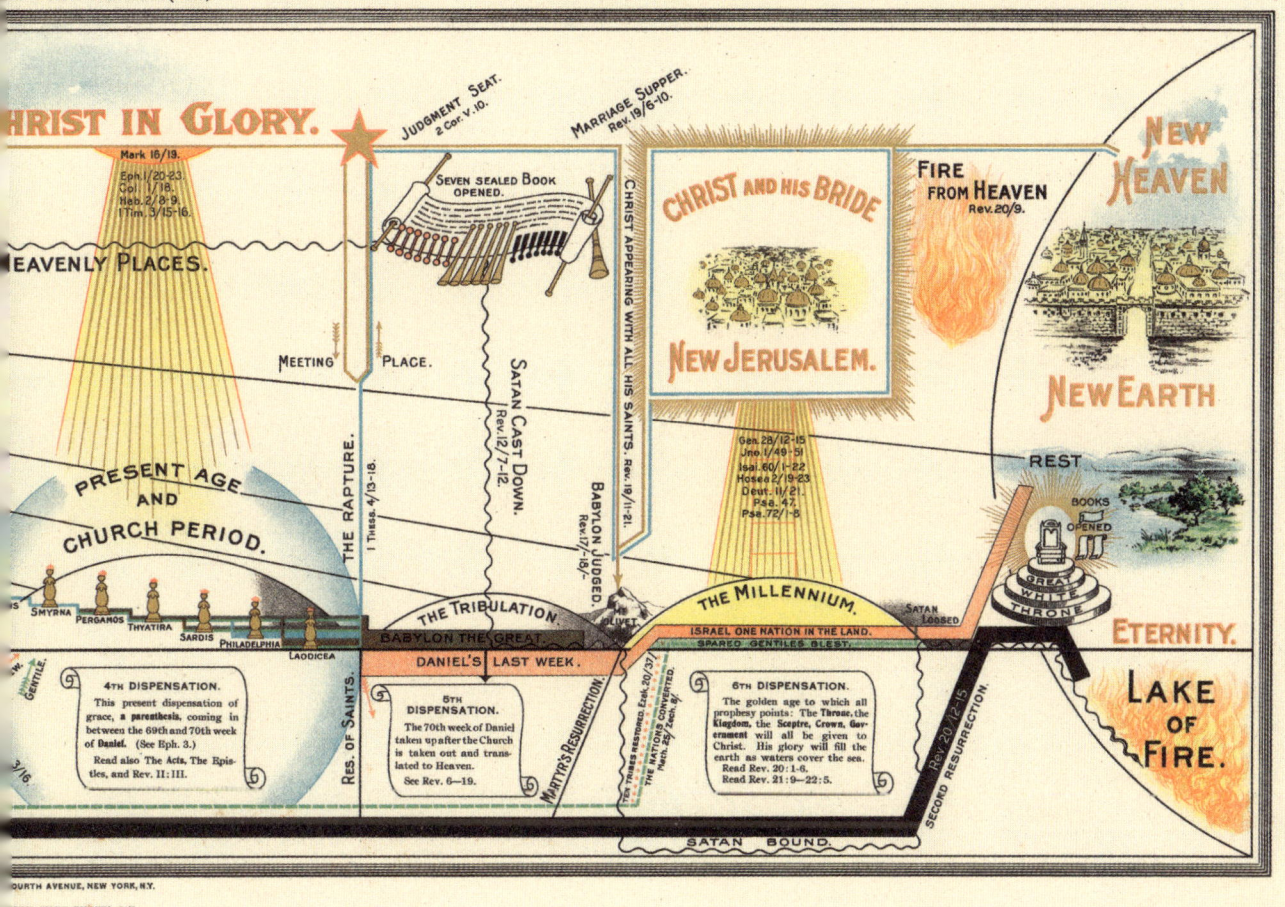

THE FLOODS OF 1524

REVELATION
Active

CHANNEL
Celestial

INTERMEDIARY
Any

CONTEXT
Societal, Personal

In February of 1524, all the planets were due to converge in a Great Conjunction and this was taken as an omen that something momentous would occur.

SINCE the Great Conjunction of planets would fall in Pisces, a 'watery' house, it was believed that there would be floods. In 1499 the German astrologers Johannes Stöffler and Jacob Pflaum were the first to predict that great change would take place on 20 February 1524. Then in 1512, Luca Gaurico (see p. 140) also published a pamphlet predicting a terrible flood, and in 1519 or 1520 Agostino Nifo published *De falsa diluvii prognosticatione* ('On the false prediction of the flood'), which challenged these notions. In fact, more than sixty writers published on the coming catastrophe, either predicting the end or claiming that nothing would happen.

The people responded with anxiety. In London it is estimated that twenty thousand citizens fled the city, expecting it to be flooded. The inhabitants of Friuli in Italy built wooden houses on mountaintops. And, perhaps most extreme, the Count von Iggleheim in Germany went so far as to construct an ark on the Rhine. The atmosphere of worry across Europe may have created a receptive audience for figures such as Martin Luther, whose Reformation movement spread the message of the need for change. Needless to say, there were no floods.

Interestingly the conjunction was also anticipated in China, but there the attitude towards it was very different. While in the West there was widespread awareness of the event thanks to the recent invention of the moveable-type printing press, in China awareness was limited to the educated classes, and as a result led to curiosity more than fear – the Great Conjunction was associated with potential dynastic changes.

RIGHT

A 1523 depiction of the predicted Great Conjunction, with the constellation Pisces depicted as a huge fish, leading to flooding.

LEFT

The 1524 floods imagined in a pamphlet from 1521, probably the first printed German-language version of this prophecy.

JOANNA SOUTHCOTT

REVELATION
Passive

CHANNEL
Divine communication

INTERMEDIARY
Mystic

CONTEXT
Personal

Joanna Southcott began writing rhyming prophecies in the late eighteenth century and foretold that the world would come to an end in 2004.

LEFT

A double-decker bus with a message imploring the bishops to open Joanna Southcott's box, from the 1920s or 1930s.

RIGHT

A bookplate depicting Joanna Southcott.

BORN in Devon, England, in 1750, Joanna Southcott declared herself to be the Woman of the Apocalypse mentioned in the biblical Book of Revelation (in that narrative she gives birth to a son, and for that reason is widely associated with the Virgin Mary). She amassed a very large following (probably in the tens of thousands) in London. Things came to a head in 1814, when she claimed that she was pregnant with the new Messiah, which was due to be born on 19 October 1814. This did not happen, and she died in December of that year.

Even her death did not entirely kill the devotion she inspired. Her followers would not let go of her body, believing that she would come back to life, and they only relented when her body started to decay. She left behind a sealed box containing prophecies. Her instructions were that it was only to be opened in times of national crisis, and only then in the presence of all the bishops of the Church of England. The precise whereabouts of the real box are today disputed, but the fact that the contents haven't been published suggests that it has not yet been opened.

MILLERISM AND THE GREAT DISAPPOINTMENT

In 1831 New York farmer and lay preacher William Miller predicted that the end of the world would come in 1843–44.

REVELATION
Passive

CHANNEL
Tool

INTERMEDIARY
Mystic

CONTEXT
Personal

LEFT

A satirical cartoon critiquing William Miller's prediction of the end of the world; a prominent follower of Miller, Joshua V. Himes, is held back by the Devil.

RIGHT

Millerism was influenced by the prophecies of Daniel, including the interpretation of Nebuchadnezzar's dream (see p. 156) illustrated here.

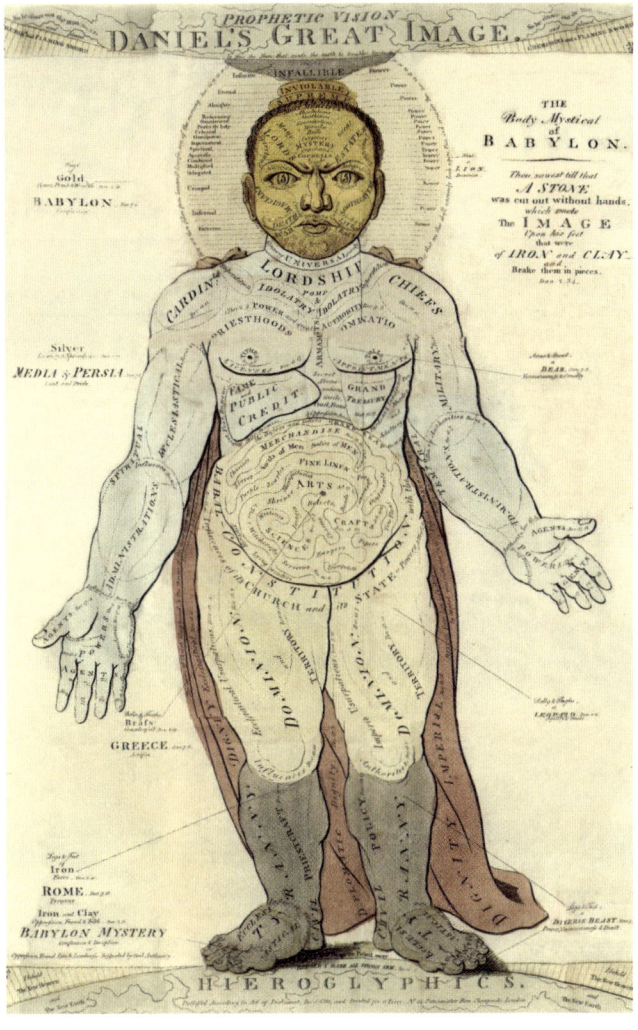

WILLIAM Miller's were among the most persuasive of the many prophecies of the nineteenth century, and he amassed a following of around 100,000 people. In predicting the date for the end of the world he used the Bible as his main source for his calculations. His followers prepared for the end, with some selling or abandoning their businesses. Various specific dates were predicted by different factions, and as each date passed a new one was proposed, until they settled on 22 October 1844.

When nothing happened on that date, it led to what has been called the 'Great Disappointment'. Miller's followers were genuinely shocked, and several left descriptions of how let down they felt. Some started to act like children, crawling around the streets, taking inspiration from Matthew 18:3: 'Truly I tell you, unless you change and become like little children, you will never enter the kingdom of heaven.' The majority left the church, some believed that the calculations were simply wrong and that the Second Coming was still imminent, and some former followers recongregated as Seventh-day Adventists. Miller accepted his error, and left the movement, dying in 1849.

SIGNS OF THE TIMES
Of the Second Coming of Christ.

J. V. HIMES, EDITOR.]   "THE TIME IS AT HAND."   [DOW & JACKSON, PUBLISHERS.

VOL. I.   BOSTON, JUNE 15, 1840.   NO. 6.

THE SIGNS OF THE TIMES

Is published on the first and fifteenth of each month, making twenty-four numbers in a volume; to which a title-page and index will be added.

TERMS.

One Dollar a year—always in advance. Persons sending five dollars without expense to the publishers, shall receive six copies; and for ten dollars, thirteen copies to one address. No subscription taken for less than one year.

DIRECTIONS.—All communications designed for the Signs of the Times, should be directed, *post paid*, to the editor, J.V. HIMES, Boston, Mass. All letters on business should be addressed to the publishers, DOW & JACKSON, No. 14 Devonshire Street, Boston.

Back numbers can be sent to those who subscribe soon.

ILLUSTRATION OF PROPHECY.

"But I will show thee what is noted in the Scripture of truth."

MR. CAMBELL ON THE RETURN OF THE JEWS.

Daniel iv. 9. " O Belteshazzar, master of the magicians, because I know that the spirit of the holy gods is in thee, and no secret troubleth thee, tell me the visions of my dream that I have seen, and the interpretation thereof. Thus were the visions of my head in my bed; I saw, and beheld a tree in the midst of the earth, and the height thereof was great. This is the interpretation, O king, and this is the decree of the Most High, which has come upon my lord the king; That they shall drive thee from men, and thy dwelling shall be with the beasts of the field, and they shall make thee eat grass as oxen, and they shall wet thee with the dew of heaven, and seven times shall pass over thee, till thou know that the Most High ruleth in the kingdom of men, and giveth it to whomsoever he will."

And "seven times shall pass over thee." This notable expression is repeated also, in verses 16, 23 and 32,—just four times, as in Leviticus xxvi. 18, 21, 24 and 28. " Seven times," which is four times repeated in those two chapters, 2520 years, constitutes the entire boundary of Daniel's evening vision. It commences with the captivity of the Jews in Babylon, and terminates with their general restoration from among all nations. The stump and roots of Nebuchadnezzar's visionary tree, which was the root of the four great empires, remain, "even with a band of iron and brass," during precisely the same period. It is true, the branches and leaves of this great tree, (Dan. iv. 14, 15,) denoted the splendor of Nebuchadnezzar's empire, and the cutting down of the tree, referred to the remarkable manner in which the king of Babylon was driven into exile "seven times," or seven literal years; but even this very strikingly accords with the period of the Jews' dispersion during the mystical "seven times," which equals 2520 literal years.

"The stump and roots" of the tree remain in the ground until "seven times pass over it." This clearly connects the three succeeding empires with the Babylonian, which are to continue precisely "seven times" before the "stone cut without hands" is to demolish them. Half of this period, that is, three times and a half, is as signed for the captivity of the Gentile church in mystical Babylon, and will be considered in its proper place.

Literal Babylon fell gradually, just in proportion as the Jewish captives were liberated, but was not utterly destroyed until the last company left, so will this tree, with mystical Babylon at its head, be destroyed, body and branch, stump and roots, just in proportion, and just as soon as the Jews are gathered from their long dispersion, and the Gentile church becomes purified from the harlotry of Rome.

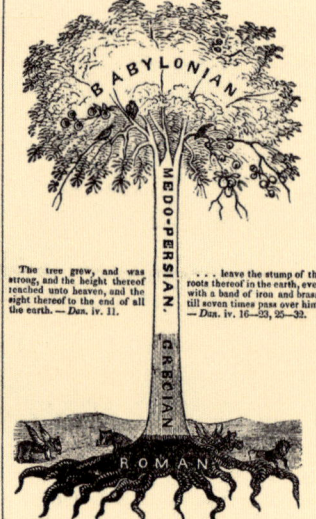

The tree grew, and was strong, and the height thereof reached unto heaven, and the sight thereof to the end of all the earth.—*Dan.* iv. 11.

... leave the stump of the roots thereof in the earth, even with a band of iron and brass, till seven times pass over him.—*Dan.* iv. 16—23, 25—32.

This tree, as before remarked, in its primary signification, certainly exhibits the punishment of the Babylonian Monarch, but it contains, also, a more deep and comprehensive meaning. The four great empires of which Babylon was the first, form a perfect parallel line with the period of Israel's captivity, 2520 years. They both commenced together and will terminate together. The rise of these empires was gradual, and the fall of Ephraim and Judah, as we *have seen*, was gradual. The downfall of the last of these empires and the liberation of the Jews will be gradual, as we *shall see* hereafter. This emblem agrees most perfectly with the history of the house of Israel, as described in all other parts of Scripture. A modern writer gives this emblem another interpretation, and identifies it with the "vine brought out of Egypt." (Psalm 80.) To this the author does not assent though the points of resemblance may hold good in some respects.

Daniel and Nebuchadnezzar were both troubled at this vision, but it is by no means to be supposed that either of them ever understood its deep and extensive meaning. It was designed for ages far future to them. Daniel sat one hour in astonishment, and his "thoughts troubled him" as the typical interpretation was revealed to him. (verse 19.) This had a direct bearing upon the person of the Babylonian monarch. Nebuchadnezzar, for his pride and arrogancy against God, one year after the vision, was driven from among men, and his dwelling was among the beasts of the field, and he was made to eat grass like oxen until seven times, or seven literal years passed over him, and until he learned that the Most High ruled. This, as a matter of history, was fulfilled in seven years, but as a beautiful allegory, it requires seven prophetic times to be fulfilled on a proud and degenerate people. God warned them repeatedly by Moses and the prophets, that if they "would walk contrary unto him," and "would not be reformed by him" they should be driven among the beasts, that is, the kings of the earth, and be punished seven times for their sins.

This is a long and dreary captivity to the Jewish church, the last half of which a degenerate Christian church suffers with her elder sister, the Jewish church, in mystical Babylon. But some few there are who have not " defiled their garments," and who have gone through the firey furnace of persecution without the smell of fire upon their garments, though the furnace has been heated "one *seven* times hotter than it was wont to be heated," like the three Hebrew captives they came out unhurt. Daniel, too, stands as a representation of all true believers during this captivity, or in the words of prophecy, while driven among the beasts of the earth, the lion's mouths are closed and harmless.

In Jeremiah v. 14, we have this remarkable prediction.

"Wherefore thus saith the Lord God of hosts, because ye speak this word, behold I will make my words in thy mouth fire, and this people wood, and it shall devour them."

How long shall they burn? Ezekiel answers, xxxix: 9.

"And they that dwell in the cities of Israel shall go forth, and shall set on fire and shall burn the weapons, both the shields and the bucklers, the bows and the arrows, and the handstaves and the spears, and they shall burn them with fire seven years."

A long trial of 2520 prophetic days, for the Lord said to Ezekiel, I have appointed thee a day for a year. Therefore this consuming fire is to last 2520 years. This would be heating the furnace " one seven times hotter than it was wont to be heated." Yet the Jews will come out of it, and a wicked world will exclaim with an astonished Nebuchadnezzar, (Dan. vi : 25,) Lo, I see four men loose, walking in the midst

BELOW

The prophecies of Daniel and John – between them, these prophecies have fuelled the majority of Christian apocalyptic thinking.

HAROLD CAMPING

REVELATION
Passive

CHANNEL
Tool

INTERMEDIARY
Mystic

CONTEXT
Personal

Harold Camping used a specific reading of the Bible, which he believed held secrets beyond the literal words, combined with numerology (belief in the mystical significance of numbers) to predict the end of the world.

HAROLD Camping was an American evangelical preacher who was convinced that Christ would return and that the world would end on 6 September 1994. He devised a new biblical chronology (for example, dating the Great Flood to 4990 BCE), and from this calculated a very specific end date of the world.

The end of the world did not come in 1994, but this did not dampen Camping's enthusiasm. In 2001 he claimed that the Great Tribulation had begun already, and then later he claimed that the Day of Judgment would start with the 'rapture' (in which believers are taken up to heaven) and huge earthquakes on 21 May 2011, with the world ending on 21 October 2011. While many were sceptical, others took it seriously. In Vietnam five thousand Hmong people gathered in May to await the event. On 23 May 2011, Camping announced that he was 'flabbergasted' that the judgment had not begun but then decided that it had been an invisible judgment, and that the physical end of the Earth would still come in October of that year. In 2012 he admitted that he had made a mistake and would not attempt to forecast the end of the world again. He died in 2013.

OPPOSITE

A banner in Manila, Philippines, publicizing the coming Judgment Day on behalf of Family Radio, Camping's radio station, claiming 'The Bible guarantees it'.

WHEN PROPHECY FAILS

DOOMSDAY CULTS

REVELATION
Passive

CHANNEL
Divine communication

INTERMEDIARY
Mystic

CONTEXT
Personal

The twentieth century saw a spike in organizations with a deep-seated belief in the coming end of the world, or some sort of transcendental event. In 1966, the sociologist John Lofland coined the term 'doomsday cult' to describe them.

LEFT

Dorothy Martin (centre) and Charles Laughead (left), founders of The Seekers, the original 'UFO cult'.

ABOVE

Members of Aum Shinrikyo march in Kumamoto, Japan, in 1990.

SOMETIMES based on religion, but sometimes drawing on UFO conspiracies (there was simultaneously a huge growth of interest in space travel and comic books), and often led by a modern-day 'prophet', dooms-day cults thrived especially in the Cold War period that followed World War II. Well-known examples are Heaven's Gate (often referred to as a 'UFO cult', it was founded in the United States in 1984 and ended with the suicide of its members in 1997), and the Japanese group Aum Shinrikyo, whose leader, Shoko Asahara, also prophesied that the end of the world would come in 1997.

In such cults many followers kept their beliefs even after the prophecy failed to materialize as predicted. Henry Riecken, Leon Festinger and Stanley Schachter, authors of the seminal work in this area *When Prophecy Fails* (1956), interviewed members of a UFO cult called The Seekers before and after a failed prophecy of a terrible flood on 21 December 1954. While some left in the aftermath, many stayed, and so Festinger tried to explain why that should be. A large part of the motivation was embarrassment and an unwillingness to confront reality when so much had already been invested.

THE 2012 PHENOMENON

REVELATION
Active

CHANNEL
Celestial

INTERMEDIARY
Priest

CONTEXT
Societal

From the 1970s, the year 2012 started to be seen as an apocalyptic or transformative year, with the date of 21 December pinpointed as the end of the world.

SOME calendars work on cycles that are longer than a year, decade or century. In Mesomerican mythology, which uses the Mesoamerican Long Count calendar, a previous world had ended after 5,126 years. The year 2012 (in the Gregorian calendar) marked the end of a cycle of the same length and so was seen as momentous. While there was no indication from Mesoamerican mythology that anything specific would happen, in 1966 the scholar Michael D. Coe suggested that the ancient Mayans may have anticipated some sort of cataclysmic event on the date (though others pointed out that cycles never actually end in the Mesoamerican Long Count calendar, and that there is no evidence that the ancient Mayans anticipated an apocalypse).

However, this idea was picked up on by various New Age thinkers, who believed that the Mayans had some arcane knowledge that would be revealed in 2012. A cottage industry grew up around this, with many publications predicting various outcomes. Certain sites with esoterica associations around the world, such as the Pic de Bugarach in France (which has an existing association with UFOs), started to receive large numbers of visitors who believed something spectacular would happen. Nothing happened, which brought disappointment to many, but also presumably relief to the 8 per cent of the world population who had reported being anxious about the date.

ABOVE

The Aztec 'sun stone', perhaps the most famous example of Mesoamerican calendar iconography. At the centre is the god Tonatiuh, and in the first ring the twenty days of the eighteen months of the Aztec solar calendar.

IX.
THE END OF THE WORLD

JUST as every culture has its creation myths, most cultures also have predictions as to how the universe or world will end. Since human life is finite, it is logical to assume that the world should also have an end. The study of the end of times in the context of religion is called 'eschatology'. Most world religions and belief systems have their own eschatologies, which attempt to answer questions around what happens to the universe, but also what happens to the individual after death: salvation, damnation or nothing?

OPPOSITE

The avatar of Vishnu Matsya fights a demon during a great deluge to save humanity.

THE end of the world is rarely the end of existence, however. Even in the most catastrophic scenarios – as found in Christianity and Islam – the end of the world is actually the beginning of a new phase. In that sense, the end is rarely the end, rather it is the end of the current state of the world, with its iniquities and injustice. The new phase will put everything right, and then it will stay right forever. This is a linear view of history, though it often contains within it echoes of the past. For example, the world is often projected to end in flood or fire, but such scenarios have precedents in ancient Mesopotamian mythology and the Bible, in which humanity had previously been wiped out by floods.

The idea of a more perfect future and a coming saviour can be found in other parts of the world. In China, the *Divine Incantations Scripture*, a Taoist writing from the fifth century CE, promises the arrival of a messiah-like figure called Li Hong. This will follow the invasion of the current world by hordes of demons who spread disease and chaos and undermine society. Only a correct understanding of Taoism will save humanity by converting the demon lords and using them to combat and drive out the lesser demons. Li Hong, the 'perfect lord', will come and usher in a new age in which people will live for three thousand years and will raise unicorns and phoenixes.

Some belief systems are more clearly cyclical. The Vedic religions that originated in South Asia – Hinduism, Jainism and Buddhism – all share the fundamental philosophy that the world will be made, sustained, un-made and then made again in cycles. In Hindu thinking these 'Yuga cycles' are typically very long, with each being 4,320,000 human years; the life of the god Brahma lasts for 72 million Yuga cycles.

More recently, concerns about the end of the world have focused on both science fiction and science. There have been speculations about impending devastating events since the early nineteenth century – for example, the English poet Lord Byron wondered about a potential world-ending comet impact. Other speculated ends have included alien invasion, zombie apocalypse and nuclear disaster –

BELOW

Thomas Burnet's *The Sacred Theory of the Earth*, showing the seven periods of cosmology (according to Burnet) that end in the transformation of the Earth into a star.

OPPOSITE

John Martin's illustration of the flood described in the Old Testament; apocalyptic predictions often contain echoes of what had happened before.

it seems that there is a deep-seated need to speculate on apocalyptic incidents, and as religion began to play a less prominent role in society, science provided fresh potential catastrophes. One of the first examples of this genre of dystopian fiction was Mary Shelley's *The Last Man*, from 1826, which tells the story of the last days of humans on Earth. In the introduction she claims that she discovered in a cave near Naples some prophetic writings of the Cumaean sibyl related to the last days of a man living in the years 2073 to 2100.

Since the late twentieth century – probably originating in Azerbaijani author Zecharia Sitchin's 1976 book *The 12th Planet* – there has been a theory about a coming collision with the 'hidden' planet Nibiru. This theory reached its zenith in 2012 when it was conflated with the so-called 'Mayan apocalypse'. While that theory has largely been debunked since, the same period has seen rising concern about more tangible threats such as climate change and the state of our environment, and, increasingly, artificial intelligence. So while cosmic calamities such as comets cannot be ruled out, science points to a future that is radically uncertain, with gradually worsening conditions rather than a specific apocalyptic 'end date'.

THE MAITREYA IN BUDDHISM

REVELATION
Passive

CHANNEL
Divine communication

INTERMEDIARY
Priest

CONTEXT
Official

The Maitreya is a bodhisattva (a person striving towards enlightenment) who would appear after a period during which the Buddha's teachings are forgotten. Maitreya can be loosely translated as 'loving friend'.

LEFT

The Maitreya depicted on a *tsakali* card that would be used, with other similar cards, to form a sacred space.

ABOVE LEFT

The Maitreya, the 'Buddha to come', also known in Tibetan as Jampa.

ABOVE RIGHT

A statue of the Maitreya from Pakistan, from the third century CE, showing Hellenistic influence.

IN Buddhism, the guiding principle is that nothing is permanent. One school of thought argues that Buddha's teachings would be forgotten after five thousand years – meaning by about 4600 CE. In that moment the Maitreya would appear to teach enlightenment to the next generation. This perspective is somewhat influenced by Chinese Taoist principles, and some scholars have pointed out that the concept of a messianic saviour exists earlier in Taoism, in the form of the figure of Li Hong (see p. 292).

However, Buddhism is a rich and varied set of beliefs, and there exist other traditions. For example, in the Buddha's sermon of the Seven Suns, found in the Pali canon, he explains that in the future it will stop raining and a second sun will appear. Then, after a long time, all streams will dry up and a third sun will appear. Then all rivers, including the Ganges, will dry up, and a fourth sun will appear. Then the great lakes will dry up, and a fifth sun will appear. The oceans will start to dry up, and a sixth sun will appear. Mountains start to quake, a seventh sun appears and the Sineru (Meru), king of mountains, explodes. Everything is engulfed in flames and no trace of the Earth is left.

THE CYCLES OF HINDUISM

REVELATION
Passive

CHANNEL
Divine communication

INTERMEDIARY
Priest

CONTEXT
Official

In Hindu thought, Kali Yuga is an age of darkness that is said to have started in 3102 BCE – meaning that we are currently in it.

As with Buddhism, Hinduism does not espouse the belief that anything ends permanently. However, there are still beliefs around how the *current* world will end, based on the concept of the 'Yuga cycle', which in total lasts for 4,320,000 years. In this cycle the world passes through four ages, going from the Satya Yuga (the age of sincerity) through Treta Yuga (when morality starts to fail), Dvapara Yuga (when people become more selfish), and finally Kali Yuga (the age of darkness and misery). Kali Yuga represents a period, lasting 432,000 years, of gradually worsening conditions, immorality, and ultimately the fall of humanity.

In Vaishnava tradition, at the end of Kali Yuga the next incarnation of Vishnu, Kalki, will be born. Riding a white horse, and carrying a fiery sword, he will purge the world of evil and bring humanity back to a new Satya Yuga. The Bah'ai faith (see p. 119) believes that Baha'u'llh was Kalki, conflating him with various other messianic figures including Jesus.

OPPOSITE

Vishnu's future incarnation as Kalki, when he will purge the world of evil and usher in an era of truth and goodness.

THE END OF THE WORLD

THE APOCALYPSE

REVELATION
Passive

CHANNEL
Divine communication

INTERMEDIARY
Prophet

CONTEXT
Official

The three main Abrahamic religions of Judaism, Christianity and Islam developed a comprehensive eschatology, though with some differences.

LEFT

The Day of Judgment, when the Quran says the sun and moon will join.

RIGHT

The Heavenly Jerusalem, as promised to the faithful after the apocalypse.

JUDAISM, the oldest of the three religions, developed the concept of the Messiah. In Jewish eschatology, the end of days will start with a war with Gog (a prince) and Magog (his land), taking place in or around Jerusalem (Ezekiel 38–39). According to some later traditions, then the Temple will be restored, the Messiah will arrive, the dead will be resurrected and a new heaven and Earth will be created.

Many of these concepts were carried across into Christian eschatology, with Jesus as the Messiah. The Book of Revelation outlines the apocalypse: it starts when a symbolic lamb with seven eyes and seven horns takes a scroll with seven seals. Events are triggered as each of the seals is broken, including the unleashing of the Four Horsemen of the Apocalypse. Humanity hides in caves, and huge earthquakes rock the world. Then 144,000 of the most faithful are chosen, and seven angels sound their trumpets. Stars collide into the Earth, the oceans and rivers are poisoned, a dragon appears, then a beast to rule over the Earth – a false prophet forces everyone to adopt the Mark of the Beast. After various other events including the fall of Babylon, Jesus returns to Earth with a heavenly army, Satan is cast into an abyss and so begins a new Earth and new Heaven.

Islamic eschatology builds on some of these themes – for example, Gog and Magog become Yajuj and Majuj. Some Hadiths give the overall lifespan of the Earth at six to seven thousand years; its final destruction will be heralded by a series of signs. Over centuries the tales of the apocalypse have been added to, but the the most important figures remain the Mahdi – the 'guided one', who will guide humanity – Isa (Jesus), the Dajjal ('deceiver') and the Beast. The world will collapse and burn and will be replaced by a new Paradise.

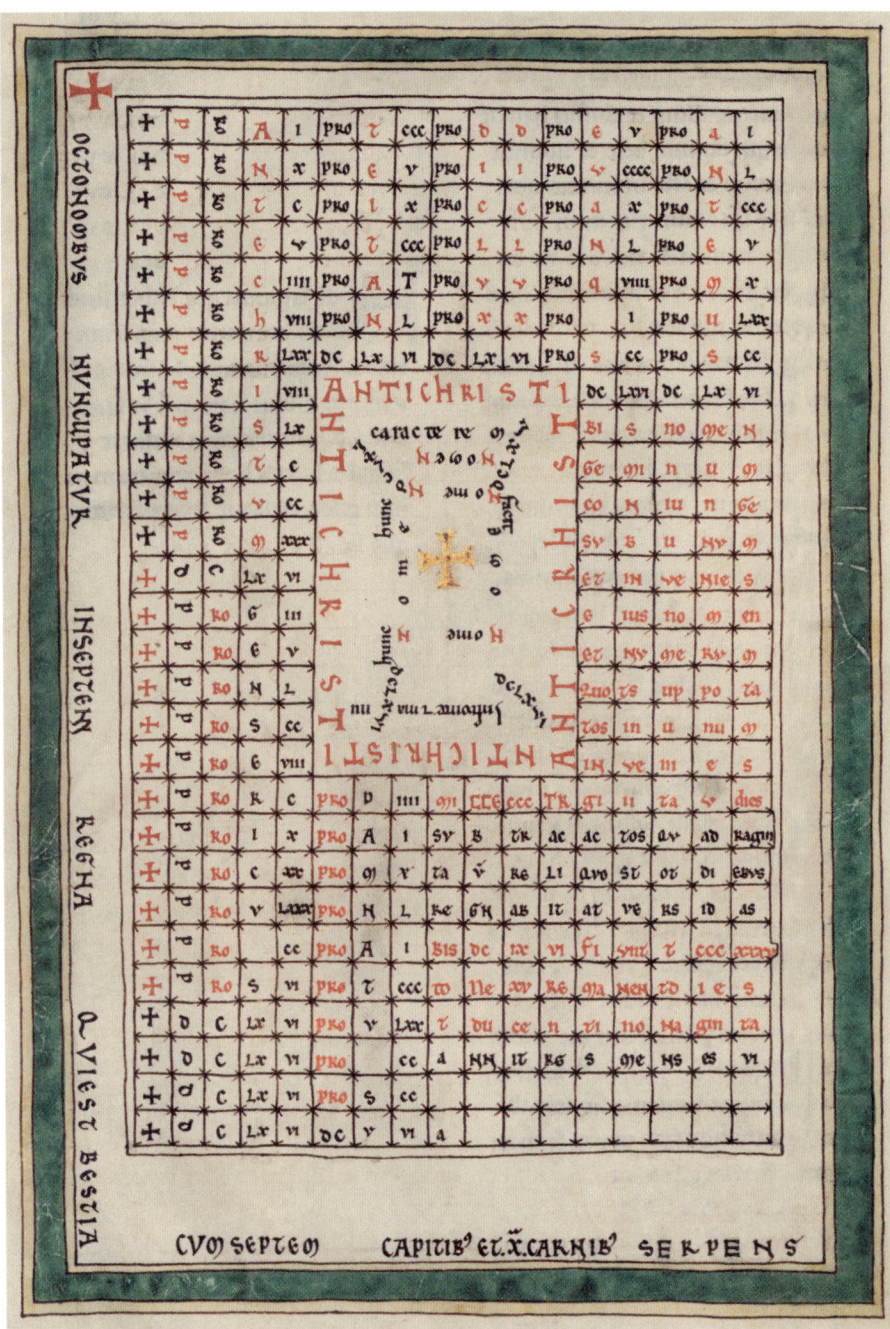

Two leaves from a Spanish commentary on the Book of Revelation, *c.* 1180.

ABOVE

'Table of the Antichrist', used to calculate the 'number of the beast'.

OPPOSITE

The eight names of the Antichrist in red and the number 666 in Roman numerals.

munera: de inferno autem illum surgere quem in prima bestia de abisso diximus suscitatur uerbo ut a qua nutriet illum et abissus hauxit illum qui tantum licet et nomine inmutato et acto inmutato uenuar. dit sps: numerus enim nois est. Et numerus eius. Sic ait ex litteris grecis in compluribus in conuenienter numeri. DCLXVI. Sub eo qui p septem capita hoc est septem regna sibi subdita septem nominibᵘ nuncipabitur et octauum nomen habebit qd supra diximus. Acxyore.

In quo nomine notam. In manu et in fronte facturus ē: et hec septem nomina caritati ure explanemus.

Idest Euantas. Quod latine dicit serpens eo qd euam primus decepit.

Sedm nomen habet Dampnatus eo qd magnum dampnum intulit mundo. Tercium nomen habet Antemus Idest abstemius a temeto idest uino. quasi abstinens a uino.

Quartum nom habet gotica lingua. G. ensericus Quintum nom hab; linguarum. Anuxps Sextum nomen habet grece. Teytan Septimum nom habet latine. Diclus

Quo nomine p antifrasin expressum intelligimus. Anuxpm Qui cum a luce supna priuatus sit atq; abscisus transfigurat tamen se in angelum lucis. presumens se dicere lucem. De eadem.

I Nomina DCLXVI

II	Euantas	DCLXVI
III	Dampnatᵘ	DCLXVI
IIII	Antemus	DCLXVI
V	Gensericᵘ	DCLXVI
VI	Anuxps	DCLXVI
VII	Teytan	DCLXVI
VIII	Diclus	DCLXVI
VIIII	Acxyore	DCLXVI

Hic est sapientia qui habet intellectum computer numerum bestie. Numerus enim hominis est idest xpi. Cuius nomen sibi facit bestia. Quantum enim adtineat p singulas litteras hunc numerum nomen quod expleunt interpretatum que sic. DCLXVI.

ABOVE AND OPPOSITE

Events during the Apocalypse as described in the Book of Revelation, from a manuscript by a group of Russian 'Old Believers' who broke with the Orthodox Church, *c.* 1800.

RAGNARÖK

REVELATION
Passive

CHANNEL
Divine communication

INTERMEDIARY
Mystic

CONTEXT
Societal

Ragnarök translates to the 'twilight of the gods' or 'the doom of the gods' and refers to catastrophic events foretold in Norse mythology.

LEFT

The blind Höðr killing Baldr with mistletoe – a key event triggering *Ragnarök*, from an eighteenth-century edition of the *Prose Edda*.

THE END OF THE WORLD

ABOVE LEFT

Valhalla, home of dead warriors until *Ragnarök*.

ABOVE RIGHT

Jörmungandr – the Midgard serpent – is caught by Thor using a giant cow's head as bait; they clash again in *Ragnarök*.

THE Icelandic *Poetic Edda* and *Prose Edda*, both likely compiled or written in the thirteenth century CE, the latter by Snorri Sturluson, describe a sequence of dramatic events that lead ultimately to the destruction of everything – though that does not mean that it is the *end* of everything. It will start with three roosters crowing, a harsh three-year winter called *Fimbulwinter*, and the breaking loose of the hound Garmr. Humanity will turn against one another, and the Midgard serpent that encircles the Earth will writhe around creating huge waves.

The Earth will be invaded by various creatures, and while the gods will fight them, they will lose: Odin to the giant wolf Fenrir and Thor to the Midgard serpent. The Earth will burst into flames and sink into the sea. This is not, however, the end of the world. After the chaos, the world tree Yggdrasil will be repaired. Two humans will survive – Líf and Lífþrasir – and they will repopulate the Earth.

THE FIVE SUNS

REVELATION
Passive

CHANNEL
Divine communication

INTERMEDIARY
Priest

CONTEXT
Societal

The Aztecs believed that four suns had existed before the current one. There would be no sixth sun, and humanity would cease to exist.

ACCOUNTS such as the sixteenth-century Codex Chimalpopoca describe the four previous worlds and how each had been obliterated and destroyed when the sun that sustained it died. In the first world, the sun was knocked from the sky and humans were destroyed by jaguars in darkness. In the second, they had been turned into monkeys and the god Quetzalcoatl, who was serving as the sun, blew them away with a hurricane. He then abdicated his role. The third sun had been extinguished by rain, thanks to the god Tlaloc. And the fourth sun was killed by a huge flood, with the humans becoming fish in order to survive.

The Aztecs believed that they lived in the era of the fifth sun, and their main priority was to sustain the sun through blood sacrifice and worship. However, it was also known that eventually the fifth sun would be destroyed by an earthquake, and that skeletal beings called Tzitzimimeh would come and devour all humans.

OPPOSITE

The current, fifth (and final) sun embodied by the god Tonatiuh.

THE END OF THE WORLD

FURTHER READING

There are very few general publications on this topic – below are listed some specialist articles and publications, as well as a selection of introductions and more accessible titles.

GENERAL

Geoffrey Ashe, *The Book of Prophecy: From Ancient Greece to the Millennium*, London: Cassell Illustrated, 1999.

Jonathan Dee, *Book of Prophecies: Discover the Secrets of the Past, Present and Future*, London: Collins & Brown, 1999.

DK, *A History of Astrology, Divination and Prophecy*, London: Penguin Random House, 2025.

Rosemary Ellen Guiley, *The Encyclopedia of Magic and Alchemy*, New York: Checkmark Books, 2006.

Peter Struck, *Divination and Human Nature: A Cognitive History of Intuition in Classical Antiquity*, Oxford: Princeton University Press, 2018.

ORACLES & SEERS

Carmen Blacker, 'Divination and Oracles in Japan', in Hugh Cortazzi (ed.), *Carmen Blacker: Scholar of Japanese Religion, Myth and Folklore: Writings and Reflections*, Amsterdam: Amsterdam University Press, 2017, 284–303.

Robert Flaceliere, *Greek Oracles*, New York: W. W. Norton and Company, 1965.

Leszek Gardeła, Sophie Bønding and Peter Pentz (eds), *The Norse Sorceress. Mind and Materiality in the Viking World*, Oxford: Oxbow Books, 2023.

Jane L. Lightfoot, *The Sibylline Oracles: With Introduction, Translation, and Commentary on the First and Second Books*, Oxford: Oxford University Press, 2007.

John Matthews, *The Book of Merlin*, Stroud: Amberley Publishing, 2024.

Michael Scott, *Delphi: A History of the Center of the Ancient World*, Princeton: Princeton University Press, 2014.

Richard Stoneman, *The Ancient Oracles: Making the Gods Speak*, New Haven: Yale University Press, 2011.

Gaëlle Tallet, 'Oracles', in Christina Riggs (ed.), *The Oxford Handbook of Roman Egypt*, online edn, Oxford Academic, 2012.

Katarina Turpeinen, 'The Soteriological Context of a Tibetan Oracle', *Himalaya, the Journal of the Association for Nepal and Himalayan Studies*, 39/1 (2019), article 8.

OMENS & PORTENTS

Amar Annus (ed.), *Divination and Interpretation of Signs in the Ancient World*, University of Chicago Oriental Institute Seminars, 6 (2010).

L. de Blois, P. Funke and J. Hahn (eds), *The Impact of Imperial Rome on Religions, Ritual and Religious Life in the Roman Empire: Proceedings of the Fifth Workshop of the International Network Impact of Empire June 30–July 4, 2004, at Westfälische Wilhelms-Universität Münster, Germany*, Leiden: Brill, 2004.

Sally M. Freedman, *If a City is Set on a Height: The Akkadian Omen Series Summa Alu*, vol. 1: tablets 1–21, Occasional Publications of the Samuel Noah Kramer Fund, Philadelphia: Penn Museum, 1998.

S. M. Moren, 'Šumma Izbu XIX: New Light on the Animal Omens', *Archiv für Orientforschung*, 27 (1980), 53–70.

Lorenzo Verderame, 'The Substitute King (Šar Pūḫi): An Assyrian Ritual of the First Millennium', in Jens E. Braarvig and Velizar Sadovski (eds), *Ritual Texts and Contexts: Philology, Pragmatics, and Cultural History*, vol. 1, Olso: Hermes, 2020.

PROPHETS & PRIESTS

D. E. Aune, *Prophecy in Early Christianity and the Ancient Mediterranean World*, Grand Rapids: William B. Eerdmans, 1983.

Mark J. Boda and Lissa M. Wray Beal, *Prophets, Prophecy, and Ancient Israelite Historiography*, University Park: Penn State University Press, 2013.

Maria Dell'Isola, 'They are not the words of a rational man: ecstatic prophecy in Montanism', in V. Gasparini et al., *Lived Religion in the Ancient Mediterranean World: Approaching Religious Transformations from Archaeology, History and Classics*, Berlin: De Gruyter, 2020, 71–86.

Anne Marie Kitz, 'Prophecy As Divination', *Catholic Biblical Quarterly*, 65 (2003).

M. Kjellgren, 'Taming the Prophets: Astrology, Orthodoxy and the Word of God in Early Modern Sweden', doctoral thesis, Lund: Sekel Bokförlag, 2011.

Barry Kogan, 'Understanding Prophecy: Four Traditions', in Steven Nadler and T. M. Rudavsky (eds), *The Cambridge History of Jewish Philosophy from Antiquity through the Seventeenth Century*, Cambridge: Cambridge University Press, 2008, 481–523.

Laura Nasrallah, *An Ecstasy of Folly: Prophecy and Authority in Early Christianity*, Boston: Harvard Divinity School, 2004.

Martti Nissinen, *Ancient Prophecy: Near Eastern, Biblical, and Greek Perspectives*, online edn, Oxford Academic, 2017

Fazlur Rahman, *Prophecy in Islam: Philosophy and Orthodoxy*, Chicago: University of Chicago Press, 1958.

Jayne Svenungsson, *Divining History: Prophetism, Messianism and the Development of the Spirit*, New York: Berghahn Books, 2016.

PREDICTIONS & REVELATIONS

Jonathan Green, *Printing and Prophecy: Prognostication and Media Change* 1450–1550, Ann Arbor: University of Michigan Press, 2011.

M. Heiduk, K. Herbers and H.-C. Lehner (eds), *Prognostication in the Medieval World: A Handbook*, Berlin: De Gruyter, 2021.

Alessandro Palazzo and Anna Rodolfi (eds), *Prophecy and Prophets in the Middle Ages*, Florence: Edizioni del Galluzzo, 2020.

Paracelsus, *The Prophecies of Paracelsus*, trans. J. K., London: William Rider & Son, 1915, online edn, https://sacred-texts.com/pro/pop/index.htm

Winfried Vogel, 'The Eschatological Theology of Martin Luther, Part I: Luther's Basic Concepts', *Andrews University Seminary Studies*, 24/3 (1986), 249–64.

Daniela Wagner, 'Prophecy and Prognostication in Visual Art of the Medieval Western Christian World', in M. Heiduk, K. Herbers and H.-C. Lehner (eds), *Prognostication in the Medieval World: A Handbook*, Berlin: De Gruyter, 2021.

DREAMS

Aristotle, *On Prophesying by Dreams*, trans. J. I. Beare, The Internet Classics Archive, https://classics.mit.edu/Aristotle/prophesying.html

Artemidorus, *The Interpretation of Dreams*, trans. Martin Hammond, Peter Thonemann (ed.), Oxford: Oxford University Press, 2020.

Samson Eitrem [and Fritz Graf], 'Dreams and Divination in Magical Ritual', in Christopher A. Faraone and Dirk Obbink (eds), *Magika Hiera: Ancient Greek Magic and Religion*, Oxford: Oxford University Press, 1991, 175–87.

Christopher A. Faraone, 'The Use of Divine Images in the Dream-Divination Recipes of the Greek Magical Papyri', in A. Mastrocinque, J. E. Sanzo and M. Scapini (eds), *Ancient Magic: Then and Now*, Stuttgart: Franz Steiner Verlag, 2020, 193–209.

Claire Hall, 'Artemidorus, Dream Exegesis, and the Case of the Interpolating Expert Dreamer', *Mnemosyne*, 76/6 (2023), 1000–25.

Ze Hong, 'Dream Interpretation from a Cognitive and Cultural Evolutionary Perspective: The Case of Oneiromancy in Traditional China', *Cognitive Science*, 46 (2022).

Bronwen Neil, *Dreams and Divination from Byzantium to Baghdad, 400–1000 CE*, Oxford: Oxford University Press, 2021.

Megan Pōtiki, 'Moemoeā', *Journal of New Zealand Studies* NS35 (2023), 46–57.

Donald A. Russell and Heinz-Günther Nesselrath (eds), *On Prophecy, Dreams and Human Imagination: Synesius, De insomniis*, SAPERE series, 24, Tübingen: Mohr Siebeck, 2014.

Synesius of Cyrene, *The Essays and Hymns*, trans. A. Fitzgerald, 2 vols, Oxford: Oxford University Press, 1930.

Brigid E. Vance, 'Deciphering Dreams: How Glyphomancy Worked in Late Ming Dream Encyclopedic Divination', *Chinese Historical Review*, 24/1 (2017), 5–20.

ASTROLOGY

Roger Beck, *A Brief History of Ancient Astrology*, Oxford: Blackwell, 2007.

Benson Bobrick, *The Fated Sky: Astrology in History*, London: Simon & Schuster, 2006.

Nicholas Campion, *A History of Western Astrology*, 2 vols, London: Continuum, 2009.

Nicholas Campion, *Astrology and Cosmology in the World's Religions*, New York: New York University Press, 2012.

Nicholas Campion and Ronnie Gale Dreyer, 'Indian Astrology', in David Kim (ed.), *Modern History of Asian Religions*, Leiden: Brill, 2015, 163–91.

Hart Defouw and Robert Svoboda, *Light on Life: An Introduction to the Astrology of India*, Delhi: Penguin Books India, 1996.

Jeffrey Kotyk, 'Buddhist Astrology and Astral Magic in the Tang Dynasty', doctoral thesis, Leiden University, 2017.

Andrea Richards and Jessica Hundley (eds), *Astrology: The Library of Esoterica*, London: Taschen, 2020.

H. Rutkin, 'Astrology', in Katharine Park and Lorraine Daston (eds), *The Cambridge History of Science*, vol. 3, Cambridge: Cambridge University Press, 2006, 541–61.

DIVINATION & FORTUNE-TELLING

Emiliano Gallaga M. and Marc G. Blainey, *Manufactured Light: Mirrors in the Mesoamerican Realm*, Boulder: University Press of Colorado, 2019.

Jue Guo, 'Divination', in Randall L. Nadeau (ed.), *The Wiley-Blackwell Companion to Chinese Religions*, Chichester: Wiley-Blackwell, 2012.

Michael Lackner (ed.), *Coping with the Future: Theories and Practices of Divination in East Asia*, Leiden: Brill, 2018.

Ai Nishida, 'Old Tibetan Scapulimancy', *Revue d'Etudes Tibétaines*, 37 (2016), 262–77

Lisa Raphals, *Divination and Prediction in Early China and Ancient Greece*, Cambridge: Cambridge

University Press, 2013.
Angela Voss, 'Scrying', in Christopher Partridge (ed), *The Occult World*, London: Routledge, 2014.
Roger D. Woodard, *Divination and Prophecy in the Ancient Greek World*, Cambridge: Cambridge University Press, 2023.

WHEN PROPHECY FAILS

Robert P. Carroll, *When Prophecy Failed*, Norwich: SCM Press, 2011.
Esther Eidinow, 'Oracular Failure in Ancient Greek Culture', in Roger D. Woodard (ed.), *Divination and Prophecy in the Ancient Greek World*, Cambridge: Cambridge University Press, 2023.
Leon Festinger, Henry Riecken and Stanley Schachter, *When Prophecy Fails*, Minneapolis: University of Minnesota Press, 1956.
Plutarch, 'The Obsolescence of Oracles', in *Moralia*, vol. 5, trans. F. C. Babbitt, Loeb Classical Library, Cambridge: Harvard University Press, 1936, 347–501.

THE END OF THE WORLD

Anonymous, *The Poetic Edda*, trans. Carolyne Larrington, Oxford: Oxford University Press, 2014.
William C. Chittick, 'Muslim Eschatology', in Jerry L. Walls (ed.), *The Oxford Handbook of Eschatology*, Oxford: Oxford University Press, 2007.
Sebastian Job and Linda Connor (eds), Online proceedings of the symposium 'Anthropology and the Ends of Worlds', Sydney: Department of Anthropology, University of Sydney, 2010.
Jonathan Kirsch, *A History of the End of the World: How the Most Controversial Book in the Bible Changed the Course of Western Civilization*, San Francisco: HarperOne, 2007.
Craig R. Koester (ed.), *The Oxford Handbook of the Book of Revelation*, Oxford: Oxford University Press, 2020.
Snorri Sturluson, *Edda*, trans. and ed. Anthony Faulkes, London: Weidenfeld & Nicolson, 2008.
Eugen Weber, *Apocalypses: Prophecies, Cults and Millennial Beliefs through the Ages*, Cambridge: Harvard University Press, 2000.

SOURCES OF QUOTATIONS

All Bible quotations are taken from the New Revised Standard Version Updated Edition. Copyright © 2021 National Council of Churches of Christ in the United States of America. Used by permission. All rights reserved worldwide.
Page 11: Cicero, *De Divinatione* (On Divination), trans. William Armistead Falconer, Loeb Classical Library, Cambridge: Harvard University Press, 1923, 1.1.
Page 16: Translations adapted from Sally M. Freedman, *If a City is Set on a Height: The Akkadian Omen Series Summa Alu*, vol. 1: tablets 1–21, Occasional Publications of the Samuel Noah Kramer Fund, Philadelphia: Penn Museum, 1998, 91.
Page 29: Cicero, *De Divinatione* (On Divination), trans. William Armistead Falconer, Loeb Classical Library, Cambridge: Harvard University Press, 1923, 1.3.
Page 36: Fragments of Heraclitus from John Burnet, *Early Greek Philosophy*, London: A & C Black Ltd, 1920, fragment 92, 133–34.
Page 48: Geoffrey of Monmouth, *Histories of the Kings of Britain*, trans. Sebastian Evans, London: Dent & Co, 1904, 172.
Page 57: Bartolomeo Platina, *Lives of the Popes* [1470], as quoted in Edwin Emerson, *Comet Lore: Halley's Comet in History and Astronomy*, New York: Schilling Press, 1910, 74.
Page 62: William of Malmesbury, *Historia Novella*, Lib. ii sec. 25, as quoted in George F. Chambers, *The Story of Eclipses*, London: George Newnes, 1899, chapter 12.
Page 69: Pliny the Elder, *The Natural History*, trans. John Bostock and H. T. Wiley, London: H. G. Bohn, 1855, book 10, chapter 9.
Page 72: Translation adapted from Sally M. Freedman, *If a City is Set on a Height: The Akkadian Omen Series Summa Alu*, vol. 1: tablets 1–21, Occasional Publications of the Samuel Noah Kramer Fund, Philadelphia: Penn Museum, 1998, 20.
Page 76: Translation adapted from J. L. Shastri and G. P. Bhatt (eds), *Garuda Purana*, part 1, AITM vol. 12, Delhi: Motilal Banarsidass, 1957, 205.
Page 92: As quoted in Aaron Schart, 'Combining Prophetic Oracles in Mari Letters and Jeremiah 36', *Journal of the Ancient Near Eastern Society*, 23 (1995), 78, based on a translation in William W. Hallo, *The Book of the People*, Atlanta: Scholars Press, 1991, 162 (57b).
Page 110: Eusebius, *Ecclesiastical History*, trans. Arthur Cushman McGiffert, Buffalo, NY: Christian Literature Publishing, 1890, 5.16.7.
Page 131: Hildegard of Bingen, *Scivias*, as quoted in Francis Mershman, 'St. Hildegard', in *The Catholic Encyclopedia*, vol. 7, New York: Robert Appleton Company, 1910, 351.
Page 134: Nostradamus, *Les Prophéties*, as quoted in Theophilus de Garencieres, *The true prophecies or prognostications of Michael Nostradamus, physician to Henry II, Francis II, and Charles IX, kings of France and one of the best astronomers that ever were a work full of curiosity and learning*, London, 1685.
Page 156: *Linga Purana*, trans J. L. Shastri, AITM vols 5 and 6, Delhi: Motilal Banarsidass, 1951, 91:15.
Page 157: Aristotle, *On Prophesying by Dreams*, trans. J. I. Beare, The Internet Classics Archive, https://classics.mit.edu/Aristotle/prophesying.html
Page 160: *The Dream of Dumuzid*, 41–55, J. A. Black et al., The Electronic Text Corpus of Sumerian Literature (http://www-etcsl.orient.ox.ac.uk/), Oxford, 1998.
Page 170: Synesius of Cyrene, *The Essays and Hymns*, trans. A. Fitzgerald, vol. 2, Oxford: Oxford University Press, 1930, 1.3.
Page 186: Translation adapted from Jeanette C. Fincke, *From Celestial Omens to the Beginnings of Modern Astrology in Ancient Mesopotamia*, The Babylonian Sky, vol. 1, Dresden: ISLET, 2024.
Page 222: *Shardulakarnavadana*, as quoted in Kenneth G. Zysk, 'Three Versions of Crow Omens', *History of Science in South Asia*, 10 (2022), 239.
Page 228: Dice oracle inscriptions translated by the author from F. Heinevetter, *Würfel- und Buchstabenorakel in Griechenland und Kleinasien*, Breslau: Grass Barth & Comp., 1912, 35.
Page 237: Rodrigo Hernández Príncipe, as quoted in Neil MacGregor, *A History of the World in 100 Objects*, London: Allen Lane, 2010, 470–75.
Page 241: The Council of Vannes canons, as quoted in James Strong and John McClintock, *The Cyclopedia of Biblical, Theological, and Ecclesiastical Literature*, New York: Harper and Brothers, 1880.

SOURCES OF ILLUSTRATIONS

a ABOVE, b BELOW, l LEFT, r RIGHT, c CENTRE

2 Bodleian Libraries, University of Oxford/Bridgeman Images; **8–9** Wellcome Collection, London; **10** Albertina Museum, Vienna; **12** Pictures from History/Bridgeman Images; **13l** Rijksmuseum, Amsterdam [RP-P-OB-53.320]; **13r** British Library, London/Bridgeman Images; **14** Brooklyn Museum, New York. Gift of Mr and Mrs Robert L. Poster [78.260.5]; **15** Private collection; **16** Photo The Trustees of the British Museum; **17** Rijksmuseum, Amsterdam [RP-P-OB-73.046]; **18, 19** The Metropolitan Museum of Art, New York; **20** Luisa Ricciarini/Bridgeman Images; **21a** Turkish and Islamic Arts Museum, Istanbul; **21b** Wellcome Collection, London; **22a** Private collection; **22b** Photo © Jon Bilous. All rights reserved 2025/Bridgeman Images; **23** Fonds Gilberte Brassaï, Paris. Photo GrandPalaisRmn/Michèle Bellot. © Estate Brassaï – GrandPalaisRmn; **24–5** Tate, N01541; **26** Musée des Beaux-Arts, Quimper. Photo GrandPalaisRmn/Michèle Bellot; **28** Art Gallery of South Australia, Adelaide. Gift of the Rt. Honourable, the Earl of Kintore 1893/Bridgeman Images; **31** The Metropolitan Museum of Art, New York. Gift of Cornelius Vanderbilt, 1880 [80.3.277]; **32a** Dennis Sumrak; **32b** Merlin74/Shutterstock; **33** Zev Radovan/Alamy Stock Photo; **34** Musée Fabre de Montpellier Méditerranée Métropole [868.1.8]. Photo Frédéric Jaulmes; **35l** Norman B. Leventhal Map & Education Center at Boston Public Library [DL31 .M26 1859]; **35r** The Árni Magnússon Institute for Icelandic Studies, Reykjavík [AM 738 4to]; **36a** Penn Libraries, Philadelphia [Inc B-720]; **36b** Scala, Florence; **37** British Library, London/Bridgeman Images; **38, 39** The Metropolitan Museum of Art, New York. Harris Brisbane Dick Fund, 1937; **40** University of Michigan Museum of Art [1968/2.75]; **41l** Photo The Trustees of the British Museum; **41r** Science History Images/Alamy Stock Photo; **42** The Cleveland Museum of Art. Leonard C. Hanna Jr Fund [1994.200]; **43l** Private collection. Photo courtesy Heritage Auctions; **43r** Photo musée du quai Branly – Jacques Chirac, Dist. GrandPalaisRmn/Pierre Verger. Photo © Fundação Pierre Verger; **44** Freer Gallery of Art, National Museum of Asian Art, Smithsonian Institution, Washington, D.C. [F1984.42]; **45a** Majority World/UIG/Bridgeman Images; **45b** V. Muthuraman/IndiaPictures/Universal Images Group/Getty Images; **47** Tokyo National Museum; **49** Lambeth Palace Library; **50** Photo © Manuel Bauer/Fotostiftung Schweiz; **51** British Library London [Add.Or.3043]; **52** Di Giacinto Morris Collection. Photo Christopher Stach/Kasmin, New York. © Theodora Allen; **54a** Municipal Museum of Piacenza; **54c** The Metropolitan Museum of Art, New York [86.11.503]; **54b** Biblioteca Nacional de España, Madrid; **55** Zentral- und Hochschulbibliothek Luzern; **56** Musée de la Tapisserie, Bayeux. Photo Ministère de la Culture – Médiathèque du patrimoine et de la photographie, Dist. GrandPalaisRmn/Jean Gourbeix, Simon Guillot; **57l** Biblioteca Apostolica Vaticana [Vat.sir.162]; **57r** Harvard College Observatory; **58, 59** Universitätsbibliothek Kassel [4° Ms. astron. 5]; **60** Zentralbibliothek Zürich [PAS II 17/3]; **61l** Österreichische Nationalbibliothek, Vienna [Cod. Theol. gr. 31]; **61r** Private collection. © 2025 John Mawurndjul/Copyright Agency. Licensed by DACS; **62** Bibliothèque nationale de France, Paris. Département des Manuscrits [Mexicain 385]; **63l** Bibliothèque nationale de France, Paris. Département des Manuscrits [Latin 7432]; **63r** New York Public Library, Spencer Collection [Persian MS. 6]; **64, 65** Bayerische Staatsbibliothek, München [Cod.icon. 181]; **66** Smithsonian American Art Museum. Gift of Eleanor Blodgett [1911.4.1]; **67** Granger/Bridgeman Images; **68** The Metropolitan Museum of Art, New York. Gift of M. Knoedler & Co., 1918; **69l** Wellcome Collection, London; **69r** Rijksmuseum, Amsterdam [RP-P-OB-44.818]; **70, 71** University of Pennsylvania, Kislak Center for Special Collections, Rare Books and Manuscripts [Ms. Coll. 390 Item 1914]; **73al** Biblioteca Medicea Laurenziana; **73ar** Catherine Shepard/Bridgeman Images; **73b** Walters Art Museum. Acquired by Henry Walters, before 1931 [22.264]; **74, 75** Courtesy of the University of St Andrews Libraries and Museums [ms32(o)]; **76** Chester Beatty, Dublin [Thi 1302]; **77, 78** Wellcome Collection, London; **79** Library of Congress, Washington, D.C. Rare Book and Special Collections Division, Jay I. Kislak Collection [Kislak MS 1025]; **80–1** Bibliothèque nationale de France, Paris. Département des Manuscrits [Mexicain 18-19]; **82** Fitzwilliam Museum, University of Cambridge/Bridgeman Images; **84, 85** University of Pennsylvania, Kislak Center for Special Collections, Rare Books and Manuscripts [Ms. Coll. 390 Item 3025]; **86** Musée Condé, Chantilly. Photo GrandPalaisRmn (Domaine de Chantilly)/Michel Urtado; **88l** The National Gallery, London/Scala, Florence; **88r** British Library, London/Bridgeman Images; **89** Rijksmuseum, Amsterdam [RP-P-1896-A-19368-1333]; **90, 91** Bayerische Staatsbibliothek München [Cod.icon 414];

93, 94, 95, 97 Photos The Trustees of the British Museum; **98, 99** The University of Manchester, The John Rylands Library [Persian MS 41]; **101a** Musée Cognacq-Jay, Paris; **101b** British Library, London/Bridgeman Images; **102–3** Rijksmuseum, Amsterdam [SK-A-1783]; **105a** Bodleian Libraries, University of Oxford/Bridgeman Images; **105b** Wellcome Collection, London; **106–7** Sandro Vannini/Bridgeman Images; **108, 109** Bodleian Libraries, University of Oxford/Bridgeman Images; **110** Wellcome Collection, London; **111** Museum für Asiatische Kunst, Staatlichen Museen zu Berlin [III 6368]; **112–13** Museum für Asiatische Kunst, Staatlichen Museen zu Berlin [III 4979 v]. Photo Scala, Florence/bpk, Bildagentur für Kunst, Kultur und Geschichte, Berlin/Iris Papadopoulos; **114, 115** Staatsbibliothek zu Berlin [Diez A fol. 3, 142v, 148r]; **116, 177** Chester Beatty, Dublin [T 423.21 recto, T 423.19 verso, T 423.18 recto, T 423.19 recto]; **118** Harold B. Lee Library, Brigham Young University, Provo; **119l** Private collection; **119r** British Library, London; **120** Bodleian Libraries, University of Oxford/Bridgeman Images; **122al** Sheridan Libraries, Johns Hopkins University; **122ar** Bodleian Libraries, University of Oxford/Bridgeman Images; **122b** British Library, London/Bridgeman Images; **123** Bernard Becker Medical Library, Washington University; **124–5** Beinecke Rare Book and Manuscript Library, Yale University, New Haven [2000 Folio 6 20]; **126, 127** National Central Library, Taipei; **128, 129** Leiden University Libraries [SINOL. Gulik E 109]; **130** Bridgeman Images; **131** Biblioteca Statale di Lucca [MS 1942]; **133l** National Museum of Indonesia, Jakarta. Photo Gunawan Kartapranata; **133r** Dewantara Kirti Griya Museum, Yogyakarta; **135a** Jean Bernard/Bridgeman Images; **135b, 136** Musée des Civilisations de l'Europe et de la Méditerranée, Marseille. Photo GrandPalaisRmn (MuCEM)/image GrandPalaisRmn; **137** Wellcome Collection, London; **139** Bibliothèque nationale de France, Paris. Département Littérature et art [16-INDOCH PIECE-875]; **140** Biblioteca comunale di Trento; **141** Biblioteca Nazionale Centrale di Firenze; **143** Zentralbibliothek Zürich [Paracelsus I, 24]; **144, 145** Getty Research Institute, Los Angeles; **146, 147l, 147r** Beinecke Rare Book and Manuscript Library, Yale University, New Haven [Nkk94 Sh5 +651, Nkk12 642T, Nkk94 Sh5 +651]; **149a** Tallandier/Bridgeman Images; **149b** Used by permission of the Edgar Cayce Foundation, Virginia Beach, VA; **150** Courtesy CSU Archives/Everett Collection/Alamy Stock Photo; **151** Ken Faught/Toronto Star/Getty Images; **153** Photo © Ivan Grigorov; **154** The Cleveland Museum of Art. Jo Hershey Selden Fund [2021.12]; **156** The Cleveland Museum of Art. Leonard C. Gift in honour of Madeline Neves Clapp; Gift of Mrs. Henry White Cannon by exchange; Bequest of Louise T. Cooper; Leonard C. Hanna Jr. Fund; From the Catherine and Ralph Benkaim Collection [2013.353]; **157a** British Library, London [Yates Thompson 36]; **157b** Gallerie dell'Accademia, Venice; **158–9** Philadelphia Museum of Art. Gift of Stella Kramrisch, 1967 [1967-226-1(12a,b)]; **161a** Photo The Trustees of the British Museum; **161b** The Israel Museum, Jerusalem. Bequest of Joseph Ternbach, New York, to American Friends of the Israel Museum [87.160.802]. Photo © The Israel Museum/Laura Lachman; **162** Granger Historical Picture Archive/Alamy Stock Photo; **163a** The Metropolitan Museum of Art, New York. Rogers Fund, 1915 [15.2.8]; **163b, 164** Photo The Trustees of the British Museum; **165** British Library, London/Bridgeman Images; **166** Bridgeman Images; **167l** Österreichische Nationalbibliothek [Cod. Theol. gr. 31]; **167r** Musée du Louvre, Paris; **168** Bridgeman Images; **169l** Manchester Central Library. Sutton Witchcraft Collection [133.4]; **169r** British Library, London [E.1158.(2)]; **170** Universal History Archive/ UIG /Bridgeman Images; **171** Bibliothèque nationale de France, Paris. Département Réserve des livres rares [RES-G-732]; **173** Private collection; **174** Detroit Institute of Arts. Founders Society Purchase [81.233.4]; **175** Fenimore Art Museum, Cooperstown, New York, Thaw Collection; **176–7** American Museum of Natural History, Department of Anthropology [50.2/4063]; **179** © Nigel Borell; **180** Universitätsbibliothek Heidelberg [Cod. Pal. germ. 833]; **182l** Wellcome Collection, London; **182r** Bibliothèque nationale de France, Paris. Département des Manuscrits [Français 9140]; **183** British Library, London [Add MS 27089]; **184–5** Musée Guimet – musée national des Arts asiatiques, Paris. Photo GrandPalaisRmn (MNAAG, Paris)/Thierry Ollivier; **186** The Israel Museum, Jerusalem. Purchase, Anna D. Ternbach Bequest Fund, in memory of Joseph Ternbach [99.81.10]. Photo © The Israel Museum/ David Harris; **187a, 187b** Vorderasiatisches Museum, Staatliche Museen zu Berlin [VAT 07847, VAT 07851]. Photos Olaf M. Teßmer; **189** Bridgeman Images; **190** Biblioteca Comunale di Trento; **191** Minneapolis Institute of Art. The Minnich Collection, The Ethel Morrison Van Derlip Fund, 1966 [P.14, 543]; **192** Musée Condé, Chantilly. Photo GrandPalaisRmn (Domaine de Chantilly)/Michel Urtado; **194, 195** Biblioteca Estense Universitaria, Modena [lat. 209=Alfa.X.2.14]. Su concessione del Ministero della Cultura – Gallerie Estensi, Biblioteca Estense Universitaria; **196** Wellcome Collection, London; **197** Musée national du château de Pau. Photo GrandPalaisRmn (Château de Pau)/René-Gabriel Ojeda; **198–9** Wellcome Collection, London; **201** University of Pennsylvania, Rare Book & Manuscript Library [Ms. Indic 3]; **202–3** Cleveland Museum of Art. Gift of Doris and Ed Wiener [1971.61]; **204, 205** Cleveland Museum of Art. Gift of Nancy and Wayne Hunnicutt [2020.432, 2014.651]; **206** Biblioteca Apostolica Vaticana [Vat.gr.1291]; **207** Su concessione del Ministero della Cultura – Archivio fotografico delle Gallerie Estensi;

208 Royal Ontario Museum, Toronto; **209l** The Dr Paul Singer Collection of Chinese Art of the Arthur M. Sackler Gallery, Smithsonian Institution; a joint gift of the Arthur M. Sackler Foundation, Paul Singer, the AMS Foundation for the Arts, Sciences, and Humanities, and the Children of Arthur M. Sackler [S2012.9.3422]; **209r** Harvard Art Museums/Arthur M. Sackler Museum, Gift of the Friends of Arthur B. Duel [1933.4.1726]. Photo President and Fellows of Harvard College; **210–11** Gallery Zacke, Lot 100, *A Museum Treasury of Buddhist and Himalayan Art: The Peter Kienzle-Hardt Collection Part I*, auction held on 07.03.2025; **212** Harvard Art Museums/Arthur M. Sackler Museum, Bequest of Abby Aldrich Rockefeller [1960.191]. Photo President and Fellows of Harvard College; **213** Wellcome Collection, London; **214, 215** Harvard Art Museums/Arthur M. Sackler Museum, Gift of Philip Hofer in memory of Eric Schroeder [1972.3]. Photos President and Fellows of Harvard College; **216, 217** Bibliothèque nationale de France, Paris. Département des manuscrits [Arabe 2583]; **218a, 219a** Bodleian Libraries, University of Oxford/Bridgeman Images; **218b, 219b** Bibliothèque nationale de France, Paris. Département des Manuscrits [Supplément turc 242]; **220** University of Pennsylvania, Kislak Center for Special Collections, Rare Books and Manuscripts [Ms. Coll. 390 Item 778]; **222a** Private collection; **222b** Photo Fortean/TopFoto; **223l** British Library, London [8610.aa.40]; **223r** Christie's Images/Bridgeman Images; **224–5** Photo © Richard Kalvar/Magnum Photos; **226, 227** Private collection; **229al** The Metropolitan Museum of Art, New York. Gift of Helen Miller Gould, 1910 [10.130.1158]; **229ar** Photo © The Board of Trustees of the Science Museum; **229b** British Library, London [Or.8212/161]; **230, 231** The Metropolitan Museum of Art, New York. Rogers Fund, 1916 [16.10.505a–c]; **232, 233** Bayerische Staatsbibliothek München [BV001551971]; **234** Wellcome Collection, London; **235l** Nationalmuseet, Copenhagen [8752]. Photo Roberto Fortuna and Kira Ursem; **235r** The Metropolitan Museum of Art, New York. Bequest of Mary Anna Palmer Draper, 1915 [15.43.285]; **236** Photo The Trustees of the British Museum; **237** Rijksmuseum, Amsterdam [RP-P-OB-56.518]; **238** Musée du Louvre, Paris. Photo GrandPalaisRmn (musée du Louvre)/Tony Querrec; **239** DeAgostini/Getty Images; **240** British Library, London/Bridgeman Images; **241l** Biblioteca Apostolica Vaticana [Vat.lat.3867]; **241r** The Khalili Collections [MSS 979]; **242, 243** The Walters Art Museum, Baltimore [Ms. W.635]; **244–5** The Walters Art Museum, Baltimore [Ms. W.569]; **247a** Photo © Abbas/Magnum Photos; **247b** Rijksmuseum, Amsterdam [RP-T-2015-32-87]; **248–9** Photo © Abbas/Magnum Photos; **251** Beinecke Rare Book and Manuscript Library, Yale University, New Haven. Cary Collection of Playing Cards [PLAYING CARDS GEN 965]; **252a, 253a** Beinecke Rare Book and Manuscript Library, Yale University, New Haven [GEN MSS 2136]. © Bea Nettles; **252b, 253b, 254** Private collection; **255a** New York Public Library, Dorot Jewish Division [b16027600]; **255b** Stiftsbibliothek, St Gallen [Cod. Sang. 756]; **256** Niedersächsische Landesbibliothek, Hannover; **257** The National Museum of Modern Art, Tokyo; **258–9** MeijiShowa/Alamy Stock Photo; **260l** Musée Guimet – musée national des Arts asiatiques, Paris. Photo GrandPalaisRmn (MNAAG, Paris)/Thierry Ollivier; **260r** National Museum of the American Indian, Smithsonian Institution [12/7199]. Photo NMAI Photo Services; **261** Gallery Zacke, Lot 63, *Asian Art Discoveries*, auction held on 18.01.2023; **262** Stiftsbibliothek, St Gallen [Cod. Sang. 756]; **263** Michel Renaudeau/Gamma-Rapho/Getty Images; **264–5** Wellcome Collection, London; **266** Bridgeman Images; **268l** The National Gallery, London [NG1034]; **268r** Galleria Nazionale dell'Umbria/with permission of the Italian Ministry of Culture/Bridgeman Images; **269** Rijksmuseum, Amsterdam [RP-P-OB-78.493]; **270** Pascal Lemaitre/Bridgeman Images; **271l** The Metropolitan Museum of Art, New York. The Elisha Whittelsey Collection, The Elisha Whittelsey Fund, 1951 [51.501.352]; **271r** Rare Book and Manuscript Library, Columbia University [PQ4302 .B68]; **273** Corpus Christi College, Oxford/Bridgeman Images; **274–5** Private collection; **277a** Staatliche Bibliothek, Regensburg [999/Philos.2280 angeb.5]; **277b** Bayerische Staatsbibliothek, Munich; **278** Photo courtesy The Panacea Charitable Trust; **279** Private collection; **280** The New York Historical/Getty Images; **281, 283** Department of Archives and Special Collections, University Libraries, Loma Linda University [IBP-II-011, 2018.001]; **282** AF Fotografie/Alamy Stock Photo; **285** Associated Press/Pat Roque/Alamy Stock Photo; **286** Associated Press/Charles E. Knoblock/Alamy Stock Photo; **287** The Asahi Shimbun/Getty Images; **289** Museo Nacional de Antropología, Mexico City; **290, 292, 293** Wellcome Collection, London; **294** The Metropolitan Museum of Art, New York. Rogers Fund, 2000 [2000.282.10]; **295l** Wellcome Collection, London; **295r** The Metropolitan Museum of Art, New York. Rogers Fund, 1913 [13.96.17]; **297** Wellcome Collection, London; **298** Staatsbibliothek zu Berlin; **299** Armenian Patriarchate of Jerusalem; **300, 301** The Metropolitan Museum of Art, New York. Purchase, The Cloisters Collection, Rogers and Harris Brisbane Dick Funds, and Joseph Pulitzer Bequest, 1991 [1991.232.13]; **302, 303** The Walters Art Museum, Baltimore [Ms. W.917]; **304** The Árni Magnússon Institute for Icelandic Studies, Reykjavík [SÁM 66]; **305** The Árni Magnússon Institute for Icelandic Studies, Reykjavík [AM 738 4to]; **307** Granger/Bridgeman Images

INDEX

Page numbers in *italic* refer to illustrations; page numbers in **bold** refer to full entries.

2012 Phenomenon 23, **288–9**, 293

abacomancy 222
Abbasid Caliphate 213
Abd al-Ghani al-Nabulsi 172
Abe no Seimei 46, *47*
Abraham 20, 100
Abu Ma'shar al-Balkhi (Albumasar) 58, 213
    Kitab al-Mawalid 214, *214–15*
Abydos 271
Achaemenid Empire 32
Achmet ibn Sirin, *Oneirocriticon* 172
Adam (biblical figure) 115
Adams, Evangeline 23
aeromancy 54, 263
Agamemnon 69, 157
Agni Purana 156
Agrippa, Marcus Vipsanius 57
Ahab 17
Aion 207, *207*
Akkadians 14, 72, 77, 88, 92, 182, 187
albatrosses 69
Alexander the Great 29, 32, 37, 169, 207, 255
Alexandria 170, 207
Allen, Theodora, *Shooting Star III 52*, 53
Alliette, Jean-Baptiste (Etteilla) 21, 250
Ambrosius Aurelianus 48
Amenemhat I 163
American Civil War *66*, 67, 118
Amsterdam 269, *269*
Amun 29, 32, *32*, 33
Anabaptists 269, *269*
angels 105, *105*, 114, *114*, 115, *115*, 118, 148, 156, *157*, 167, 299, *299*
    Gabriel 88, *88*, 115
    Moroni 118, *118*
Anishinaabe people 175
Antichrist 105, *106–7*, 300, *300*, *301*
Aotearoa *see* Maori
Apis bull 33, *33*
apocalypse 21, 89, 96, 104–5, *105–9*, 131, 272, *273*, 279, 283, 292–3, **298–303**
Apollo 20, 41, 110
Aristander of Telmessos 169
Aristotle and Aristotelianism 157, 207, 255
Artemidorus 72, **168–9**
Arthur, King 48
Asahara, Shoko 287
Asclepius 156
Ashurbanipal 61
    Library of 92, *94–5*
Assyrians 14, 63, 88
astragalomancy 222, **228–33**, 263
astronomy 54, 127, 182, *183*, **188–91**, 200
Athanasius, St 69, *69*
Athena 69
Athens 170
Atlantis 148

augurs 30–1, 222, 237
Augustine, St 89, 197, 207
Augustus 271
Aum Shinrikyo 287, *287*
auroras **66–7**
Australia 61, 67, 269
Ayyub (Job) 115, *115*
Aztecs 12, 14, 54–5, *54*, 62, *62*, 73, *73*, 79, *80–1*, 187, 235, 289, *289*, 306, *307*

Báb **119**
Baba Vanga 23, **152–3**
babaláwos 29, **42–3**
Babylonians 61, 88, 92, 161, 236, *236*
    astrology 182, *186*, 187, 188, 206
    omen compilations 14–16, *16*, 54, 63
Baghdad 20, 213
Baha'i faith 119, 296
Baha'u'llah 119, 296
Balaam 100, *101*, *101*
Balak, King 100
Baldr 304, *304*
Baltimore 269
bamboo 246
Bangkok 72
Bar-Jesus 270, *270*
Bayeux Tapestry *56*, 57
bazi (Four Pillars of Destiny) 20, 209
beans 222
Bentivoglio, Giovanni II 140
Bes 162, 271
Best, Elsdon 178
Bhadrakali 44, *44*, 45
Bible 88, *89*
    apocalypse in 21, 89, 96, 104, 131, 279, 283, 284, 292, **298–303**
    casting of lots in 246
    dreams in 17, 89, *156*, 166–7
    omens in 61
    prophets and prophecy in 13, 17, *17*, 36, *36*, 37, 54, *86*, 88–9, 92, 100, 104, 268, *270*, 271, *271*
    Second Coming in 272, 281
    use in bibliomancy 241
bibliomancy 89, 221, **226–7**, **240–5**
birds 20, 30, **68–71**, 72, 160, 221, 222
Black Hawk 175, *175*
black magic 263
Bodhisattva Avalokiteshvara 246
Bologna 140
bones, use in divination 16, *18–19*, 187, 222–3, *222*, 228, *229*, **230–1**, 260–1, 263
Book of Thoth 250
Booth, A. E., 'Chart of the Ages' 274, *274–5*
Borell, Nigel, *Talking to the Moon 179*
Botticelli, Sandro 268–9
Brahan Seer 122
Brahma 44, *44*, 292
Brassaï 23

Buddha *8–9*, 11, 111, 164, *164*, 165, 293, 294, 295
Buddhism 29, 51, 111, 222, 246, 292
    and dreaming 164–5
    Maitreya **294–5**
Bulgaria 152–3
Burnet, Thomas, *The Sacred Theory of the Earth* 292, *292*
Byron, Lord 292

Caligula 207
Cambyses II 32
Cameroon 12, 222
Camping, Harold 268, **284–5**
Canada 223, 261
capnomancy 221
Cardano, Girolamo 141
Cary–Yale Tarot deck 251, *251*
Cassandra 271
Cassius Dio 35
casting of lots *see* cleromancy
Catherine of Siena, St 21
catoptromancy *see* mirrors and mirror divination
Cayce, Edgar 23, **148–9**
Cellarius, Andreas, *Harmonia Macrocosmica* 190, *190–1*
Celts 156
Chad 263
chains, use in divination 29, 43, 222
Chaldeans 16, 160
Chartres Cathedral 166, *166*
Cheiro (William John Warner) 255
Childeric I, King 223, 235
chiromancy *see* palmistry
Church, Frederic Edwin, *Aurora Borealis 66*, *66*
Cicero, *On Divination* 11, 20, 29
Cihuacoatl 73, *73*
Claudius 237
Claudius Gothicus 241
cleromancy 221, 222, **246–9**, 257
cobras 72, 73, *73*
Coe, Michael D. 288
coffee-ground reading 223
Cold War 287
comets 54–5, *55*, **56–9**, 96, 100, 182, 202, *203*, 292, 293
Confucianism 20, 138, 256
Constantine 271
Constantinople (Istanbul) 141, *141*, 170, 172
Court de Gébelin, Antoine 250
cowrie shells 222
crabs 222
Cree people 223
Croesus 29
Crow people 175
crows 69, *69*, 222
crystal balls 223, *223*, 234, 235, *235*

Cuauhtemoc 235
Cumaean sibyl 36, *36*, 37, *39*, 293

Dalai Lama 29, 51, 228
Daniel (prophet) 89, 96, 104, 156, *157*, 160, 281, *282*, 283
Dante Alighieri, *Divine Comedy* 157, *157*, 271, *271*
days, auspicious and inauspicious 55, 78–81, 210, *210–11*
Dee, John 223, 235
Deir el-Bahari 29
Delphi *41*
    oracle 20, *20*, 28, *28*, 40–1
    sibyl 36, *39*, 41
'Dendera zodiac' 182, *182*
Denmark 235, *235*
Devil 69, 105, *106*, 280, *280*, 299
dice 222, **228–33**, 263
Dieri people 67
Dixon, Jeane 23, 123, **150–1**
Domitian 35
doomsday cults **286–7**
doppelgängers 82, 83
Dumuzid 160
Dune (film) 123
Dunhuang 228
dust 222

earthquakes 16, 108, *109*, 148, 284, 299, 306
East Java 132–3
eclipses 16, 54, **62–5**, 202, *203*
Eddic writings 35, *35*, *304*, 305
Edward, Prince of Wales 255
Egypt, ancient 12, 14, 72, 131, 250
    astrology and astronomy 182, *182*, 187, **206–7**
    dream interpretation 156, **162–3**
    oracles 29, **32–3**
    temple practices 13, 156, 207
Ellison, Raniera 178
Elymas 270, *270*
Enlightenment, Western 21, 183, 188
entrails, consultation of 20, 53, *54*, 100, 221, **236–9**
Enuma Anu Enlil 14, 54, *54*, 63
Ephesus 168
eschatology 21, 89, 96, 104, *105–9*, 123, *124–5*, 142, 147, 278, 281, 284, **286–7**, 288, **291–307**
Etruscans 54, *54*, 237, *239*
Etteilla (Jean-Baptiste Alliette) 21, 250
Eusebius 110
Ezekiel *13*

face reading 77, *77*, *78*
Falnamas 241, *241*
false prophets 104, 110, *266*, 267, 268, 270–1, 299
Fates (Moirai) 14
favomancy 222
Festinger, Leon 287
Finland 13, 67
five phases *see* wuxing
Five Suns 306–7
floods 287, *290*, 291, 292, 306
    of 1524 276–7

Great Flood 284, 292, *293*
Florence 269
Four Horsemen of the Apocalypse 89, 299
Four Pillars of Destiny *see* bazi
Franks 235
French Revolution 67
Freud, Sigmund 157, 169
Friday the 13th 55, 79

Gabriel (angel) 88, *88*, 115
Gadong oracle 51
Game of Thrones (Book and TV series) 123
Ganna 35
Gara divination 263
Garuda Purana 76
Gaurico, Luca 140–1, 276
Geoffrey of Monmouth 48
geomancy 255, **262–5**
Gerard of Cremona 263
Geshtinanna 160
Gildas 48
Gilgamesh, Epic of 160
Gnosticism 111
Gog and Magog 299
Goya, Francisco, 'Los Caprichos' 68, *68*
'great chain' concept 21, *211*
Great Conjunction 269, 276, *277*, *277*
Great Disappointment 21, 281
Great Tribulation 269, 284
Gregoras, Nicephorus 183
Gregory XI, Pope *122*, 123
Gutenberg, Johannes 122–3

Hadrian 241
Hafez, *The Divan* 241, *242–3*
Haggai 36, *36*
hakata 222, *222*, 228, 229, *229*
Halley's Comet 54, 56, *56*, 57, *57*
halomancy 222
Han dynasty 209
Hananiah 268
Harold, King 54, *56*, 57
Harry Potter (book and film series) 123
Hastings, Battle of (1066) 54, *56*, 57
Hatshepsut 29, 32
Heaven's Gate (cult) 287
Hebrew sibyl *see* Persian sibyl
hemerology *see* days, auspicious and inauspicious
Henry I, King of England 63
Henry II, King of France 141, *141*
Henry IV, King of France 197, *197*
Henry VIII, King of England 147
Heraclitus 36
Hermes Trismegistus 182
Hernández Principe, Rodrigo 237
Hildegard of Bingen 21, **130–1**
Himes, Joshua V. 280, *280*
Hinduism *14*, **44–5**, 63, 132, 133, *133*, 156, 193, 197, **200–3**, *290*, 291
    cycles of 292, **296–7**
Hitler, Adolf 136
Hittites 69
Hmong people 284
Höðr *304*, *304*
Homer 240, *240*
    Iliad 69, 156–7

horoscopes 14, *14*, 23, 79, 134, 141, *141*, 182, 193, **196–9**
Hugh of Santalla 263
hydromancy 263
Hypnos *170*, 171

I Ching (*Book of Changes*) 16, 29, 46, 127, 138, 209, 222, **256–9**
Ibn al-Muqri 172, *173*
Ibn Sirin of Basra 172, *173*
Iceland 35, 305
Ifá divination 29, **42–3**, 222, 263
Iggleheim's Ark 276
Inca 14, 54, 63, 237
Indonesia 132–3
Innu people 223, *260*, 261
Inquisition, Catholic Church 20–1
Iran 87, 114, 197, 241, 263
    see also Persia
Ireland 61
Irk Bitig (*Book of Omens*) 228, *229*
Ishtar 187
Iskandar 197, *198–9*
Islam 20, 88, 89, 96, 114–16, 271, 292, 298, 299
    astrology in 20, **212–19**
    dream interpretation in 172–3
    see also Quran

Jainism 111, *154*, 155, 158, *158–9*, 292
Japan 55, 83, 136, 223, *224–5*
    astrology and astronomy 182, 188, 208, 209, *209*
    doomsday cults 287, *287*
    Onmyōryō (Bureau of Divination) 29, **46–7**
    sacred lots 246, *247*, *248–9*
Java 132–3
Jayabaya 132–3
al-Jazari, Ismail 212, *212*
Jerusalem 115, 119, 299
Jesus Christ 20, 79, 88–9, *90–1*, 100, 104, 111, *116*, 123, *266*, 267
    birth 21, 37, 167
    Second Coming 21, 89, 104, 131, 268, 272, 274, *274–5*, 281, *282*, *282*, 284, 299
Jibra'il *see* Gabriel (angel)
Joachim of Fiore 272, *273*
Job (Ayyub) 115, *115*
John of Patmos, St *86*, 89, 110, 283
Jonah (Yunus) 114, *114*
Joseph (Yusuf, prophet) 17, 89, 104, 156, *156*, 167, *167*
Joseph, St 167, *167*
Josephus 100
Judaism 20, 88, 104, 115, 298, 299
Judgment Day 284, *285*, 298, *298*
Jung, Carl 157
Jupiter (planet) 63, 187, *194*, 209

Kabbalah 183, *183*, 255, *255*
Kalki 296, *297*
Kannon 246
Karnak *32*, 33
Kashmir 54, 57
kau chim 246, *247*
Kazan, Emperor 46

Kediri kingdom 132–3
Kennedy, John F. 151
Kerala 44–5
Korea 13, 20, 208, 257, 261
Kumalak divination 263

Lakota people 175, 176, *176–7*
Latter-day Saint movement *see* Mormonism
Laughead, Charles 286, *286*
Leibniz, Gottfried Wilhelm 256, *256*
Leo (zodiac sign) 187, *187*
Leo VI, Emperor 122, *122*
Leo Tuscus 172
Leowitz, Cyrian, *Eclipses luminarium* 64, *65*, 66
Li Chunfeng 127
Li Hong 292, 295
Libya 170
lightning 30, 54, 55, 72
Linga Purana 156
Little Big Horn, Battle of the (1876) 175
Liu Bowen 122
livers 236, *236*, 237
London 276, 279
    Great Fire (1666) 134, 136, 147
Lord of the Rings (book and film series) 123
Los Angeles 148
lottery books 226, *226–7*
Lucas van Leyden *38–9*
Luther, Martin 276
Lycurgus 40, *40*

Madagascar 263
Madden, Samuel, *Memoirs of the Twentieth Century* 21
Mahabharata 132
Maitreya **294–5**
Malachi 100
Mali 263, *263*
Mandate of Heaven 209
Mani and Manichaeism 111–13
Manila 284, *285*
Manilius, Marcus, *Astronomica* 207
al-Mansur 213
Maori 60, *60*, 61, 67, **178–9**
Marduk 187
Mari 92
Maricopa people 175
Mars (planet) 79, 182, *182*, 194, *194*, 202, *203*, 218, *218*
Martin, Dorothy 286, *286*
Martin, John 292, *293*
Mary, Virgin 167, 279
Mashallah ibn Athari 213
Mata Hari 255
Mathys, Jan 269
Matrix (film series) 123
Mawurndjul, John, *Ngalyod the Rainbow Serpent* 61, *61*
Maximilla 110
Maya, Queen 164, *164*, 165, *165*
Mayans 14, 23, 235, 288, 293
Mecca 115
Medici, Catherine de' 134, 135, *135*, 137, *137*, 141
Melba, Dame Nellie 255
Memphis 33

Mercury (planet) *194*, 202, *202*, 218, *218*
Merlin 48–9, 146, *146*
Mesopotamia 12, 14–16, 54, 72, 77, 87, 88, 92, 160–1, 182, 187, 200, 236, 268, 292
metoposcopy 77
Micaiah 17
Michelangelo 36
Midgard serpent 305, *305*
Millennialism 21, **272–5**
Miller, William and Millerism 21, 22, **280–3**
Mimir 29
Mirabilis Liber 134
mirrors and mirror divination 12, 55, 221, 228, 234, *234*, 235, *235*
Mo divination 228
Moctezuma II *54*, 55
Moirai (Fates) 14
Mömpelgard altarpiece *266*, 267
Mongolia 12, *12*, 261
'Monster of Ravenna' 54
Montanus and Montanism 110, 272
Mormonism 21, 118, 148
Moroni 118, *118*
Moses 54, 88, 89, 100, *101*, 102, *102–3*
Mother Shipton 122, **146–7**
Mountain Dream Tarot 252, *252–3*
Muhammad, Prophet 20, 88, *88*, 89, 114, 115
Münster 269
Myrddin 48

Nabu 92, 93, *93*
Nanshe 161, *161*
Naples 293
Napoleon I 136
Napoleon III 119
Naskapi people 223
Native Americans 83, **174–7**, 223, 260, 261
Nawbakht 213
Nebuchadnezzar II 89, 156, *157*, 160, 281, *281*
Nechung oracle 29, 50, *50*, 51, *51*
Nettles, Bea 252
New Age thinking 23, 149, 288
New York 148, 269
    World Trade Center attack (2001) 136
New Zealand *see* Maoris
Nezahualpilli, King *54*, 55
Nggàm 222
Nguyen Binh Khiem 122, **138–9**
Nibiru 293
Nifo, Agostino 276
Nigeria 222, 263, 269
nigromancy 263
Nineveh 92, 94
Nixon, Richard 151
Noboru, Kitawaki 257, *257*
Norns 14, 35, *35*
Northern Lights *see* auroras
Norway 35, 67
Nostradamus *13*, 21, 48, 123, 127, **134–7**, 138
numerology 138, 210, 284
Nuremberg 61, *61*

Odin 29, 305
Odysseus *10*, 11
Oedipus 14
Olivet discourse 272
Olodumare 43
omikuji 246, *247*, **248–9**
Onmyoryo (Japanese Bureau of Divination) 29, **46–7**
Orestes 20, *20*, 41, *41*
ornithomancy *see* birds
Orunmila 42, *42*, 43
Ottoman Empire *21*, 136, 218–19, 222, *222*
owls 68, *68*, 69, 160

Pakistan 295, *295*
palmistry 16, 76, 220, 221, 223, 224, **254–5**, 263
Paracelsus 123, *123*, **142–5**
Pascalis Romanus, *Liber thesauri occulti* 172
Pasenadi, King 165
Paul, St 168, *168*, 270, *270*, 272
Paul the Octopus 23
Pausanias 37, 235
peacocks 69
Pehar Gyalpo 51
Pepuza 110
Pepys, Samuel 147
Persia 29, 96, 115, 119, 207, 213, *213*, 241, 255
    see also Iran
Persian sibyl 37, *39*
Peru 13, 237
Pflaum, Jacob 276
Philip II, King 196, *196*
Philippines 284, *285*
physiognomy 76–7, 147
Pic de Bugarach 288
Pisces (zodiac sign) 276, 277, *277*
planispheres 13, 190, *191*
plastromancy 15, 46, 247, *247*, 260–1
Platina, Bartolomeo, *Lives of the Popes* 57
Plenty Coups 175
Pliny the Elder 69, 77
Poe divination 222
printing, development of 122–3
Priscilla 110
Ptolemais 170
Ptolemy 58, 213
    Almagest 213
    Tetrabiblos 21, *206*, 207
'purple star astrology' *see* ziwei doushu
pyromancy 263
Pythia (Delphic oracle) 20, *20*, 28, *28*, 40–1

al-Qazwini, *Wonders of Creation* 214, *214–15*
Qing dynasty 55, *126*, 127
Quetzalcoatl 306
Quran 74, 89, 115, 156, 212, 241, 271, 298

Ragnarök 304–5
Rahu 63, 202, *203*
rainbows 54, 60–1
Rama I, King 72

Rapture 268, 284
Ravenna, Battle of (1512) 54
Reagan, Nancy 123, 151
Reagan, Ronald 123, 151
Reformation, Protestant 269, 276
Rembrandt, *Balaam and the Ass* 101, *101*
Renaissance 37, 172, 255
Rider–Waite–Smith Tarot deck 250, 252, *252–3*
Riecken, Henry 287
Romani people 255
Romulus and Remus 20, 30, *31*
Roosevelt, Franklin D. 151
Rossetti, Dante Gabriel, *How they Met Themselves* 82, *82*
Russia 67, 261, 302, *302–3*
Ryogen 246

sacred lots *see* cleromancy
sacrifice:
    animal 20, 29, 237, *237*, 238, *238*
    human 63, 306
Sahl ibn Bishr 213
salt:
    halomancy 222
    spilling 83
Sami people 67
Samuel (biblical figure) 17
San Francisco 148
Sarawak 69, *69*
Satan *see* Devil
Saturn (planet) 15, *15*, *195*, 202, *202*
Saudi Arabia 269
Saul, King 16, 17, *17*
Savonarola, Girolamo 268, *268*, 269
Saxons 48, 235
scapulimancy 222 3, 260 1, 263
Schachter, Stanley 287
scrying 12, 223, **234–5**
    see also crystal balls; mirrors and mirror divination
Second Great Awakening 118
seeds 29, 35, 43, 222
Seekers, The 286, *286*, 287
Senusret I 163
serpents *see* snakes and serpents
Seventh-day Adventists 281
Severus, Septimius 271
Shakespeare, William 69, 169
Shamash-shum-ukin, King 61
Shang dynasty 12, 14, 16, **18–19**, 29, 222, 261, *261*, *262*
Shaobing Ge ('Pancake poem') 122
Shardulakarnavadana 222
Shelley, Mary, *The Last Man* 293
shells 43
    see also cowrie shells; turtle shells
Shinto 46
Shipton, Mother 122, **146–7**
Shiva 44, *44*
Shona people 228
Short Bull 176, *176–7*
Shreyamsa, Prince *154*
Shrivara 54, 57
Shumma alu 16, *16*, 72
sibyls **36–9**, 41, 91, *91*, 123, 146, *146*, 293
Sikidy divination 263
Sin (moon god) 186, *186*
Sioux 83, 174, *174*

Sitchin, Zecharia, *The 12th Planet* 293
Sitting Bull 175
Siwa 29, 32, *32*
Smith, Joseph 21, 118, *118*, 148
smoke divination 221
snakes and serpents 16, *16*, 40, 60, 61, *61*, 69, **72–5**, 209, *209*, 305, *305*
Solomon (Suleyman) 89, *116*
Song dynasty 20
Southcott, Joanna **278–9**
Southern Lights *see* auroras
spider divination 12, 222
Star Wars (film series) 123
Stöffler, Johannes 276
Stoicism 207
Sturluson, Snorri 305
Suddhodana, King *8–9*, 11
Sukarno 132
Sumerians 14, 92, 160
Sweden 35, 67
Synesius of Cyrene 170–1

Tages 237
Taiwan 222
Tajikistan 269
Tang dynasty 20
Taoism 77, 292, 295
Tarot cards 21, *23*, **250–3**
Tarquinius Superbus 36, *36*, 37
tasseography 223
tea-leaf reading 223
Termessos 228
Thailand 72, 76, *76*, 79, 83, **184–5**, 208, *208*
Theyyam rituals 45, *45*
Thor 305
Thoth, Book of 250
Thrasyllus of Mendes 207
Thutmose IV *162*, 163
Tiberius 207
Tibet 29, **50–1**, 78, *78*, 182, **210–11**, 228, 261, 295
Tiburtine sibyl 37, *38*
Timur 197
Tinnin 63, *63*
Tiresias 10, 11, 69
Tlaloc 306
Tonatiuh 289, *289*, 306, *307*
Tournai 223
Trajan 241
Trang Trinh *see* Nguyen Binh Khiem
Trishala, Queen 158, *158–9*
Trojan Horse 271
Troy 69, 271
Tui Bei Tu 122, **126–9**
Tung Shing (Chinese Imperial Calendar) 55, 79
Turkey 110, 223, 228, 235
    see also Constantinople (Istanbul); Ottoman Empire
Turkic peoples 228, 229, *229*
turtle shells 16, 46, 247, *247*, **260–1**
Twain, Mark 255
Tymion 110
Tzitzimimeh 306

Uenuku 61
UFO cults 286, *286*, 287

UFOs 287, 288
Urim and Thummim 17, 118
Ursula, St 156, *157*

Valhalla 305, *305*
Valmiki 16, 255
Vannes, Council of (465) 241
Varro 36
Vedic religions 14, 16, 182, 193, **200–3**, 254, *254*, 292
    see also Buddhism; Hinduism; Jainism
Veleda 26, 27, 34, *34*
Velichappadu **44–5**
Venus (planet) 182, *182*, 186, 187, *195*, 218
Vergil *241*, 242
Victoria, Queen 119
Vietnam 83, 122, **138–9**, 182, 208, 284
Vishnu 44, *44*, 133, *133*, *290*, 291, 296
Völuspá ('Prophecy of the *völva*') 29, 35
volvelles *180*, 181, 188, *188*, 226, *227*
Vortigern, King 49, *49*

Wadjet 72, 73, *73*
Waluburg 35
Warner, William John (Cheiro) 255
Warren Field 187
Waterhouse, John William 23, *24–5*, 223, *223*
weather 30, 53, 54, 134, 263
wheels of fortune 223, *223*
Wilde, Oscar 255
William of Malmesbury, *Historia Novella* 62
Witch of Endor 16, 17, *17*
Wolsey, Thomas *146*, 147
wuxing (five phases) 183, 208, 209

Yajuj and Majuj 299
Yggdrasil 35, *35*, 305
yin-yang 183, 208, 209, 257
Yoruba people 14, 29, **42–3**, 263
Young, Brigham 118
Yuan Tiangang 127
Yuga cycles 292, 296
Yunus (Jonah) 114, *114*

Zarathustra *see* Zoroaster and Zoroastrianism
Zayn al-Abidin, Sultan 57
Zeus 156–7
Zhou dynasty 29, 256
Zimbabwe 222, *222*, 228
ziwei doushu ('purple star astrology') 20, 209
zodiac:
    Chinese 12, 182, 184, *184–5*, 193, 197, **208–11**
    Hellenistic 21, *180*, 181, 182, *182*, 183, *183*, 187, *187*, 190, *190*, 193, 194, *194–5*, *198–9*, 200, 206–7, 212, *213*, *214–15*
    Vedic 193, **200–5**
Zoroaster and Zoroastrianism **96–9**, 104, 111, 119
Zuleykha 156, *156*

AUTHOR BIOGRAPHY

Christopher Dell holds a degree in the History of Art from the Courtauld Institute, London. He has written and edited many bestselling titles on art, the occult and visual culture, including *Monsters*, *Mythology*, *What Makes a Masterpiece?* and *The Occult, Witchcraft & Magic*, all published by Thames & Hudson.

ACKNOWLEDGMENTS

I want to thank my commissioning editor, Philip Watson, for the ongoing support, encouragement and interest in somewhat eccentric topics. Emma Barton, my editor, was a phenomenal fount of knowledge and a much-needed voice of common sense. I leant heavily on her background in the Classics to avoid some of the more obvious errors – needless to say, any errors that may remain are my responsibility. The designer, Agatha Smith, has done a beautiful job of bringing this potentially dusty topic to life – I love the planisphere! This book is the first for which I've handed over responsibility for finding images to someone else – Nikos Kotsopoulos, you've done a wonderful job, thank you. Finally, I want to thank my family and friends for their curiosity, ideas, patience and support as I've worked on this book, in particular Swati and Silky!

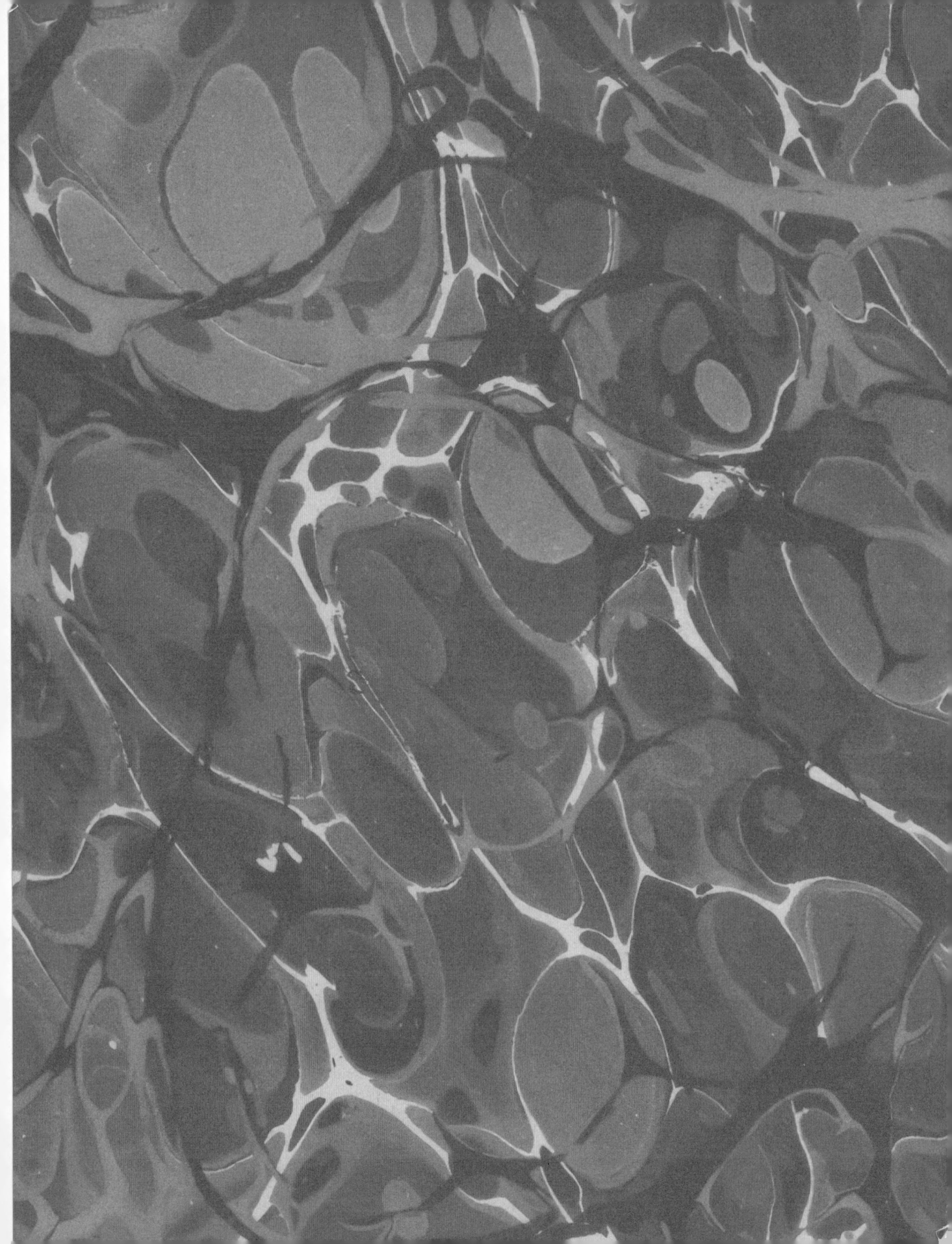